CW00689254

Modular A-Level and AS Mathematics

Aiming High

*A Flexible Learning Course for the new
AS and A–Level Mathematics Syllabuses*

S1

by
Barbara Young
and
Brian Law

Tarporley Community High School, Cheshire

Cartoons by Jenny Smith and Matthew Staff

AUTHOR'S ACKNOWLEDGEMENTS

Many thanks to all those Y12-13 Tarporley High School students who have borne the brunt of the experimentation which has gone with the development of these texts, over a period of 5-6 years. Their patience, good humour and positive criticism has been excellent, and we cannot thank them enough for the many good ideas that they have given us.

Thanks also to Linda Goodwin, for her help with allocating exam questions to the relevant part of the syllabuses.

The publishers would like to thank the following examination boards for their kind permission to include questions from past examination papers: OCR, AQA and Edexcel.

Thanks to the Official for National Statistics for permission to use statistical data from Social Trends 24 and 30.

© The 'Maths Is ...' Jugglers
2, Millview Close, Bulkeley, Malpas, Cheshire, SY14 8DB

This edition was first published in Great Britain 2001
British Library Cataloguing in Publication Data

ISBN   1 – 874428 – 83 – 2

Printed and bound by PRINTCENTRE WALES, Mold, Flintshire

CONTENTS

> This book can be used as a standard text book.
> All topics are developed using a structured approach.

However, it was developed as a Flexible Learning course.

Features of the Flexible Learning Course

- Each module is divided into units, lasting 3-5 weeks.
- Students work through each unit on their own, asking for help from the teacher as it is required. This way students get individual tuition as and when they need it. However, the teacher can teach some or all of the material to the whole class or to groups of students, using their experience and expertise to judge what is best for their group of students.
- At the end of each unit, the student does a competence test, using the text for reference, if needed. The competence tests are in the text, at the end of each unit. When the teacher has marked this, the teacher discusses it with the student, looking for weaknesses in understanding and/or explanation, and hands it back to the student for corrections to be done. In extreme cases, the student knows that the teacher may ask to see the student's file of work on this topic. This picks up the cases where a student has not done all of the work ! [The answers to the competence tests are not included, as students need to be able to do this test without access to any answers.]
- Only when all corrections are done to the teacher's satisfaction, can the student sit the end-of-unit test, which is done under standard test conditions. Marks below 70% trigger an investigation into what has gone wrong and, eventually, a re-test.
- Each student is also given a booklet containing study advice, which comes complete with due dates for each competence test, and for the modular exams. As soon as the competence test has been handed to the teacher for marking, the student starts the next unit.
- At the end of each module will be a selection of exam questions for the relevent board, organised into topics.

Advantages of the Flexible Learning Course

- Students take responsibility for organising their own work. Having due dates for the whole module, and the date for the modular exam, they can see that there is little room to get behind.
- University visits, field trips, etc. do not disrupt the course. Since students have dates to work to, they organise their work to fit round these interruptions.
- Individual tuition means that students get help as and when they need it.
- Able students have everything they need here to work on their own. Let them go and watch them fly.

AIMING HIGH

S1

Unit 1
Representation of data

CONTENTS

	OCR	AQA	Edexcel
Section 1	All	All	All
Section 2	All	All	All
Section 3	All	All	All
Section 4	All	All	All
Section 5	All	All	All
Section 6	All	All	All
Section 7	All	All	All
Section 8	All	All	All
Section 9	All	All	All
Section 10	All	All	All

Unit 1: Representation of Data
Section 1 : Mathematical models

In this section you will meet mathematical models.

DEVELOPMENT
D1.1: What is a mathematical model ?

Modelling is a vital activity in engineering, science, economics, technology, business, ... any field where mathematics is applied.

A mathematical model is a simplified representation of a real-life problem.

The degree of simplification will depend on the purpose for which the solution of the problem is required.

1. A ship is travelling directly towards a port at a speed of 10 knots (nautical miles per hour). The ship's master radios for a tug to escort the ship into port. When the ship is 12 nautical miles away, the tug leaves port and sails directly towards the ship at 5 knots.

   (a) Work out how far out from the port the tug should meet the ship.

   (b) When should the tug start looking out for the ship ?

In order to solve the real-life problem, it has been simplified. For simplification, certain **modelling assumptions** have been made.
However, the estimates produced by this model will be sufficiently accurate for the tug master to find the ship.
The two variables used to solve the mathematical problem were distance from port and time. These variables are called **the relevant variables** .

2. The following **mathematical assumptions** have been made in question 1:
   A: both vessels travel a constant speeds (whereas the tug will, in fact, have to accelerate up to the cruising speed of 5 knots)
   B: both vessels are assumed to be points
   C: both vessels are travelling directly towards each other
   D: both ships sail in a straight line
   E: tidal flow and currents do not affect the speeds of the two vessels
   F: the depth of the water does not affect the speeds of the ships
   G: the wind speed and direction do not affect the speeds of the ships

   If you needed to make a more accurate mathematical model of this situation, which three of the above assumptions would be the most important to change.

If the tug had been required to find and intercept a ship whose path was not directly towards the tug, the model would have needed to be a little more accurate. If it had been a space ship trying to rendez-vous with Jupiter on its orbit round the sun, the model would have had to be far more accurate. So, the purpose for which the model is to be used dictates the level of simplification of the model.

Section 2 : Working with Data

In this section you will:
* meet various types of data
* review the use of frequency tables.

DEVELOPMENT

D2.1: Types of data

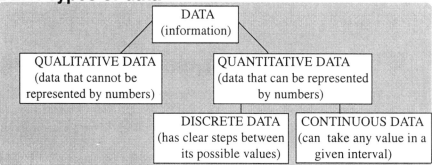

DATA
(information)

| QUALITATIVE DATA (data that cannot be represented by numbers) | QUANTITATIVE DATA (data that can be represented by numbers) |

| DISCRETE DATA (has clear steps between its possible values) | CONTINUOUS DATA (can take any value in a given interval) |

State whether each of these sets of data is qualitative (QL) or quantitative (QN):

1. favourite football teams
2. length of golf shots
3. temperature of the bath water
4. countries in Europe

State whether each of these sets of data is discrete (D) or continuous (C):

5. number of golf shots for each hole
6. lengths of golf shots
7. noonday temperatures
8. number of items in schoolbags
9. how old schoolbags are
10. sizes of shoes

* *Check your answers.*

D2.2: Ungrouped frequency tables

1. Here are a set of test scores for a mental arithmetic test.

   5   4   9   8   7   5   6   9   3   7
   6   8   4   6   9   6   4   9   10   8

   Put these scores into an ungrouped frequency table.

   *This is a set of **raw data.** Putting it into a frequency table usually clarifies the data.*

2. Here are a set of exam marks

   55   64   39   78   97   45   66   29   43   27
   36   48   84   66   59   46   94   89   76   82
   48   72   51   68   77   45   88   92   58   63

   Explain why putting these scores into an ungrouped frequency table would not make the data much clearer.

   * *Check your answers.*

Section 3 : Stem-and-Leaf diagrams

In this section you will meet and use stem-and-leaf diagrams.

DEVELOPMENT

D3.1: Stem-and-leaf diagrams

A stem-and-leaf diagram is way of organising ungrouped data so that it shows up any patterns. It can also be used to compare two sets of data.

EXAMPLE   Ages of fathers of Y12 students

37 49 43 38 56 46 42 50 35 61 47

(a) Put this data onto a stem-and-leaf diagram which is
(i) unordered   (ii) ordered

(b) What do you notice about the ages ?

(a) (i) Underlined: Unordered stem-and-leaf diagram

Ages of fathers of Y12 students   3|7 means 37 years ◄ key

```
3 | 7  8  5          (3)
4 | 9  3  6  2  7    (5)
5 | 6  0             (2)
6 | 1                (1)
```
stem   leaves

The numbers in brackets tell us how many leaves belong to each stem. It is not essential to have them, but they are often useful. Their total provides a check that no data value has been missed out.

(ii) Underlined: Ordered stem-and-leaf diagram

Ages of fathers of Y12 students   3|7 means 37 years

```
3 | 5  7  8          (3)
4 | 2  3  6  7  9    (5)
5 | 0  6             (2)
6 | 1                (1)
```

To make an ordered stem-and-leaf diagram, it is usually easier to make an unordered one first.

(b) Either :   There are more fathers in their 40s than in their 30s
    or   :   Few of these fathers are over 50

1. The ages of mothers of the Y12 students are:

    39 50 40 33 48 51 37 41 35 37 40

    Construct an ordered stem-and-leaf diagram, complete with a key for this data.

    Stack the leaves in precise columns.

2. The lengths of feet, in cm, of a sample of men who wore a size 9 shoe are:

    | 27.2 | 27.4 | 27.5 | 28.2 | 26.9 | 28.1 | 28 | 27.6 | 26.8 | 27.1 |
    | 27.4 | 27.6 | 28 | 27.9 | 27.7 | 27.7 | 26.9 | 28.2 | 28.1 | 27.5 |
    | 27.8 | 26.6 | 27.5 | 27.8 | 28.1 | 28.2 | 29 | 28.3 | 26.8 | 27.7 |

    (a) Using a key where 27|2 means 27.2, construct an ordered stem-and-leaf diagram for this data.

    (b) One length seems out of place. Which length would you measure again ?

> **Stem-and-leaf diagrams** have the clarity of the shape of a bar chart
> plus   the detail of the original data.
>
> Their stems may have more than one digit
> BUT   their leaves can have only one digit.
>
> Lines with a lot of data in them can be split
> eg   3 | 0 0 1 1 2 2 2 2 3 3
>   3 | 4 5 5 6 6 6 7 8 8 9
>
> Continuous data can be displayed on a stem-and-leaf diagram, provided each piece
> of data is rounded to the same number of decimal places or significant figures.

3. Number of days that patients have waited for a first appointment with an orthopaedic consultant at Brambley Road Hospital ßis shown on this stem-and-leaf diagram:

Number of days										Key 4|2 = 42
1	0	1	2	4						(4)
2	0	1	5	7	9					(5)
3	1	4	6	8	8					(5)
4	0	1	2	2	3	5	7	8	9	(9)
5	2	4	5	8	9	9				(6)
6	1	4	5							(3)
7	1	2								(2)

A doctor wants to give his patient an estimate of how long they are likely to have to wait for an appointment.

What estimate would you give ?

4. Weights of sampled packets of soap powder in kilograms are given here:

weights of packets									Key 362|2 = 3.622 kg
362	8	9							(2)
363	1	4	4	5	6	7	7	8 9	(9)
364	0	1	2	2	3	3	4	5 5	
	6	6	7	7	9				(14)
365	0	1	3	5	8	9			(6)
366	5								(1)

Quality control at this factory states that all packets in a sample of 32 should be within ±0.5% of the target weight of 3.645 kg.

How many of these packets are outside the permitted weight range ?

5. The results of the GCSE mock examination in mathematics in January 2000, for higher tier students, are given here (as percentages):

Mock results										Key 4|2 = 42%
2	3									(1)
3	1	3	6	7	8	8	8	9	9	(9)
4	1	1	2	3	3	5	5	6	6 7	(10)
5	1	1	4	4	4	6	6	6	9	(9)
6	0	0	0	3	3	5	6	7	7 9	(10)
7	0	0	1	1	2	4	5	5		(8)
8	0	2	5	6	6	6	7	7	8 9	(10)

(a) Students who got 60% or more in the mock exam were given a predicted GCSE grade of A. How many students were predicted an A ?

(b) Students who got less than 35% in the mock exam were given a predicted GCSE grade of D. How many students were predicted a D?

• *Check your answers.*

3.2 : Back to back stem-and-leaf diagrams

> Direct comparison of two sets of data can be achieved by placing two
> stem-and-leaf diagrams back-to-back.

EXAMPLE   This back to back stem-and-leaf diagram shows the GCSE higher tier exam marks for boys and girls.

Key $3/9 = 39\%$ Boys   Higher Level GCSE Maths   Girls   Key $4|0 = 40\%$

	Boys			Girls	
(1)	9	2		
(1)	9	3	3 6 7 9	(4)
(5)	8 8 4 4 2	4	0 0 2 2 5 6 8 8	(8)
(6)	9 7 5 4 2 1	5	0 4 4 5 6 7 8	(7)
(4)	8 5 2 2	6	0 1 2 7 1 6	(6)
(5)	9 7 7 5 0	7	6 6 9 9	(4)
(5)	8 8 4 0 0	8	1	(1)

(a) What was the lowest mark ?

(b) Who got the better marks, the boys or the girls ?

(c) Marks 60% and over earned a grade A or A*. How many pupils got A or A* ?

(a) 29   (b) Boys   (b) 25

1. (a) Combine the ages of fathers and mothers of Y12 students in a back to back stem-and-leaf diagram.(Data in Example and Q1 both in D3.1)

   (b) Compare the ages of the fathers and the mothers. What do you notice ?

2. The number of days that patients have waited for a first appointment with an orthopaedic consultant at Stone Wall Hospital:

43	15	73	67	30	15	27	35	48	51	20	32
16	45	51	73	31	44	71	48	54	62	16	72
64	43	37	29	26	55	47	28	41	32	39	26

   Construct an ordered back to back stem-and-leaf diagram for this data and the data for Brambley Road Hospital (Data in D3.1 Q3)

   (b) Which hospital would you prefer to be referred to, and why ?

3. The results of the GCSE examination in mathematics in June 2000, for the higher tier students whose mock results were given in Q5 in D3.1, are :

	Mock exam		GCSE exam	
(1)	3	2	9	(1)
(9)	9 9 8 8 8 7 6 3 1	3	3 6 7 9 9	(5)
(10)	7 6 6 5 5 3 3 2 1 1	4	0 0 2 2 2 4 4 5 6 8 8 8 8	(13)
(9)	9 6 6 6 4 4 4 1 1	5	0 1 2 4 4 4 5 5 6 7 7 8 8 9	(14)
(10)	9 7 7 6 5 3 3 0 0 0	6	0 2 2 2 3 5 6 7 8 9	'(10)
(8)	5 5 4 2 1 1 0 0	7	0 5 6 6 7 7 8 9 9	(9)
(10)	9 8 7 7 6 6 6 5 2 0	8	0 0 1 4 8	(5)

   (a) GCSE students generally improve between the mock and the GCSE exam. Did they appear to do so here ?

   (b) Do you think the mock paper was easier to get high marks on, or harder, than the GCSE paper ?   • Check answers.

Section 4 : Working with secondary data

In this section you will read information from tables and statistical diagrams.

DEVELOPMENT
D4.1: Information from tables

Source: Census, Office for National Statistics

1. Population of Metropolitan Counties in Great Britain (in millions)

	1891	1911	1931	1951	1971	1991
Greater London	5.6	7.2	8.1	8.2	7.5	6.4
West Midlands	1.4	1.8	2.1	2.5	2.8	2.5
Greater Manchester	2.2	2.6	2.7	2.7	2.7	2.5
West Yorkshire	1.6	1.9	1.9	2.0	2.1	2.0
Merseyside	1.1	1.4	1.6	1.7	1.7	1.4
South Yorkshire	0.7	1.0	1.2	1.3	1.3	1.3
Tyne and Wear	0.8	1.1	1.2	1.2	1.2	1.1
All metropolitan counties	13.2	16.9	18.9	19.6	19.2	17.1
Great Britain	33.0	40.8	44.8	48.9	54.0	54.2

(a) The largest of these urban areas is Greater London.
Which are the next two urban areas with the highest populations ?

(b) In 1991, Greater London had about two and a half times the population of each of the next two urban areas. True or false ?

(c) In 1971, what percentage of the population resided in metropolitan counties ? (Give your answer to the nearest one per cent.)

(d) 'In 1891 a larger proportion of the total population were resident in these areas than in 1991.' Is this statement true or false ? Justify your conclusion.

(e) During the 1980s there was a trend for people to move out from metropolitan areas to smaller areas and rural settlements. Urban decentralisation was particularly clear in four metroplitan areas. State which four areas this refers to and justify your choice.

2. The following table shows the average number of persons per household in the United Kingdom in each of seven consecutive years.

	1985	1986	1987	1988	1989	1990	1991
Males	1.258	1.236	1.229	1.217	1.229	1.193	1.169
Females	1.339	1.317	1.310	1.288	1.292	1.281	1.253
All	2.596	2.554	2.533	2.516	2.509	2.475	2.422

© G. Dennis (ed), *Annual Abstract of Statistics 1993, Central Statistics Office)*

(i) Give a reason why, for some years, the value in the third row is not the exact sum of the values in the first and second rows.

(ii) State briefly two distinct features of the data.

(iii) State why it is not possible to deduce from the above data that the population of the U.K. decreased between 1985 and 1991.   (OCR)

• *Check your answers.*

D4.2: Statistical diagrams

1. Relative price levels : EU comparison 1997   Indices (UK = 100)

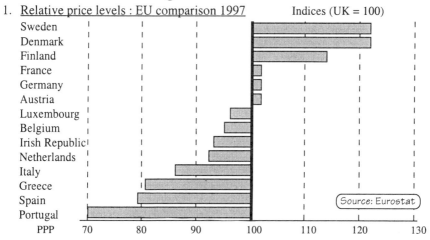

The purchasing power of the pound abroad is measured by Purchasing Power Parities (PPPs). A PPP between the UK and another country is the exchange rate that would be required to purchase the same quantity of goods or services costing £1 in the UK

(a) Which three countries' price levels would have appeared similar to that of the UK?

(b) Which three countries' price levels would have appeared dearer to that of the UK?

(c) Would price levels in Greece have appeared lower or higher to an Italian ?

(d) Would an Irish holiday maker's money have bought more or less in the UK than in the Irish Republic ?

(e) Spain, Portugal and Greece are among the most popular holiday destinations for UK residents. Give one reason why you think this might be so.

2. (a) Did more burglaries occur during the evening/night or during the day ? Justify your answer.

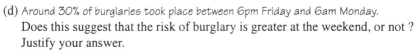

(b) Two sectors are labelled evening/night and morning/afternoon. Why do you think these sectors were required ?

(c) During what period did the least number of burglaries occur ?

(d) Around 30% of burglaries took place between 6pm Friday and 6am Monday. Does this suggest that the risk of burglary is greater at the weekend, or not ? Justify your answer.

(e) A similar survey in 1990 found that 65% of burglaries that year took place in the evening/night. Explain why this does not necessarily mean that there were more burglaries during that period of the day in 1990 than in 1997.

3. Percentage of adults with a full car driving licence: by gender and age,

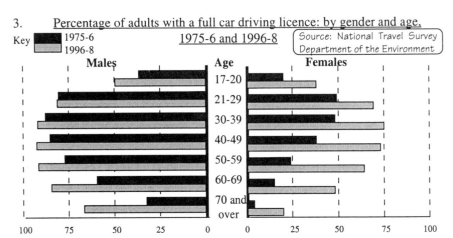

Key ▓ 1975-6   1975-6 and 1996-8   Source: National Travel Survey
    ░ 1996-8   Department of the Environment

Between 1975-6 and 1996-8, for both genders and all age groups, there was a marked increase in the proportions that hold licences.

(a) For people aged 70 and over, which gender showed the bigger increase ?

(a) For which gender was the most marked increase overall ?

(b) Which two age groups saw the overall biggest increases ?

4. Plastic card transactions

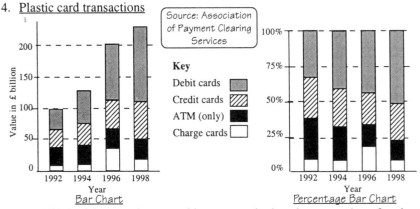

Source: Association of Payment Clearing Services

Key
Debit cards ░
Credit cards ▨
ATM (only) ■
Charge cards ☐

Bar Chart   Percentage Bar Chart

(a) Which of the two charts would you use to look at the proportion of each type of transaction ?

(b) Which of the two charts would you use to look at the value of each type of transaction ?

(c) Between which two of these years did the overall value of plastic card transactions double ?

(d) Between which two of these years did the proportion of one type of transaction almost double, and what kind of transaction was it ?

(e) Which kind of transaction has maintained a steady value ? Has its percentage share of the total transactions risen or fallen ?   • Check your answers.

Section 5 : Histograms

In this section you will:
- read data from and construct histograms
- work with relative frequency histograms
- review and use frequency polygons

DEVELOPMENT

D5.1: Histograms

A **histogram** is used to illustrate continuous data, or discrete data which has been grouped, and is therefore treated as if it were continuous data.

The area of each block represents the frequency.

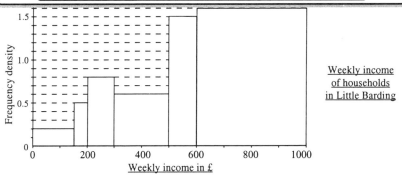

Weekly income of households in Little Barding

1. *Copy and complete this frequency table for the above histogram:*

Weekly income (£)	Width of class	Frequency density	Frequency
0–150	150	0.2	30
150-200	50		
200-300			
....			

2. (a) *Copy and complete this table:*

Weekly income for households in Great Barding			
Weekly income (£)	Width of class	Frequency density	Frequency
0–150	150		45
150-200	50		60
200-300			90
300-400			110
400-600			160
600–1000			440

(b) Draw a histogram for the household incomes of Great Barding.

(c) Which is the wealthier, Little or Great Barding ?

• Check your answers.

5.2: More about histograms

Points to note:
- The data is split into groups, which are more usually called **classes**.
- There are no gaps between the classes.
- The lower class boundary (LCB) is the lowest possible value that any number in that class could take.
- The upper class boundary (UCB) of one class is the LCB of the class above
- The LCB is in the class. The UCB is not in that class.
- The scale across the page is continuous.
- The classes may, or may not, have equal class widths.
- The area of each block is proportional to the frequency (and usually equal to it).
- Unless stated otherwise, frequency = frequency density x class width.

Classes are described in one of two ways:

Type 1 : (where the LCBs and the UCBs are the given endpoints of each class – often called true classes)

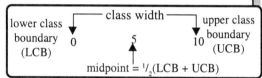

eg

    0–10   or $0 \le x < 10$

    10–20   or $10 \le x < 20$

lower class boundary (LCB) $\quad 0 \qquad 5 \qquad 10$ upper class boundary (UCB)

class width

midpoint = $\frac{1}{2}$(LCB + UCB)

Type 2 : (where the LCBs and the UCBs are NOT the given endpoints of each class, and which will need to be calculated)

eg   0–10   which is equivalent to the true class $-0.5 \le x < 10.5$

      11–20   which is equivalent to the true class $10.5 \le x < 20.5$

given classes   –   which must be rewritten using LCBs and UCBs

there appear to be gaps between these classes

lower class boundary (LCB) $-0.5 \qquad 10.5$ upper class boundary (UCB)

class width

given endpoints of the class

1. (a) *Copy and complete this table:*

Length of fish in the pond to the nearest centimetre				
Length	frequency	true classes	class width	frequency density
0-5	150	$-0.5 \le x \le 5.5$	6	25
6-10	75			
11-20	60			
21-36	48			
37-60	48			

(b) Draw a histogram for this distribution.

Even though the lengths cannot be negative, numerically the class 0-5 can take values $-0.5 \le x \le 5.5$ and it will overlap the vertical axis.

2.

Survey of distance of homes of shoppers from the hypermarket						
Distance	0-1	2-6	7-10	11-20	21-35	36-60
Frequency	20	65	48	60	24	20

(a) Make a table to calculate the frequency densities for this distribution.

(b) Draw a histogram for this distribution.

> *Grouped discrete data*
> Histograms always stand on a continuous scale.
> So, grouped discrete data is treated exactly as if it were continuous.

3.

Number of faulty light bulbs in weekly sample batches of 500					
Number faulty	1 - 2	3 - 5	6 - 10	11 - 20	21 - 50
Frequency	8	15	16	5	6

(a) Make a table to calculate the frequency densities for this distribution.

(b) Draw a histogram for this distribution.

> *When one (or both) of the end classes is open-ended*
> A frequently used 'rule of thumb' is to make the width
> of this class twice that of the one before (or after) it.

4. The speeds, in miles per hour, of vehicles travelling on a motorway, were measured by the police.

Speed	30 - 50	50 - 60	60 - 70	70 - 80	over 80
Frequency					

The histogram to illustrate this data is shown below.

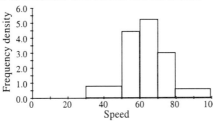

Use the histogram to complete the frequencies in the table above.

> *Using common sense rather than the above 'rule of thumb'*
> Use common sense to work out the width of the end class(es).
> For instance, if the classes are ages and the top class is 'over 70'
> then common sense tells us that a better class to replace this
> with is 70 - 100, as this would cover all the likely ages.

5. The inhabitants of the village of Muckle were asked how old they were.

Age given	under 5	5 - 15	15 - 30	30 - 50	50 - 80	over 80
Frequency	12	30	44	32	18	6

(a) Make a table calculating the frequency densities for each class.

(b) Would the age given be 'the age to the nearest year' or 'the age at the last birthday'?

(c) In a survey of a nother village Mickle, these villagers were also asked how old they were. The classes of ages were recorded as 5 and under, 6-20, 21-50, 51-90.
Write down the class boundaries for each of these classes.

• Check your answers.

5.3: Getting the words right

Population or sample

It is sometimes important to know whether the data you are working with is drawn from the whole population or just a sample of the population.

A survey is to be done to find out what proportion of the students eat in the school canteen. Adi wants to ask all students whether they eat in the school canteen. Jumila wants to ask the first five students in each tutor group.

Adi's is a population survey.
Jumila's is a sample survey.

Task 1: Look at each of questions 1-5 in D5.2. For each question, state whether the data given is drawn from the whole population or is just a sample.

Primary and secondary data

Primary data comes directly from the original source. If it is edited, commented on, added to, summarised or ..., it becomes **secondary data**.

A policemen witnesses a crime. He records what he sees in his pocket book. This is primary data.

A policeman interviews a witness to the crime. He records what he is told in his pocket book. This is secondary data.

Task 2: Look at each of the following cases.
State whether the data is primary or secondary.

A : The raw data from a survey of favourite pop groups in Y7.

B: The display of the results from the Y7 survey in A.

C: The table of data on populations of Metropolitan Counties in D4.1.

D: The form filled in by each household for the Census.

E: The summary of findings from the Census.

F: Data found on the Internet on the first week's sales of a CD.

• Check your answers.

D5.4: Relative frequency histograms

A **relative frequency histogram** is drawn like an ordinary histogram,
but the frequencies are replaced by relative frequencies.
Relative frequencies are obtained by expressing each frequency
as a proportion of the total frequency.
The total area under the histogram is equal to 1.00

1. Height of sunflower plants to the nearest cm

Height	0 - 19	20 - 39	40 - 79	80 - 119	120 - 139
Frequency	1	3	7	18	21

Draw a relative frequency histogram for this data.

• *Check your answers.*

D5.5: Frequency polygons

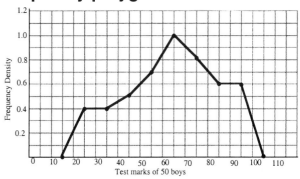

Test marks of 50 boys

This is a frequency polygon showing the test marks for 50 boys.
The marks were grouped into classes of width 10, 20-30, 30-40,40-50, ... 90-100
Note that the intervals below the first value and
above the last value are drawn as having zero frequency.

Frequency polygons can be superimposed on histograms,
by joining the midpoints of the tops of the blocks.
However, to draw a frequency polygon without drawing the histogram,
plot the frequency densities against the class midpoints.

1. The equivalent test marks for the girls are:

Class	30-40	40-50	50-60	60-70	70-80	80-90	90-100
Freq.	4	6	7	10	12	8	3

(a) Draw a frequency polygon for the girls' test marks.

(b) Use the two frequency polygons to determine the truth of each of these:
   A: More boys than girls' scored over 90
   B: The lowest few marks were boys' marks.

• *Check your answers.*

Section 6: Cumulative frequency

(In this section you will review working with cumulative frequency.)

DEVELOPMENT

D6.1: Cumulative frequency diagrams

The correct mathematical term for a set of running totals is
cumulative frequency

A lot more information is available from cumulative frequencies,
if they are put onto a cumulative frequency diagram.

A **cumulative frequency diagram** is obtained by

plotting | the upper class boundary | against | the cumulative frequency. |

The points are usually joined with straight lines, which implies that the data is
evenly spread within each group.

However, sometimes, the points are joined with a smooth curve (an ogive).

Tom works in the office of a company that owns a public car park. His boss is trying to get a picture of how long cars stay in the car park. Then they can use the information to work out a new price charging structure. Tom takes the receipts for the previous Saturday and notes the length of stay of each car. This is what he found:

Make a cumulative frequency diagram using this information. Use the diagram to investigate the truth of these four hypotheses that his boss has made:

A: Around half the cars stay for between 80 and 145 minutes.

B: Around one third of the cars stay for between 40 and 90 minutes.

C: Around 10% of the cars are in the car park for 30 minutes or less.

D: Around 10% of the cars are in the car park for 3 hours or longer.

Length of stay (in minutes)	Number of cars (frequency)
$0 \le$ time < 20	1
$20 \le$ time < 40	17
$40 \le$ time < 60	46
$60 \le$ time < 80	39
$80 \le$ time < 100	58
$100 \le$ time < 120	72
$120 \le$ time < 150	70
$150 \le$ time < 180	52
$180 \le$ time < 210	23
$210 \le$ time < 240	11
$240 \le$ time < 270	17

You need to quote figures to back up each of your conclusions.
It is not sufficient to say whether each hypothesis appears to be true or false.

• *Check your answers.*

D6.2: Britain's population outlook ⟨Source: Social Trends⟩

The two cumulative frequency diagrams show the mid-year population estimates for 1961 and 1991. It is on figures like these that the government bases its planning for such services as education, hospitals, care for the elderly ...

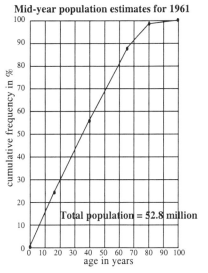

Mid-year population estimates for 1961

Total population = 52.8 million

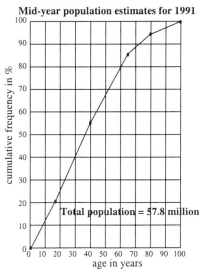

Mid-year population estimates for 1991

Total population = 57.8 million

Mid-year population predictions for 2021						
	less than 16	at least 16 & under 40	at least 40 & under 65	at least 65 & under 80	at least 80 & under 95	pop. in millions
2021	18.5%	30.0%	32.3%	14%	5.2%	62.0

1. Estimate the percentage of the population below 50 in 1961.

2. Estimate the percentage of the population below 20 in 1991.

3. Estimate the number of people over 65 in 1961.

4. Estimate the number of people below 40 in 1991.

5. Draw a cumulative frequency diagram for the predicted population in 2021.

6. Assuming the potential working population is the population between the ages of 18 and 65, work out what percentage of the total population is the working population for each of these three years.

7. Estimate the number of the potential working population for each of these years.

8. If the retirement age in 2021 was to be 60, estimate what percentage of the population would be retired in 2021.

• Check your answers.

Section 7: Median and quartiles

In this section you will:
- find the median and quartiles of raw data and from stem-and-leaf diagrams
- find the median and quartiles from frequency tables (ungrouped/grouped)
- use cumulative frequency diagrams to calculate medians, quartiles and percentiles

DEVELOPMENT

D7.1: Ordered raw data

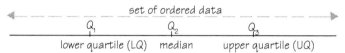

set of ordered data

Q_1 Q_2 Q_3

lower quartile (LQ)   median   upper quartile (UQ)

The **median** is the middle value of a set of ordered data.
The **lower quartile** is the value one quarter from the bottom of the ordered data.
The **upper quartile** is the value one quarter from the top of the ordered data.

EXAMPLE   Find the median of each set of data values:

(a)   2   3   5   7   9   11   11

          median = 7

(b)   3   5   7   8   9   10   11   13

          median = 8.5

(c)   1   2   4   4   5   9

          median = 4

1. *Write down the median of each set of data values:*
   (a) 2   3   5   6   7   (b) 8   10   11   12   14   14   17   20
   (c) –2   –1   0   0   2   3   (d) 48   50   59   63   67   71   75

The **lower quartile** is the middle value of the bottom half of the data values.
The **upper quartile** is the middle value of the top half of the data values.

For an EVEN number of data values:
- split the data into lower and upper halves
- the median of the lower half is Q_1
- the median of the upper half is Q_3

     2   3   5   6   6   7

     $Q_1 = 3$ $Q_3 = 6$

For an ODD number of data values:
- find the median and remove from list
- split the data into lower and upper halves
- the median of the lower half is Q_1
- the median of the upper half is Q_3

     2   3   5   6   6   7   8   9   9

     $Q_1 = 4$ $Q_3 = 8.5$

2. *Find the median and quartiles of each set of data values:*
   (a) 55 56 60 62 68 80 82 90 95
   (b) 3   5   2   3   1   6   7   8
   (c) 96 98 94 88 92 86 84 90 91 89 88
   (d) 43 62 41 65 47

3. Ages of fathers of Y12 students   3|7 means 37 years

3	5 7 8	(3)
4	2 3 6 7 9	(5)
5	0 6	(2)
6	1	(1)

   (a) How many fathers are listed in this stem-and-leaf diagram.

   (b) Find the median and quartiles of this set of data values.

   (c) What is the interquartile range ?

4. Number of motorists who fill up with 'lead replacement' petrol
   each day at the Starlight Filling Station for three weeks:

   | 23 | 31 | 27 | 35 | 42 | 59 | 64 | 32 | 56 | 49 | 52 |
   | 35 | 22 | 30 | 41 | 39 | 62 | 54 | 68 | 47 | 34 |

   (a) Make an ordered stem-and-leaf diagram for this data.
       Add a cumulative frequency column on the right of this diagram.

   (b) Find the median and quartiles of this set of data values.

   (c) What is the interquartile range for this data set ?

   (d) At least 48 people filled up with 'lead replacement' petrol on more than half
       of the days during the three weeks. True or false ?

   • *Check your answers.*

D7.2: Median and quartiles from frequency tables

For larger numbers of data values, there are several methods that are used for working out which values to take for the median and the lower and upper quartiles. The one we show here is one of the simplest ways, and accurate enough for our purposes.

For n data values:
- the lower quartile is the $\frac{1}{4}$(n + 1)th value
- the median is the $\frac{1}{2}$(n + 1)th value
- the lower quartile is the $\frac{3}{4}$(n + 1)th value

EXAMPLE   Find the median and quartiles of the Number of GCSE A*–C passes given in the table below.

A*–C passes	Freq.	Cu. Freq.
4	5	5
5	6	11
6	7	18
7	5	23
8	5	28
9	3	31
10	1	32

$n = 32$

$Q_1 = \frac{1}{4}$(n + 1)th value = 8.25th value
The 8.25th value lies in the group of 5 passes
$Q_2 = \frac{1}{2}$(n + 1)th value = 16.5th value
The 16.5th value lies in the group of 6 passes
$Q_3 = \frac{3}{4}$(n + 1)th value = 24.75th value
The 24.75th value lies in the group of 8 passes

Add a cumulative frequency column to the frequency table.

$Q_1 = 5$, median = 6, $Q_3 = 8$

1. Number of goals scored by Hazelbank Harriers F.C. in matches in 2000-2001

Number of goals	Frequency
0	6
1	5
2	4
3	4
4	3
5	0
6	0
7	1

(a) How many matches were played ?

(b) Work out the median number of goals.

(c) Work out the quartiles for this distribution.

(d) What is the inter-quartile range ?

2. Number of people living in each house on the Barleyfield Estate

Number in each house	1	2	3	4	5	6	7	8
Frequency	4	8	10	15	11	4	2	1

Work out the median and quartiles for this distribution.

• *Check your answers.*

7.3: Interpolation

EXAMPLE

The cormorant dives under the water to catch fish.
The length of time that the cormorant is underwater
is measured each time the cormorant dives.
The times are recorded in the table below.

(a) In which class is the median time ?
(b) Use interpolation to work out a more accurate estimate
of the median time.

Time in s	Freq.	Cu Fr
$0 \le t < 10$	3	3
$10 \le t < 20$	6	9
$20 \le t < 30$	9	18
$30 \le t < 50$	15	33
$50 \le t < 60$	3	36
over 60	2	38

(a) Median = $\frac{1}{2}$ x 39 th value = 19.5th value
19.5th value is in class $30 \le t < 50$

(b) There are 18 data values below this class.
We need the 1.5th value in this class.
$d = \dfrac{1.5}{15}$ x 20 = 2

$\Rightarrow$ time $\approx$ 30 s + 2 s = $\boxed{32 \text{ s}}$

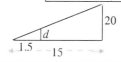

1. (a) In the example above state the classes which contain the lower and upper
quartiles.
(b) Use interpolation to work out reasonable estimates for the lower and upper
quartiles.

2. Lengths of garden slugs in centimetres (1999 study)

Length	$3.0 \le l < 3.5$	$3.5 \le l < 4.0$	$4.0 \le l < 4.5$	$4.5 \le l < 5.0$	$5.0 \le l < 3.5$
Freq.	32	40	48	70	10

(a) Use interpolation to work out estimates to 3 d.p. for the median and the
lower and upper quartiles for the lengths of the slugs.

(b) A similar study was done on garden slugs in 2000.
For this group, the median was 4.15, and the quartiles were 3.76 and 4.64.
(i) In which year were the slugs longer ?
(ii) In which year were the lengths more consistent ?

3. Body temperatures of 50 Y12 students, measured to the nearest 0.1°C

Temp.	36.0-36.5	36.6-36.7	36.8-36.9	37.0-37.1	37.2-38.0	over 38.0
Freq.	5	8	20	14	2	1

(a) Use interpolation to work out estimates to 2 d.p. for the median and the
lower and upper quartiles for the temperatures. Note that these are not true
classes.

(b) Estimate the number of students whose temperature was 36.8 or below.

• *Check your answers.*

7.4: Using cumulative frequency diagrams

The simplest and most accurate way of evaluating medians and quartiles
from grouped data, is to read them off a cumulative frequency diagram.

EXAMPLE The table below gives the heights of 200 Y9 students in cm.
Draw a cumulative frequency diagram for
this data and use it to work out the median
and quartiles.

Heights	Freq.	Cu. Freq.
$100 \le h < 110$	7	7
$110 \le h < 120$	20	27
$120 \le h < 130$	27	54
$130 \le h < 140$	42	96
$140 \le h < 150$	51	147
$150 \le h < 160$	38	185
$160 \le h < 170$	11	196
$170 \le h < 180$	4	200

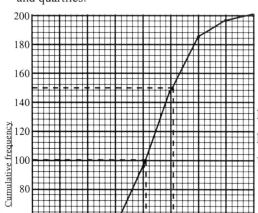

Median ≈ 100th value ≈ 141 cm

LQ ≈ 50th value ≈ 128 cm

UQ ≈ 150th value ≈ 151 cm

Remember:
the cumulative
frequencies are
plotted against
the TOP of each
interval.

Chyps

1. Weekly income for households in Littlehaw

Income (£)	0–150	150-200	200-300	300-400	400-600	600–1000
Freq.	54	64	105	140	152	85

(a) Draw a cumulative frequency diagram for this distribution.
(b) Work out the median and quartiles from the diagram.
(c) What is the range of income of the middle 50% of these households ?

QUARTILES are the values you find when the data is split into four equal parts.
The first quartile is the lower quartile, the second quartile is the median and
the third quartile is the upper quartile.
If the data is split into ten equal parts, these are called **DECILES**.
The first decile is the value one tenth of the way from the bottom. ...
The ninth decile is the value one tenth of the way from the top.

2. (a) Using the cumulative diagram that you drew for question 1, find the values of
the first, fourth and ninth deciles of this distribution.

(b) John Sawyer lives in Littlehaw. His family's income lies between the fourth and fifth deciles. State his family's weekly income, I, in the form $a \le I < b$.

(c) What is the range of incomes of the middle 80% of these households.

PERCENTILES are the values you find when the data is split into 100 equal parts.

3. The marks obtained by candidates in a Statistics exam

Marks	0 - 40	40 - 50	50 - 60	60 - 70	70 - 80	80 - 100
Freq.	12	33	110	90	73	32

(a) Draw a cumulative frequency diagram for this distribution.

(b) Work out the median and quartiles from the diagram.

(c) Work out the 95th percentile mark.

(d) Work out the 20th percentile mark.

(e) "Students who achieved ......marks or less will be invited to discuss their lack of progress with the Head of Studies." 15% of the students received this invitation. What was the mark stated in the above notice.

(f) Students achieving above the 90th percentile mark received a commendation. What mark did they have to achieve to be commended ?

4. Income range of tax payers (1993-94)

Source: Inland Revenue
[Social Trends 24 (1994)]

Annual Income(£)	Number of taxpayers (millions)	Total annual income (£ million)
3 500 – 5 000	2.2	9 400
5 000 – 7 500	3.9	24 700
7 500 – 10 000	4.0	34 900
10 000 – 15 000	6.1	75 900
15 000 – 20 000	3.9	68 000
20 000 – 30 000	3.2	77 400
30 000 – 40 000	1.0	33 600
40 000 and above	0.8	61 500

(a) The first £3 500 of income was tax free.
There were 2.2 million people who earned between £3 500 and £4 000.
What was the mean income of this group ?

(b) There were 0.8 million taxpayers who earned £40 000 or above.
What was the mean income of this group ?

(c) Taking the upper class boundary of the top group as £100 000, draw a cumulative frequency graph for the annual incomes.

(d) Work out the median income of the taxpayers.

(e) What was the lower boundary of the incomes of the top decile group ?

(e) What was the upper boundary of the incomes of the bottom decile group ?

• *Check your answers.*

Section 8: Averages

In this section you will:
- review mean, median and mode as measures of the centre of a data set
- meet and use sigma (Σ) notation
- estimate the mean and median from histograms
- meet a shortcut to simplify calculation of the mean

DEVELOPMENT

D8.1: What is an average ?

> Calculation of the median was covered in Section 7.

An **average** is a measure of the centre of a data set.
There are three measures that we use as averages.

The **median** is the middle value of a set of ordered data.
The **mode** is the most common value of a set of data.
The **mean** is the sum of all the values divided by the number of values.

For any set of data values, we use the average that is most representative of the set.

1. The weekly wages in a small factory are :

   £120   £120   £135   £135   £135   £135   £135   £150   £285

   (a) Work out the mean, the median and the mode of these wages.

   (b) In this situation, the mean is not a representative value for this data. Explain why.

   (c) What has distorted the value of the mean, so that it is not a representative value ?

   (d) Which average would you use as the most representative value here?

2. Number of children in families in Hazelbank Close

Number of children (x)	Frequency (f)	$f \times x$
0	3	
1	8	
2	9	
3	5	
4	3	
5	1	
8	1	
	$\Sigma f =$	$\Sigma fx =$

The sigma (Σ) notation

Σf = the sum of the frequencies

Σfx = the sum of the fx values

The symbol Σ means 'the sum of'

Big Edd

   (a) Copy and complete this table and use it to find the mean, the mode and the median of this data.

   (b) Which value would you use as the most representative value here ?

   (c) How many families are there ?

   (d) How many children are there ?

IMPORTANT NOTE

If you give the correct answer to a question, to the required degree of accuracy, with no working shown, it will earn you full marks. However, if you make just one slip, in either the calculation or the accuracy of the answer, you will get no marks.

To maximise your examination marks, it is advisable to show all working clearly, so part marks can be awarded for method and accuracy within the working, in the case that you do not give the correct answer.

Driller

3.

Ages of children of families in Hazelbank Close			
Ages	Frequency (f)	Midpoint (x)	$f \times x$
$0 \le age < 5$	20	2.5	
$5 \le age < 7$	9	6	
$7 \le age < 11$	15		
$11 \le age < 14$	8		
$14 \le age < 16$	7		
$16 \le age < 18$	7		
	$\Sigma f =$		$\Sigma fx =$

It is not known how the data is distributed within each class.

The midpoint is chosen as the representative value for each class.

Any average that is calculated from this data can only be an estimated value.

(a) What is the modal class for this data ?

(b) Complete this table and use it to find an estimate for the mean of this data.

(c) Use linear interpolation to find an estimate for the median of this data.

4.

Ages of mothers of families in Hazelbank Close	Key 1|9 = 19
1 | 9	(1)
2 | 0 2 4 7 8 9 9 9	(8)
3 | 1 1 2 3 5 5 7 8 8	(9)
4 | 1 2 3 4 6 6 6 9	(8)
5 | 2	(1)

(a) State the modal ages.

(b) What is the median age ?

(c) Calculate the mean age.

(d) Which average would be a good representative value for these ages ?

• *Check your answers.*

The standard symbol for the mean is $\overline{x}$ (read as x bar)

For n values of raw data, the mean value $= \overline{x} = \dfrac{\Sigma x}{n}$

$\Sigma =$ sigma

For ungrouped data in a frequency table, $\overline{x} = \dfrac{\Sigma fx}{\Sigma f}$

For grouped data in a frequency table, $\overline{x} = \dfrac{\Sigma fx}{\Sigma f}$ (x is the class midpoint)

D8.2: Using statistical calculator functions

1. Find out how to put your calculator into statistical mode.

EXAMPLE   Use your calculator to work out the mean:
(a) 2 4 6 7 9   (b) 3 4 4 4 5 8 8 8

(a) **Simple data list**
Put the data in: *either* 2 M+ 4 M+ 6 M+ 7 M+ 9 M+
      or   2 DATA 4 DATA 6 DATA 7 DATA 9 DATA

RCL $\bar{x}$ gives the mean = $\boxed{5.6}$

(b) **Grouped data list**
To enter three lots of 4: *either* you key in 4 x 3 and either M+ or DATA
      or   you key in 4,3 DATA

Hint: when you have keyed in all the data, call up *n* (the number of items entered).
If *n* is not the same as the number of items, then you have probably entered
frequency , data instead of data , frequency

RCL $\bar{x}$ gives the mean = $\boxed{5.5}$

NOTE: Make sure you clear the memory contents before entering new data.

Find the mean for each set of data values (to 2 d.p.)

2. 51   57   62   49   57   58   53   63   48

3. 63   63   65   66   68   68   68   73

4.

x	36	38	41	42	46	49	50	51
f	1	3	4	5	7	9	5	3

5.

x	23	24	25	26	27	28	29	30	31
f	315	321	356	378	372	350	345	323	301

In questions 5 – 7, find the values of n, Σx, Σx^2, and $\bar{x}$, to 2 d.p.

6. 55   57   54   48   49   60   41   45

7. 742 741 753 756 748 744 749 750 752

8. 103 111 99   104 103 108

9. Data set: $\boxed{67 \quad 69 \quad 63 \quad 72 \quad 65 \quad 69 \quad 72 \quad 70 \quad 65}$

Use the calculator to work out the value of $\left[\dfrac{\Sigma x^2}{n} - \bar{x} \right]$

The techniques used to calculate the values questions 5 – 8
will be used later in this unit. Here they are used purely to
familiarise you with some statistical functions on your
calculator.

Driller

• *Check your answers.*

D8.3: Mean and median from histograms

EXAMPLE   Estimate the median and the mean for the data given in this histogram.

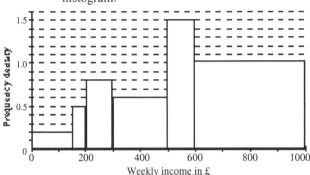

Median : The frequency for each block is given by the area of the block.
⇒ Σf = 45 + 25 + 80 + 120 + 150 + 400 = 820
⇒   median value ≈ 410th value and this lies in the block standing on 500-600. The lowest value in this block is the 270th value
⇒   median value = (410 – 270)th value in this block = 140th value
⇒   median value = 500 + $^{140}/_{150}$ x 100 ≈ 500 + 93
⇒   median value ≈ £593

Mean : $\overline{x}$ = $\dfrac{\Sigma fx}{\Sigma f}$ where $\overline{x}$ = midpoint value of each interval

Σf = 45 + 25 + 80 + 120 + 150 + 400 = 820
Midpoint values are 75, 175, 250, 400, 550, 800
⇒ Σfx = 45x75 + 25x175 + 80x250 + 120x400 + 150x550 + 400x800
⇒ Σfx = £478 250
⇒ $\overline{x}$ = £478 250 ÷ 820 ≈ £583

1. (a) What was the maximum length of call ?

   (b) How many telephone calls were made last Wednesday ?

   (c) Show that the mean length of call was roughly 6 minutes.

   (d) Estimate the median length of call to the nearest second.

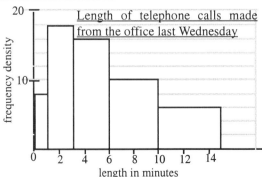

Length of telephone calls made from the office last Wednesday

2. The table gives the ages, in completed years, of the population in a particular region of the United Kingdom.

Age	0–4	5–15	16–44	45–64	65–79	80 and over
Number (in 1000s)	260	543	1727	756	577	135

A histogram of this data was drawn with age along the horizontal axis. The 0-4 age group was represented by a bar of horizontal width 0.5 cm and height 5.2 cm.

(a) Find the widths and heights, in cm to 1 decimal place, of the bars representing the following age groups:

(i) 16 – 44   (ii) 65 – 79

(b) Taking the midpoint of the last group to be 90 years, write down the midpoints of the other age groups and estimate the mean age of the population in this region of the United Kingdom.   *(Edexcel June 95 S1 Q5)*

• *Check your answers.*

D8.4: A shortcut to finding the mean

1. (a) Work out the mean of:

(i)   4   5   7   6   9

(ii)   24   25   27   26   29

(iii) 104   105   107   106   109

(b) Explain how you can deduce the mean of   54 55   57 56   59
from the mean of   4   5   7   6   9

> Mean shortcut
>
> $$\bar{x} = \frac{\sum (x - a)}{n} + a$$

2. Show how to find the mean of 857   859   854   853   860   853
by first subtracting 850 from each number.

3. Show how to find the mean of 134   132   128   135
137   129   126   135
by first subtracting 130 from each number.

4. (a) Find the mean of   2   –3   –1   5   6   –7   –4   –2

(b) Use the result to deduce the mean of
202 197 199 205 206 193 196 198

• *Check your answers.*

> This method is sometimes called **'scaling'** or **'coding'**.
> We will see it in action later.

Section 9: Simple measures of spread

In this section you will:
- work with range and interquartile range
- meet and use box-and-whisker plots
- understand skewness and outliers

DEVELOPMENT

D9.1: Range and interquartile range

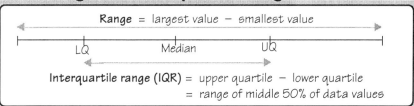

Range = largest value − smallest value

LQ   Median   UQ

Interquartile range (IQR) = upper quartile − lower quartile
= range of middle 50% of data values

1. In the GCSE mock exams, Mary's results were:
   38% 55% 60% 62% 74% 42% 68% 46% 70%
   In the same exams, James' results were:
   46% 50% 68% 38% 95% 76% 50% 60% 52% 56%

   (a) Copy and complete this table:

	Range	IQR	Median	Mean
Mary				
James				

   (b) Which value for which student has distorted the mean ?

   (c) Does this value also distort the range for this student ?

   If there are extreme values (called **outliers**) that distort the mean and range, then the median is a better representative value for the centre of the data, and the inter-quartile range is a better representative value for the spread of the data.

   (d) Which student had the better average GCSE mock mark ?
   Which average did you use to decide ?

   (e) Which student had the most consistent set of marks.
   Which measure of spread did you use to decide ?

2. Mock GCSE
   results for Y11

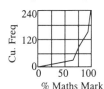
% Maths Mark

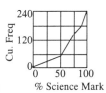
% Science Mark

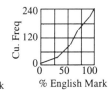
% English Mark

   (a) How many students took these mock exams ?
   (b) In which subject was the median mark the highest ?
   (c) In which subject was the inter-quartile range of the marks the least ?

• Check your answers.

D9.2: Box-and-whisker plots (a.k.a box plots)

A box-and-whisker plot is a diagram which shows the relative positions of the extreme values of the data and the median, Q_2, and quartiles, Q_1 & Q_3.

EXAMPLE   In the GCSE mock exams, Mary's results were:

38%   55%   60%   62%   74%   42%   68%   46%   70%

Draw a box-and-whisker plot for these results.

Min value = 38   Max value = 74

$Q_1 = 44$ $Q_2(\text{median}) = 60$ $Q_3 = 69$

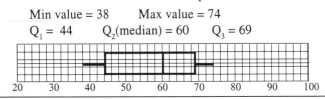

1. (a) Copy the box-and-whisker plot for Mary's results (above).

Below it, draw a box-and-whisker plot for James' results in the same exams:

46%   50%   68%   38%   95%   76%   50%   60%   52%   56%

(b) Using the two box-plots only, say whether each of the following statements is true (T) or false (F):

A: The range of James' results is greater than the range of Mary's results.

B: The IQR of James' results is greater than the IQR of Mary's results.

C: The middle 50% of Mary's results is evenly spaced about the median.

D: The middle 50% of James' results is evenly spaced about the median.

E: The median for James' results is skewed towards the minimum value.

F: Overall, Mary did better than James.

2. The children in classes A and B were each given a set of arithmetic problems to solve. Their times, to the nearest minute, were recorded and they are summarised in the tabel below.

	Class A	Class B
Smallest value	5	10
Largest value	27	26
Q_1	9	13
Q_2	15	15
Q_3	18	22

(a) On graph paper and using the same scale for both, draw box plots to represent these data.

(b) Compare and contrast the results for the two classes.   (Edexcel)

• Check your answers.

D9.3: A mixture of techniques

92 students in Y7 at Turnberry School did three maths tests in the Summer Term.

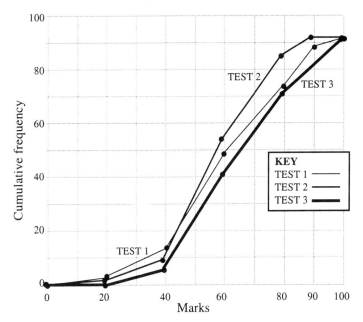

1. Which test was the most difficult ?

2. Which test had at the smallest spread of the middle 50% of marks ?

3. In Test 1, the bottom ten pupils scored less than 30 marks.
   How did the bottom ten pupils do in the other two tests ?

4. In Test 1, the top ten pupils scored more than 86 marks.
   In which test did the top ten pupils do best ?

5. Estimate the values of the medians and quartiles for each test.

The Head of Maths at Turnberry School wants to use one of the above tests as next year's Y7 end-of-year exam. He wants to use the results of this exam to put pupils into sets, so he needs a good spread of marks. He also would like an exam that leaves most pupils with a sense of achievement – not failure.

6. Make box-and-whisker diagrams (side-by-side) for all three tests.
   Which test would you use for the exam ? Explain why you chose it.

• *Check your answers.*

D9.4: Skewness

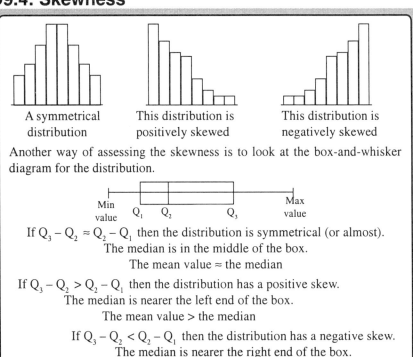

| A symmetrical distribution | This distribution is positively skewed | This distribution is negatively skewed |

Another way of assessing the skewness is to look at the box-and-whisker diagram for the distribution.

If $Q_3 - Q_2 \approx Q_2 - Q_1$ then the distribution is symmetrical (or almost).
The median is in the middle of the box.
The mean value $\approx$ the median

If $Q_3 - Q_2 > Q_2 - Q_1$ then the distribution has a positive skew.
The median is nearer the left end of the box.
The mean value > the median

If $Q_3 - Q_2 < Q_2 - Q_1$ then the distribution has a negative skew.
The median is nearer the right end of the box.
The mean value < the median

1. The following stem and leaf diagram summarises the blood glucose level, in mmol/l, of a patient, measure daily over a period of time.

Blood glucose level   5|0 means 5.0   Totals

														Totals
5	0	0	1	1	1	2	2	3	3	3	4	4		(12)
5	5	5	6	6	7	8	8	9	9					(9)
6	0	1	1	1	2	3	4	4	4	4				(10)
6	5	5	6	7	8	9	9							( )
7	1	1	2	2	2	3								( )
7	5	7	9	9										( )
8	1	1	1	2	2	3	3	4						( )
8	7	9	9											(3)
9	0	1	1	2										(4)
9	5	7	9											(3)

(a) Write down the numbers required to complete the stem-and-leaf diagram.
(b) Find the median and quartiles of this data.
(c) On graph paper, construct a box plot to represent this data.
  Show your scale clearly.
(d) Comment on the skewness of the distribution.   *(Edexcel)*

Section 10: Standard deviation

In this section you will:
- understand and calculate standard deviation for raw and tabulated data
- use a calculator to find the mean and standard deviation of a set of data

DEVELOPMENT

D10.1: The standard deviation from the mean

or **standard deviation (SD)**, for short, gives a measure of the dispersion/spread about the mean value.

Standard deviation is best used when considering the dispersion of a large amount of data, but, in order to understand exactly how standard deviation is calculated, we will first find the standard deviation of a very small sample.

1. 5 ball-bearings have these diameters: 2.6 cm, 2.9 cm, 3 cm, 3.2 cm, 3.3 cm

    (a) Calculate the mean diameter

    (b) *Copy and complete this table:*

diameter	2.6	2.9	3.0	3.2	3.3
deviation from mean	−0.4	...	...	...	+0.3

    (c) We need some measure of the amount of deviation from the mean.
    The total deviation from the mean is no use. Why is it no use ?

    (d) It is the size of the deviation that is important – not whether it is positive or negative. Calculate the sum of the squares of the deviations from the mean.

    (e) The mean square deviation from the mean is 0.06. Show how it is calculated.

    (f) But, to balance the squaring effect from earlier, we now find the square root.

    The standard deviation = $\sqrt{\text{mean square deviation from the mean}}$

    Give its value to 3 d.p.

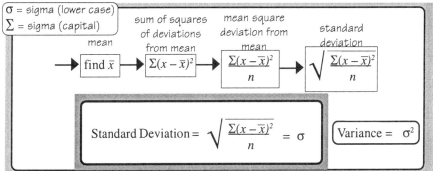

2. Calculate the mean and standard deviation of these test marks.
   Test marks: 11, 12, 15, 16, 17, 18, 19, 20   Show your working.

3. Find the mean, variance and standard deviation of 23, 27, 31, 35, 36
   Give the variance and standard deviation to 2 d.p.

When either the data or the mean are not integers, the formula is more difficult to use. There is an alternative formula which is easier.

$$\sigma = \sqrt{\frac{\Sigma x^2}{n} - \bar{x}^2}$$

This is the most usual, and the most useful, equation for standard deviation for raw data.

4. Use this formula for the data in question 3. Show that it gives the same standard deviation.

5. Calculate the mean, the variance and the standard deviation (to 2 d.p.) of
    15, 19, 20, 20, 21, 21, 27, 29

6. $\bar{x} = 60.8$ $\Sigma x^2 = 56628$ $n = 15$.   Work out the value of σ.

7. $\bar{x} = 56.576$ $\Sigma x^2 = 969696$ $n = 28$.   Work out the value of σ.

8. $\sigma = 1.9773$ $\Sigma x^2 = 7799$ $n = 12$.   Work out the value of $\bar{x}$.

9. $\bar{x} = 98.875$ $\sigma = 23.393$ $n = 16$.   Work out the value of Σx^2.

10. $\bar{x} = 75.25$ $\Sigma x^2 = 45396$ $\sigma = 3.455$.   Work out the value of n.

• *Check your answers.*

D10.2: Standard deviation of tabulated data

An agricultural chemical firm has an experimental farm where it grows potatoes on 25 hectare plots of land. The yields for each plot are given in tonnes/hectare to the nearest 0.1 tonne.

1. (a) *Copy this table and complete the second, third and fourth columns:*

Yield	Frequency f	Midpoint x	fx	$(x - \bar{x})^2$	$f(x - \bar{x})^2$
3.4 – 3.6	3				
3.7 – 4.0	5				
4.1 – 4.4	9				
4.5 – 4.9	8				
	$\Sigma f = \ldots\ldots$		$\Sigma fx = \ldots\ldots$		$\Sigma f(x - \bar{x})^2 = \ldots\ldots$

(b) $\bar{x} = \dfrac{\Sigma fx}{\Sigma f}$ *Evaluate $\bar{x}$*

(c) *Complete the last two columns of the table.*

standard deviation = $\sigma = \sqrt{\dfrac{\Sigma f(x - \bar{x})^2}{\Sigma f}}$ or $\sigma = \sqrt{\dfrac{\Sigma fx^2}{\Sigma f} - \bar{x}^2}$

basic formula   alternative formula

Variance = σ^2

The alternative formula is the most usual, and the most useful, equation for standard deviation for tabulated data.

(d) Calculate the standard deviation of the yields using each of the formulae.

2. A year after the first families moved into the new town, a survey of the ages of the children gave the following results:

Age	under 1	$1 \leq$ age < 2	$2 \leq$ age < 3	$3 \leq$ age < 5	$5 \leq$ age < 7	$7 \leq$ age< 10
f	20	25	19	46	62	38

Calculate the mean, the variance and the standard deviation of this distribution.

• *Check answers.*

D10.3: Using the calculator

> Using statistical functions on a calculator was met in D8.2.

RCL $\bar{x}$ gives the mean

RCL σ_x gives the standard deviation

NOTE: Make sure you clear the memory contents before entering new data.

Find the mean and standard deviation for each set of data values (to 2 d.p.)

1. 51 57 62 49 57 58 53 63 48
2. 63 63 65 66 68 68 68 73
3.

x	36	38	41	42	46	49	50	51
f	1	3	4	5	7	9	5	3

4. Set of GCSE mock marks:

55 64 39 78 97 45 66 29 43 27 36 48 84 66 59
94 89 76 82 48 72 51 68 77 45 88 92 58 63 46

Work out the mean and standard deviation for these exam marks.

• *Check your answers.*

E10.4: Miscellaneous Challenges

1. Machine A is set to cut lengths of wood 100 mm long. To test the accuracy of the machine, a random sample is taken from the output. The sample size is denoted by n and the length in millimetres of each piece of wood is denoted by x. The results are summarised by $n = 50$ $\Sigma x = 5035$ $\Sigma x^2 = 508033$

Calculate the mean and standard deviation of the lengths in the sample, giving your answers correct to 1 d.p.

Machine B is also set ot cut lengths of wood 100 mm long. A random sample of 50 items from this machine has mean 100.2 mm and standard deviation 1.1 mm.

Giving your reasons, comment briefly on the accuracy of the two machines.

(OCR)

2. 2 sets of marks are given in summarised form as follows:

For set X: $n = 20$ $\Sigma x = 1150$ $\Sigma x^2 = 68100$

For set Y: $n = 30$ $\Sigma y = 1800$ $\Sigma(y - y)^2 = 6000$

Calculate the mean and standard deviation of each set of marks and of the combined set of 50 marks.

Section 11: Related sets of data

In this section you will look at what happens to central measures and measures of spread, when all items in the data set are altered in the same way.

DEVELOPMENT
D11.1: What happens when ... ?

1.   5   6   8   9   11
   (a) Calculate the mean and median of this data set.
   (b) Calculate the range and the standard deviation of this data set.

2.   55   56   58   59   61
   This set is formed by adding 50 to each datapoint in the set in question 1.
   (a) Write down what you think the new mean and median will be.
   (b) Calculate the mean and median of this data set.

   (c) Write down what you think the new range and standard deviation will be.
   (d) Calculate the range and the standard deviation of this data set.

3.   45   54   72   81   99
   This set is formed by multiplying each datapoint in the set in question 1 by 9.
   (a) Write down what you think the new mean and median will be.
   (b) Calculate the mean and median of this data set.

   (c) Write down what you think the new range and standard deviation will be.
   (d) Calculate the range and the standard deviation of this data set.

                                             • *Check your answers.*

D11.2: Related data sets

For any set of data:
* the median and the mean are both measures of the centre of the data
* the range, the inter-quartile range and the standard deviation are all measures of the spread of the data about the centre.

If a constant amount p is added to each value in the set, then the spread is unchanged – BUT the mean and the median will be increased by p.

If every value is multiplied by a constant factor k, then the spread will be k times the original spread – AND the mean and the median will be multiplied by k.

1. A box of sweets should contain 30 sweets. A random sample of 50 boxes were tested which had a mean of 30.76 sweets and a standard deviation of 1.05.
   (a) 3 extra sweets are added to each pack for a '10% extra' promotion.
       What should the new mean and standard deviation be ?
   (b) A new 'GIANT' pack is produced which should contain three times the number of sweets. What should the new mean and standard deviation be ?
   (c) What should the new mean and standard deviation be if the number in the '10% extra' box in (a) was doubled ?

S1: Unit 1: Representation of data

Facts and formulae you need to know:

$$\text{Mean} = \bar{x} = \frac{\Sigma x}{n} \qquad \text{Mean} = \bar{x} = \frac{\Sigma fx}{\Sigma f}$$

$$\text{Standard deviation} = \sigma = \sqrt{\frac{\Sigma(x-\bar{x})^2}{n}} \quad \text{or} \quad \sqrt{\frac{\Sigma x^2}{n} - \bar{x}^2}$$

Competence Test S1.1

Body temperatures of 52 Y11 students at Bradfield School, measured to nearest 0.1°C

Temperature	36.0 – 36.3	36.4 – 36.5	36.6 – 36.8	36.9 – 37.1	37.2 – 37.4
Frequency	4	6	18	21	3

1. Is this data discrete or continuous ?   (1A) ①

2. (a) Make a frequency density table for the temperatures.   (2M,5A) ⑭
   (b) Draw a histogram for this distribution.   (2M,5A)

3. (a) Draw a cumulative frequency diagram for this data.   (2M,2A) ⑭
   (b) Estimate the value of the median and the quartiles.   (1M,3A)
   (c) Draw a box-and-whisker diagram for this data.   (3A)
   (d) Estimate how many students had temperatures of 36.75 or above. (1M,1A)
   (e) Comment on the skewness of this data.   (1A)

4. The body temperatures of some Y11 students at Carton High School were measured. ⑤
   Their results are given below:

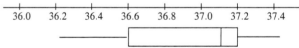

   (a) One of the two groups of students had been doing step-tests just before their
   temperatures were taken. Was this the Bradfield or the Carton students ?
   Explain why you think so.   (2M,1A)
   (b) Comment on the skewness of the Carton H. School distribution.   (2A)

5. Find the mean and standard deviation of the temperatures   (3M,4A) ⑪
   at Bradfield to 3 d.p.

6. Derva High School students did a step-test and their pulse rates   ⑨
   were measured five minutes after the test.

Pulse rate	120-150	150-170	170-180	180-210	210-250
Frequency	5	7	8	12	3

   (a) Estimate the mean of this distribution.   (2M,2A)
   (b) What is the modal class ?   (1A)
   (c) Use interpolation to estimate the median pulse rate.   (2M,2A)

Total = 50

AIMING HIGH

S1

Unit 2
Probability

CONTENTS

	OCR	**AQA**	**Edexcel**
Section 1	All	All	All
Section 2	All	All	All
Section 3	All	All	All
Section 4	All	All	All
Section 5	All	All	All
Section 6	All	All	All
Section 7	All	—	—
Section 8	All	—	—
Section 9	All	—	—

Unit 2: Probability
Section 1 : Basic ideas

In this section you will review:
- basic probability theory and terminology
- notation used in probability formulae

DEVELOPMENT

D1.1 Review

Probability is a measure of likelihood.
To say that the probability that tomorrow will be sunny is 70% or 0.7 means that we would expect, in the long run, 7 out of 10 days to be sunny under the same conditions. This kind of probability would be estimated from statistical weather records.

Experimentally, the probability of an outcome A can be estimated as:

the number of trials for which the outcome A occurred
the total number of trials

A probability obtained from an experiment or a survey can only be an estimate of the true probability. The larger the number of trials there are, the more confident we can be in our estimates.

In some cases, the probabilities can be found theoretically.
If all possible outcomes are EQUALLY LIKELY then the probability of A, denoted by $P(A)$ can be stated as:

$$P(A) = \frac{\text{number of outcomes for which A occurs}}{\text{total number of possible outcomes}} = \frac{n(A)}{n(S)}$$

where **S = the sample space** of all possible outcomes.

An event is a group or set of outcomes. The set can include several outcomes, only one outcome, or even no outcomes.
The list of outcomes making up an event is written in brackets.
The probability $P(A)$ of an event A is the sum of the probabilities that make up A.

EXAMPLE   A dice is tossed For each of the following events, list the outcomes that make up the event and find the probability of the event:
     (a) score = 5   (b) score is more than 3   (c) score = 7
(a) The event A = {5} $P(A) = \frac{1}{6}$
(b) The event B = {4, 5, 6} $P(B) = \frac{3}{6} = \frac{1}{2}$
(c) The event C = { } $P(C) = 0$

Some important results
(1)   The probability of an outcome/event is a number between 0 and 1. $0 \leq P(A) \leq 1$
(2)   A' (A dash) is the event "A does not occur". $P(A') = 1 - P(A)$
(3)   A cannot possibly occur or A is IMPOSSIBLE $\Rightarrow$ $P(A) = 0$
(4)   A must occur or A is CERTAIN $\Rightarrow$ $P(A) = 1$

1. A pupil is to be chosen from among two boys (Matthew and Mark) and three girls (Emily, Mary and Jane). Their names are put onto pieces of paper and drawn at random. What is the probability that the person chosen :
   (a) is a girl   (b) is Mark   (c) has a name not beginning with M ?

2. A counter is drawn at random from a box containing 8 red, 4 blue, 2 green counters. Find the probability that the counter chosen is:
   (a) red   (b) red or green   (c) not red   (d) not green or blue

3. A card is drawn at random from an ordinary pack of 52 playing cards. Find the probability that the card chosen :
   (a) is a red queen   (b) is the 2 of spades   (c) is not a nine
   (d) is the King of Hearts or an ace   (e) is the ace of clubs or any spade.

4. A set of cards is numbered 1 to 25. From this set, one card is drawn at random. Find the probability that the number chosen is :
   (a) greater than 17   (b) a multiple of 3   (c) a multiple of 3 greater than 17

5. Students in a Y12 class were asked how many cups of coffee they had drunk the previous day. The results are given in this table:

Number of cups	0	1	2	3	4	5	6 or more
Number of students	1	3	5	7	5	3	2

   One of these students is chosen at random.
   What is the probability that the student chosen had drunk:
   (a) 3 cups   (b) more than 3 cups   (c) 3 cups or less ?

6. Another group of Y12 students were given the coffee survey. If one student is chosen at random from this group, the probability that they had drunk less than four cups was $^{16}/_{21}$. What was the probability that the student chosen had drunk four cups or more ?

7. Two ordinary dice are thrown. The two scores are recorded.
   (a) How many equally likely outcomes are there ?
   The two scores are added. What is the probability that the total score is:
   (b) 3   (c) less than 5   (d) 10 or more   (e) 7   (f) 1

8. A counter is drawn at random from a box containing 10 red, 6 blue, 5 yellow and 3 white counters. Find the probability that the counter chosen is:
   (a) white   (b) not yellow   (c) red, white or blue   (d) green

9. On a board game, you have to toss an ordinary dice when you reach the entrance to the Caves of Doom. The results of your throw are given here:

Score	1 or 5	2	3	4 or 6
Result	Eaten by monster	pass freely	wait	thrown to wolves

   What is the probability that (a) the monster gets you   (b) you do not die ?

   • Check your answers.

D1.2: Sample space diagrams

Results of combined events

If two events are combined, it often helps to display the results of all the possible combined outcomes on a **Sample Space Diagram**.
Note that the results must all be EQUALLY LIKELY OUTCOMES.

EXAMPLE   Two dice are rolled. Event A is 'the sum of the two numbers obtained'. Display the equally likely outcomes in a sample space diagram and find the probability of getting: (a) a 7   (b) a 12   (c) at least 9

A: Possible outcomes are {2, 3, 4, 5, 6, 7, 8, 9, 10, 11, 12} but these are not equally likely – so you cannot use these on a sample space diagram !

The sample space contains 36 equally likely outcomes.

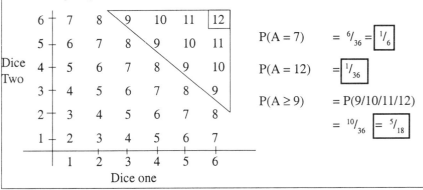

$P(A = 7)$ $= {}^6/_{36} = {}^1/_6$

$P(A = 12)$ $= {}^1/_{36}$

$P(A \geq 9)$ $= P(9/10/11/12)$

$= {}^{10}/_{36} = {}^5/_{18}$

For each of the following problems, draw a sample space diagram to help you find the probabilities asked for.

1. Two dice are thrown. Find the probability that :
   (a) the sum of the two numbers is 5
   (b) the two dice show the same number
   (c) the sum of the two numbers is less than 6

2. Two dice are thrown. Find the probability that :
   (a) the numbers on the two dice differ by 3
   (b) the numbers on the two dice differ by more than 3

3. A dice and a fair coin are thrown together. Find the probability that you get:
   (a) a head and a 5   (b) a tail and less than 5   (c) a head and an odd number

4. A dice and two fair coins are thrown. List all equally likely possible outcomes on a sample space diagram and find the probability of getting:
   (a) two heads and a number more than 4
   (b) a head, a tail and an even number
   (c) a 5 and at least one tail
   (d) an odd number and the coins showing the same face.

• *Check your answers.*

Section 2: The addition rule

In this section you will :
* meet and work with set notation;
* use the addition rule to calculate probabilities.

DEVELOPMENT

D2.1: Using set diagrams

This diagram represents a Y12 tutor group.
It shows the number of students who got high
GCSE grades (A or B) in French and German .

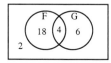

How many students …
1. … got a high grade in both French and German ?
2. … got a high grade in French only ?
3. … got a high grade in French ?
4. … got a high grade in either French or German or both ?
5. … did not get a high grade in either French or German ?
6. … are there in this Y12 tutor group ?

A student is chosen at random from this tutor group.

What is the probability that the student chosen …
7. … got a high grade in both French and German ?
8. … got a high grade in French only ?
9. … got a high grade in French ?
10. … got a high grade in either French or German or both ? • *Check answers*
11. … did not get a high grade in either French or German ? *before continuing.*

This kind of diagram is called a **Venn Diagram.**
It is useful for displaying overlapping sets of data.

In this tutor group, S is the set of students who play for a school
sports team and O is the set of students who play for a sports team
outside school.

How many students…
12. … are there in the group ?
13. … play for a school team <u>and</u> a team outside school ?
14. … play for a school team <u>or</u> a team outside school ?

A student is chosen at random from this tutor group.

What is the probability that the student chosen …
15. … plays for a school team <u>and</u> a team outside school ?
16. … plays for a school team <u>or</u> a team outside school ?
17. … plays for a team outside school but not for a school team ?
18. … plays for a team outside school ?
19. … plays for a school team ? • *Check answers.*

D2.2: The addition rule for probability

We know that: $P(A) = \dfrac{n(A)}{n(S)}$ where $n(A)$ = number of elements in A
and $n(S)$ = number of elements in the sample space

We also know that: ⬤ = ⬤ + ⬤ − ⬤

Set notation
∪ ≡ 'union' but is usually read as 'or'.
∩ ≡ 'intersection' but is usually read as 'and'.

$n(A \text{ or } B) = n(A) + n(B) - n(A \text{ and } B)$

$\Rightarrow \quad \dfrac{n(A \text{ or } B)}{n(S)} = \dfrac{n(A)}{n(S)} + \dfrac{n(B)}{n(S)} - \dfrac{n(A \text{ and } B)}{n(S)}$

Hence

$$P(A \text{ or } B) = P(A) + P(B) - P(A \text{ and } B)$$

Or, in set notation,

$$P(A \cup B) = P(A) + P(B) - P(A \cap B)$$

This is **the addition rule**. It is ALWAYS true for any events A and B.

EXAMPLE   In a group of students, 3 of the 9 female students wear glasses, as do 4 of the 11 male students.
What is the probability that a student chosen at random from this group is either female or wears glasses ?

A: Let F = "female students" and G = "students who wear glasses"

$n(F) = 9$ ⎤ $P(F) = {}^9/_{20}$
$n(F \text{ and } G) = 3$ ⎬ $\Rightarrow$ $P(F \text{ and } G) = {}^3/_{20}$
$n(G) = 7$ ⎦ $P(G) = {}^7/_{20}$

$P(F \text{ or } G) = P(F) + P(G) - P(F \text{ and } G) = {}^9/_{20} + {}^7/_{20} - {}^3/_{20} = \boxed{{}^{13}/_{20}}$

Use the addition rule to solve each of these problems :

1. A octahedral dice is thrown. Its faces are numbered 1, 2, ... 8.
   What is the probability that the numbered obtained is:
   (a) even   (b) prime   (c) even and prime   (d) even or prime ?

2. 24 families live in one street. 8 of these families have a computer.
   17 families have a video recorder. 6 families have both. A family is chosen at random. What is the probability that the family chosen will have neither ?

3. The probability that a boy in 11BL is in the basketball team is 0.4. The probability that he is in the football team is 0.3. The probability that he is in both teams is 0.15. Find the probability that a boy chosen at random from 11BL is in the basketball team or the football team.

4. In 10BY, 10 of the 30 students take Spanish. 4 of the 17 boys take Spanish, What is the probability that a student chosen at random from 10BY is either a boy or takes Spanish ?

D2.3: Probabilities of mutually exclusive events

$P(A \cap B)$
$\equiv P(A$ and $B)$

Mutually exclusive events cannot occur together.
If A and B are mutually exclusive events, $p(A \cap B) = 0$

$P(A \cup B)$
$\equiv P(A$ or $B)$

If A and B are mutually exclusive events $P(A \cup B) = P(A) + P(B)$

1. *Write down the probability of getting:*
   (a) a black counter (B).
   (b) a white counter (W).
   (c) Does P(B or W) = P(B) + P(W) ?
   Explain why or why not.

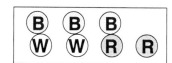

2. *Write down the probability of getting:*
   (a) a red counter (R).
   (b) not a white counter (not W).
   (c) Does P(R or not W) = P(R) + P(not W) ?
   Explain why or why not.

3.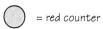

   Write down the probability of getting:
   (a) a white counter (W)
   (b) a red counter (R)
   (c) a 2
   (d) a 1
   (e) a 1 or a 2

   Key: ⬤ = red counter
          ◯ = white counter

   (f) Does P(1 $\cup$ 2) = P(1) + P(2) ?
   Explain why or why not.
   (g) Does P(red $\cup$ 1) = P(red) + P(1) ?
   Explain why or why not.

4. In the Gartside Youth Club:
   • P(girl wears glasses) = 0.2
   • P(girl has dark hair) = 0.4
   • P(girl has red hair) = 0.15

   (a) Explain why P(girl has dark hair or red hair) = 0.4 + 0.15

   (b) Explain why P(girl has dark hair or wears glasses) ≠ 0.2 + 0.4

* Challenge !

   You are also given the information that
   P(girl has dark hair <u>and</u> wears glasses) = 0.05

   (c) Work out P(girl wears glasses and does not have dark hair)

   (d) Work out P(girl has dark hair or wears glasses)

   • *Check your answers.*

Section 3: Tree diagrams

In this section you will:
- decide whether events are independent
- review the use of tree diagrams to calculate probabilities of both independent and dependent compound events.

DEVELOPMENT

D3.1: Independent events

Two events are **independent** if the probability of each event is unaffected by the result of the other event.

EXAMPLE   Three names are put onto pieces of paper and put into a box. One piece of paper is drawn out at random. The name is recorded. A second draw is made at random from the box. The second name is recorded.

Case 1:   After the first draw, the piece of paper is put back into the box. The second draw is not affected by the result of the first draw. The two events <u>are independent.</u>

Case 2:   After the first draw, the piece of paper is NOT put back into the box. The second draw IS affected by the result of the first draw. The two events <u>are not independent.</u>

For each pair of events, state whether they are independent (I) or not independent (N).

1.   Throw a dice. Toss a coin.

2.   Oversleep. Miss the school bus.

3.   Oversleep. Get a good mark for an English essay.

4.   Take one card unseen from a shuffled pack of cards.
     Look at it and replace it. Take another card.

5.   Take one card unseen from a shuffled pack of cards.
     Look at it but do not replace it. Take another card.

6.   Throw a dice. Throw the dice again.

7.   15 cans of drink are for sale. Bob chooses one and buys it. Ann chooses a can.

8.   15 cans of drink are for sale. Bob chooses one and then puts it back.
     Ann chooses a can.

9.   Choose a counter from a box of counters. Put it back. Choose a second counter.

10. Choose a counter from a box of counters. Do not put it back.
     Choose a second counter.

11. Listen to the weather forecast. Take an umbrella when you go out.

• *Check your answers.*

D3.2: Tree diagrams

Remember:
A' (A dash) is the event
"A does not occur".
$P(A') = 1 - P(A)$

1. On Wednesdays, Fred goes to Bingo.
The probability he will win a prize at Bingo is 0.15.
The probability that he will win a raffle prize is 0.1

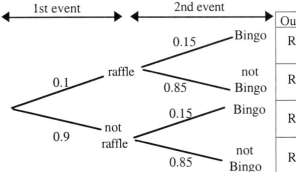

	1st event	2nd event		
			Outcomes	Probabilities
			R and B	0.015
			R and B'	0.185
			R' and B	....
			R' and B'	....

(a) Copy the tree diagram and fill in the two missing probabilities.

Use your copy of the tree diagram to find the probability that:

(b) Fred does not win either prize.

(c) Fred wins just one prize.

2. Packet of flower seeds
It is known that:
- $^2/_3$ will have white flowers
- $^1/_3$ will have yellow flowers
- $^3/_5$ of white flowers will germinate
- $^9/_{10}$ of yellow flowers will germinate

(a) *Copy and complete this tree diagram.*

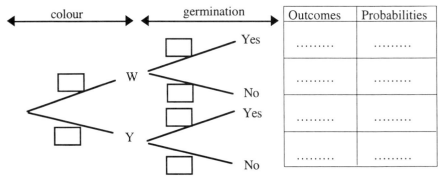

	colour	germination	Outcomes	Probabilities
			Yes	....
			No	....
			Yes	....
			No	....

(b) Calculate the probability that any seed, chosen at random, will germinate.

D3.3: Tree diagrams for dependent events

These tree diagrams are constructed and used in the exactly
the same way as for independent events
EXCEPT THAT
**the outcomes of the first event affect the probabilities of the
second, and any subsequent, events.**

1. One counter is chosen and not replaced.
A second counter is chosen.

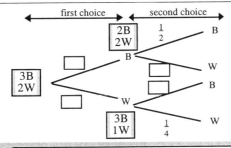

Note: the boxes like 3B/2W are not essential but are useful
when calculating the probabilities at each stage.

(a) *Copy and complete this tree diagram.*

Use the tree diagram to calculate these probabilities:
(b) p(two the same colour)   (c) p(just one counter is black)
(d) p(at least one counter is white)

2. A bag of sweets contains 2 orange, 4 white and 6 green sweets.
The wrapped sweets are identical until opened.
Dwork chooses one and eats it.
Dwork   Gorbag then takes one.   *Gorbag*

(a) *Copy and complete this tree diagram:*

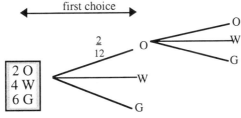

Calculate the probability that:
(b) both choose orange   (c) both sweets are the same colour
(d) at least one green one is chosen.   • *Check answers.*

D3.4: Dependent and independent events

1. A survey showed that:
   - $2/5$ of the population wear glasses
   - $1/9$ of the population is left handed

   (a) Draw a tree diagram to illustrate this information.
   (b) What is the probability that anyone selected at random
      (i) is right handed and does not wear glasses ?
      (ii) is left-handed and wears glasses ?

2. The probability that it will be sunny tomorrow is $1/3$.
   If it sunny, the probability that Juno will play tennis is $4/5$.
   If it is not sunny, the probability that she plays tennis is only $2/5$.
   Draw a tree diagram and work out the probability that she plays tennis tomorrow.

3. The probability that I am late for work each morning is 0.1.
   Draw a tree diagram and find the probability that, on two consecutive mornings,
   I am late (a) twice (b) once (c) at least once.

4. At the end of extra time, in a football semi-final, the score is 3-3. A penalty shoot out
   takes place, where five players from each team take a penalty shot at goal.

   (a) In a simple model, it is assumed that each player has a probability of 0.8 of
       scoring a goal.

   | 1st shot | 2nd shot | Outcomes | Probability |

   G

   G'

   If G means 'goal' then G' means 'not a goal'

   (i) Complete this tree diagram to show the outcomes and probabilities after the
       first two penalties for one of the teams.
   (ii) What is the probability that just one goal is scored ?
   (iii) What is the probability that at least one goal has been scored ?

   (b) When each team has taken three penalty shots, the score is 2-2. The tension is
       mounting. For the last two shots, the simple model needs to be refined.
       For the fourth shot, assume the probability of scoring is 0.7.
       If a goal is scored, the probability of scoring on the fifth shot remains 0.7.
       If the fourth player misses, the probability of scoring on the fifth shot falls to 0.6.

   (i) Draw a tree diagram to show the outcomes and probabilities for the fourth and
       fifth penalty shots for one of the teams.
   (ii) What is the probability that just one goal is scored from the last two shots ?
   (iii) Show that the probability that the fifth player scored is $6/13$, given that there
         was just one goal from the last two shots.

• Check your answers.

Section 4: The multiplication rule

In this section you will:
* meet and use the multiplication rule for independent events
* use the multiplication and addition rules for independent exclusive events

DEVELOPMENT

D4.1: The multiplication rule for independent events

If A and B are independent events

$$P(A \text{ and } B) = P(A) \times P(B)$$

or $P(A \cap B) = P(A) \times P(B)$

$\cap$ = and
$\cup$ = or

EXAMPLE   A coin is tossed. A dice is thrown.
Calculate the probability of getting a 'head' and a '5 or 6'

$P(H) = \frac{1}{2}$ $P(5 \text{ or } 6) = \frac{2}{6} = \frac{1}{3}$

$P(H \text{ and } 5 \text{ or } 6) = P(H) \times P(5 \text{ or } 6) = \frac{1}{2} \times \frac{1}{3} = \boxed{\frac{1}{6}}$

1. | Boys: Mark Adam   Clint | | Girls: Ellen   Sue |

   One boy and one girl are chosen at random.
   (a) Work out the probability that Adam and Sue are chosen.
   (b) Work out the probability that Ellen and anyone but Adam are chosen.

2.

   P(1st set of traffic lights is green) = 0.3 P(2nd set of traffic lights is green) = 0.4
   Work out the probability that:
   (a) Phil can cycle through both sets of lights without stopping.
   (b) Phil has to stop at both sets of lights.

3. | A counter is chosen from these at random. |
   | Its colour is recorded. It is replaced. |
   | A second counter is chosen. |

   (a) What is the probability that two blue counters were chosen ?
   (b) What is the probability that two red counters were chosen ?

4. Beryl challenges Sara to a tennis match and a swimming race.
   The probability that Beryl will win the tennis match is 0.6
   The probability that Sara will win the swiiming race is 0.7
   (a) What is the probability that Beryl wins both ?
   (b) What is the probability that Sara wins both ?

5. A fair dice is thrown four times.
   What is the probability of getting four sixes ?

   • *Check your answers.*

D4.2: Using the multiplication and addition rules

If A and B are independent events $\quad$ P(A and B) = P(A $\cap$ B) = P(A) x P(B)

If C and D are mutually exclusive events $\quad$ P(C or D) = P(C $\cup$ D) = P(C) + P(D)

If E and DF are NOT mutually exclusive events $\quad$ P(E $\cup$ F) = P(E) + P(F) – P(E $\cap$ F)

Both these rules can be extended to any number of events.

If A' is the event that A does not happen $\quad$ P(A') = 1 – P(A)

$\cap$ = and
$\cup$ = or

EXAMPLE $\quad$ The probability of getting a 'head' with a biased coin is $\frac{1}{3}$
The coin is tossed three times.

Work out the probability of getting :

(a) 3 heads $\quad$ (b) exactly one head $\quad$ (c) no heads $\quad$ (d) at least one head

(a) P(HHH) = P(H) x P(H) x P(H) = $(\frac{1}{3})^3$ = $\boxed{\frac{1}{27}}$

(b) P(exactly 1 head) $\quad$ = P(HTT) + P(THT) + P(TTH)

$\quad = \frac{1}{3} \times \frac{2}{3} \times \frac{2}{3} + \frac{2}{3} \times \frac{1}{3} \times \frac{2}{3} + \frac{2}{3} \times \frac{2}{3} \times \frac{1}{3}$

$\quad = 3 \times \frac{4}{27} = \boxed{\frac{4}{9}}$

(b) P(no heads) $\quad$ = P(TTT) = $\frac{2}{3} \times \frac{2}{3} \times \frac{2}{3}$ = $\boxed{\frac{8}{27}}$

(d) P(at least one head) = 1 – P(no heads) = 1 – $\frac{8}{27}$ = $\boxed{\frac{19}{27}}$

1. A fair dice is tossed three times. Work out the probability of getting:
   (a) three sixes $\quad$ (b) exactly two sixes $\quad$ (c) no sixes $\quad$ (d) at least one six

2. A pair of fair dice is thrown.
   (a) What is the probability of getting a double 6 ?
   (b) What is the probability of getting no double sixes in 25 throws ?
   (c) A 17th century gambler used to bet his friends that he would get at least one double six in 25 throws of a pair of dice.
   Work out the probability of this happening.

3. A fair dice has its faces labelled 1,1,1,2,2,3.
   (a) What is the probability of getting two 2s in two throws ?
   (b) What is the probability of getting exactly two 2s in three throws ?
   (d) What is the probability of getting no 2s in three throws ?
   (b) What is the probability of getting at least one 2 in three throws ?

4. When Ella serves during a game of table tennis, the probability that she wins the point is 0.6.
   For the first two points of any game, calculate the probability that:
   (a) she wins both points $\quad$ (b) she wins exactly one point $\quad$ (c) she loses both points

5. Assume that birthdays are spread evenly over a year of 365 days.
   (a) Work out the probability that: (i) two people have different birthdays
   $\hspace{6.5cm}$ (ii) three people have different birthdays
   (b) What is the probability that 10 people all have different birthdays ?
   (c) What is the probability that, in a group of 10 people, at least 2 of them have the same birthday ?
   (d) Show that, if there are 23 in the group, the probability of at least two of them having the same birthday would be more than 0.5

Section 5: Conditional probability

In this section you will:
* meet conditional probability
* meet and use the multiplication rule for dependent events

DEVELOPMENT

D5.1: Conditional probability

1. A group of 30 students put themselves into the
   following categories according to whether they had
   fair hair (F), long hair (L), or blue eyes (B)
   One student is chosen at random.
   The probability that the student has fair hair is $^{15}/_{30}$ or $^1/_2$

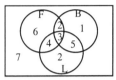

Work out the probability that the student chosen:
(a) has blue eyes   (b) has blue eyes and fair hair
(c) has long fair hair and blue eyes (d) has blue eyes and short hair

The probability that the student has long hair given that (s)he has fair hair is $^7/_{15}$
[7 out of the 15 fair haired students has long hair]
Work out the probability that the student chosen:
(e) has blue eyes, given that (s)he has long hair
(f) has long hair, given that (s)he has blue eyes
(g) has fair hair, given that (s)he has blue eyes
(h) has long hair, given that (s)he does not have blue eyes

> The last four probabilities are called **conditional probabilities**.

2. A card is picked at random from a standard 52 card pack.
   Work out:
   (a) P(heart)   (b) P(King)   (c) P(King, given that it is a heart)
   (d) P(Heart, given that it is a King)   (e) P(King, given that it is not a heart)

> The shorthand notation for P(A, given B) is P(A/B)

3. f= female students   b = has blue eyes   A student is chosen at random.
   Work out:

   (a) P(f)   (b) P(f')   (c) P(b)   (d) P(b /f)
   (e) P(f/b)   (f) P(b/f')   (g) P(f/b')   (h) P(f'/b')

4. A bag contains 3 white counters and 5 green counters. 2 counters are chosen at random.
   Work out: (a) P(second is W/ first is G)   (b) P(second is G/ first is G)
   (c) P(second is G/ first is W)

5. One house in Mulberry Street is chosen at random.

   (a) Given that the house chosen has a computer,
       the probability that it also has a video recorder is $^4/_9$.
       Show how this is calculated.
   (b) Given that the house chosen has a video recorder,
       what is the probability that it also has a computer ?   • *Check your answers.*

D5.2: The multiplication rule for dependent events

> Independent events
>
> $P(A \cap B) = P(A) \times P(B)$
>
> Dependent events
>
> $P(A \cap B) = P(A) \times P(B$, given that A has already occurred)
>
> $P(A \cap B) = P(A) \times P(B/A)$ This is the more general form
> or $= P(B) \times P(A/B)$ for the multiplication rule.

> $P(A \cap B)$
> $\equiv P(A$ and $B)$

EXAMPLE

$P(BB) = P(B) \times P(B/B) = \frac{4}{7} \times \frac{3}{6} = \boxed{\frac{2}{7}}$

$P(WW) = P(W) \times P(W/W) = \frac{3}{7} \times \frac{2}{6} = \boxed{\frac{1}{7}}$

$P(\text{one of each}) = P(B/W) + P(W/B)$
$= [P(B) \times P(W/B)] + [P(W) \times P(B/W)]$
$= [\frac{3}{7} \times \frac{4}{6}] + [\frac{4}{7} \times \frac{3}{6}]$
$= \frac{12}{42} + \frac{12}{42} = \frac{24}{42} = \boxed{\frac{4}{7}}$

(B) (B)
(B) (B)
(W) (W)
(W)

1. A bag contains 4 red counters and 6 white counters. A counter is picked at random from the bag and not replaced. A second counter is then chosen.
   Calculate the probability that:
   (a) the second counter is white, given that the first counter is white
   (b) both counters are white
   (c) the counters are of different colours.

2. Two students are to be chosen at random from this group of eleven students.
   Calculate the probability that:
   (a) the first student chosen is a girl

Boys		Girls		
Ian	Peter	Joanne		Nic
John	Rob	Laura	Catherine	
		Liz	Ruth	Sue

   (b) the second student chosen is a girl, given that the first choice was a girl
   (c) both students are girls
   (d) one boy and one girl are chosen, in either order

> Note that you cannot choose both together.
> You must always choose one, then the other.

3. Two cards are dealt from a shuffled pack of 52 cards.
   Work out the probability that:
   (a) both cards are diamonds
   (b) the first card is a diamond and the second is a spade
   (c) the second card is a diamond, given that the first is a club
   (d) the second card is a diamond, given that the first is a diamond

• *Check answers*

Section 6: Putting it all together

In this section you will:
- work with probability relationships and tree diagrams
- work with probability rules and other relationships
- apply probability rules and relationships to contextual problems
- calculate conditional probabilities in a variety of contexts

DEVELOPMENT

D6.1: Probability relationships and tree diagrams

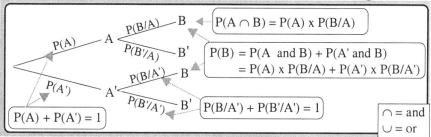

$P(A \cap B) = P(A) \times P(B/A)$

$P(B) = P(A \text{ and } B) + P(A' \text{ and } B)$
$= P(A) \times P(B/A) + P(A') \times P(B/A')$

$P(B/A') + P(B'/A') = 1$

$P(A) + P(A') = 1$

$\cap$ = and
$\cup$ = or

For each question, draw a tree diagram and use it to work out the probabilities:

1. Given: $P(A) = 0.7$ $\quad P(B/A) = 0.4$ $\quad P(B'/A') = 0.8$

   Work out: (a) P(A and B) (b) P(A') (c) P(B/A')
   (d) P(B'/A) (e) P(A' and B') (f) P(B)

2. Given: $P(R') = 0.6$ $\quad P(S/R') = 0.4$ $\quad P(R \cap S) = 0.04$

   Work out: (a) P(R) (b) P(S/R) (c) P(S ∩ R')
   (d) P(S) (e) P(S') (f) P(S'/R')

3. Given: $P(X) = \frac{1}{4}$ $\quad P(Y/X) = \frac{4}{5}$ $\quad P(Y'/X') = \frac{3}{7}$

   Work out: (a) P(Y/X') (b) P(X ∩ Y) (c) P(X' ∩ Y)
   (d) P(Y)

4. Given: $P(R) = \frac{7}{25}$ $\quad P(S/R) = \frac{5}{7}$ $\quad P(S) = \frac{11}{25}$

   Work out: (a) P(R and S) (b) P(S/R')

5. Given: $P(C) = 0.7$ $\quad P(C \text{ and } D) = 0.35$ $\quad P(D) = 0.56$

   Work out: (a) P(D/C) (b) P(C and D') (c) P(C' and D)
   (d) P(D/C') (e) P(D'/C') (f) P(C' and D')

• Check your answers.

D6.2: Probability rules and relationships

Addition rule	$P(A \cup B)$	$= P(A) + P(B) - P(A \text{ and } B)$

If C and D are **mutually exclusive events** then $P(C \text{ and } D) = 0$

$$\Rightarrow \quad P(C \cup D) = P(C) + P(D)$$

A or B ≡ A or B or both

Multiplication rule	$P(A \cap B)$	$= P(A) \times P(B/A)$
or		$= P(B) \times P(A/B)$

Chyps

If C and D are **independent events** then $P(D/C) = P(D)$

$$\Rightarrow \quad P(C \cap D) = P(C) \times P(D)$$

$$P(B/A) = \frac{P(A \text{ and } B)}{P(B)}$$

Complementary events

If A' is the event that A does not happen then $P(A') = 1 - P(A)$

$$P(B) = P(A \text{ and } B) + P(A' \text{ and } B)$$
$$= P(A) \times P(B/A) + P(A') \times P(B/A')$$

$\cap$ = and
$\cup$ = or

Use the above rules to work out the exact values of the probabilities:

1. | Given: | $P(A) = 0.4$ | $P(B) = 0.7$ | $P(B/A) = 0.35$ | $P(C \text{ and } A) = 0.2$ |

   Work out: (a) $P(A \text{ and } B)$ (b) $P(A/B)$ (c) $P(C/A)$

2. | Given: | $P(M) = {}^{7}/_{20}$ | $P(N) = {}^{9}/_{20}$ | $P(M/N) = {}^{4}/_{9}$ |

   Work out: (a) $P(M \cap N)$ (b) $P(N/M)$ (c) $P(M \cup N)$

3. | Given: | $P(A) = 0.9$ | $P(B/A) = 0.4$ | $P(B/A') = 0.3$ |

   Work out: (a) $P(A')$ (b) $P(B)$ (c) $P(B')$
              (d) $P(A \text{ and } B)$ (e) $P(A/B)$

4. | Given: | $P(R) = 0.6$ | $P(T) = 0.4$ | $P(R \text{ or } T) = 0.8$ |

   Work out: (a) $P(R \text{ or } T)$ (b) $P(R/T)$ (c) $P(T/R)$
              (d) $P(R')$ (e) $P(T/R')$

5. | Given: | $P(A) = {}^{1}/_{4}$ | $P(B) = {}^{2}/_{5}$ | B is independent of A |

   Work out: (a) $P(A \text{ and } B)$ (b) $P(A \text{ or } B \text{ or both})$
              (c) P(both A and B occur given that A occurs)

6. | Given: | $P(M) = {}^{1}/_{4}$ | $P(N) = {}^{1}/_{3}$ | $P(M \text{ or } N) = {}^{5}/_{12}$ |

   Work out: (a) $P(M \text{ and } N)$ (b) $P(M/N)$
              (c) P(M given that N does not occur)

• *Check your answers.*

D6.3: Conditional probability problems

EXAMPLE   Mike and Abe are taking the last two shots in a football penalty shoot out. The probability that Mike will miss is 0.2
If Mike scores, the probability that Abe will also score is 0.7
If Mike misses, the probability that Abe will also miss is 0.4

Work out the probability that : (a) they both score
    (b)   Abe scores a goal   (c) they both score, given that Abe scores

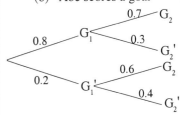

(a) P(both score) $= 0.8 \times 0.7 = \boxed{0.56}$

(b) P(Abe scores) $= P(G_1,G_2) + P(G_1',G_2)$
$= 0.56 + 0.12$
$= \boxed{0.68}$

(c) P(both score given that Abe scores) $= \dfrac{\text{P(both score and Abe scores)}}{\text{P(Abe scores)}}$

Hint: Conditional probability calculations often involve values calculated earlier in the problem.
These are easier to pick up if labellled clearly
- for example : (a) P(both score) = 0.56,
rather than   (a) 0.56,

$= \dfrac{\text{P(both score)}}{\text{P(Abe scores)}} = \dfrac{0.56}{0.68} = \dfrac{14}{17}$

In this case the event 'both score and Abe scores' is the same as 'both scores'. It is not always so.

1. A box contains 12 milk chocolates and 8 dark chocolates.
Two chocolates are taken at random, one after the other.
Calculate the probability that :
    (a) both are milk chocolates   (b) one of each kind is taken
    (c) both are milk chocolates, given that the second is a milk chocolate.

2. Ellie plays regularly at the Ashlands Golf Club. She finds the drive to the number seven green particularly tricky. Over several years, she calculates that she hits a straight drive 80% of the time when the weather is not windy, but only 30% of the time when it is windy. The weather is windy on 55% of all days.
    (a) Calculate the probability that, on any day picked at random, she will hit a straight drive.
    (b) Given that she fails to hit a straight drive, show that the probability that it is windy is 0.811.

3. A die is biased so that, when it is rolled, the probability of obtaining a score of 6 is $\frac{1}{4}$. The probabilities of obtaining each of the other five scores 1, 2, 3, 4, 5 are all equal.
Calculate the probability of obtaining a score of 5 with this biased die.
    (i) The biased die and an unbiased die are now rolled together. Calculate the probability that the total score is 11 or more.
    (ii) The two dice are rolled again. Given that the total score is 11 or more, calculate the probability that the score on the biased die is 6.   *(OCR)*

4. 0.04% of the population are carriers of the rare disease TDQ. A test has been developed to detect carriers of TDQ so that they may be offered treatment before the disease develops to its fatal stage. The test always gives a positive response to carriers but it also gives a positive response to 2% of the non-carriers.

(a) Calculate the probability that the test will give a positive response to a person chosen at random.

(b) The test is applied to a person chosen at random. Given that the response is positive. work out, to 4 d.p., the probability that the person tested is not a carrier.

(b) Is this test suitable for mass screening purposes ? Explain why or why not.

5. A company makes light meters, and the probability that a randomly chosen meter is faulty is 0.04. In a quality control process, each meter is checked and either accepted or rejected. For a faulty meter, the probability that it will be rejected is 0.84. For a meter with no faults, the probability that it will be rejected is 0.01.

Find the probability that :

(i) a randomly chosen meter will be faulty and will be accepted

(ii) a randomly chosen meter will be accepted

(iii) a randomly chosen meter will be faulty, given that the quality control process rejects it. *(OCR)*

6. The probabilities of events A and B are P(A) and P(B) respectively.

$$P(A) = \frac{5}{12} \qquad P(A \cap B) = \frac{1}{6} \qquad P(A \cup B) = q$$

Find, in terms of q,   (a) P(B)   (b) P(A/B)

Given that A and B are independent events   (c) find the value of q. *(Edexcel)*

7. A club social committee consists of eight people, two of whom are Nicky and Sam. Two of the eight committee members are to be chosen at random to organise the next club disco.

By considering the tree diagram, or otherwise,

(i) find the probability that both Nicky and Sam are chosen

(ii) find the probability that both Nicky and Sam are chosen, given that at least one of Nicky and Sam is chosen. *(OCR)*

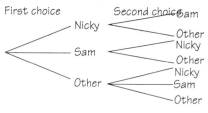

8. A group of girls at a school is entered for Advanced Level Modules. Each girls takes only module M1 or only module M2 or both M1 and M2. The probability that a girls is taking M2 given that she is taking M1 is $\frac{1}{5}$ The probability that a girls is taking M1 given that she is taking M2 is $\frac{1}{3}$

Find the probability that

(a) a girl selected at random is taking both M1 and M2

(b) a girl selected at random is taking only M1   *(Edexcel)*

9. Last year, the employees of a firm either received no pay rise, a small pay rise or a large pay rise. The following table show the number in each category, classified by whether they were weekly paid or monthly paid.

	No pay rise	Small pay rise	Large pay rise
Weekly paid	25	85	5
Monthly paid	4	8	23

A tax inspector decides to investigate the tax affairs of an employee selected at random.
D is the event that a weekly employee is selected.
   E is the event that an employee who received no py rise is selected.
   D' and E' are the events "not D" and "notE" respectively.
Find: (a) P(D)   (b) P(D∪E)   (c) P(D'∩E')
F is the event that an employee is female.
 (d) Given that $P(F') = 0.8$, find the number of female employees.
 (e) Interpret P(D/F) in the context of this question.
 (f) Given that $P(D∩F) = 0.1$, find P(D/F)   *(AQA)*

10. Two events A and B are such that $P(A \text{ or } B) = \frac{5}{8}$ $P(A) = \frac{7}{12}$ $P(\text{not } B) = \frac{3}{4}$
 (a) Calculate: (i) P(B)   (ii) P(A and B) (iii) P(A/B)
 (b) Determine, with a reason, wheterh A and B are independent. *(AQA)*

11. A maker of telescopes uses three suppliers of lenses, A, B and C. The maker receives 40% of her lenses from A, 35% from B and the rest from C. Of the lenses, 2% of those supplied by A are faulty, 1% of those supplied by B are faulty and $1\frac{1}{2}$% of those supplied by C are faulty. One lens is to be selected at random from the maker's stock of lenses.
 (a) Calculate the probability that the lens selected is faulty.
Given that the lens selected is *not* faulty   *(Edexcel)*
 (b) calculate, to 3 d.p., the probability that the lens selected was supplied by B.

12. Two dice are numbered 1, 2, 3, 4, 5, 6. They appear identical. However, one is fair and, with the other dice, probability of getting a 6 is $\frac{1}{2}$
 (i) A dice is chosen at random and thrown once.
  (a) What is the probability of choosing the fair dice ?
  (b) If the fair dice is chosen, what is the probability of getting a 6 ?
  (c) What is the probability of choosing a fair dice and getting a six ?
  (d) What is the probability of getting a six ?
  (e) What is the probability that the dice is biased, given that a 6 is thrown ?
 (ii) A dice is chosen at random and thrown twice.
  (a) What is the probability of choosing the fair dice and getting a double 6 ?
  (b) What is the probability of choosing the biased dice and getting a double 6 ?
  (c) What is the probability of getting a double 6 ?
  (d) What is the probability that the dice is biased, given that a double 6 is thrown ?
 (iii) A dice is chosen at random and thrown n times.
  (a) Show that the probability of getting n sixes is $\frac{1}{2} (\frac{1}{12})^n (2^n + 1)$
  (b) Show that the probability that the dice is biased, given that n sixes is thrown
   is $\frac{1}{(2^n + 1)}$

Section 7: Permutations

In this section you will meet and work with:
- factorials
- permutations of distinct items
- permutations of items that are not all distinct
- permutations where unlimited repetition is permitted

DEVELOPMENT

D7.1: Factorials

$$n! = n \times (n-1) \times (n-2) \times (n-3) \times \ldots \times 3 \times 2 \times 1$$
$n!$ is read as "n factorial"

1. *Evaluate:*   (a) 3!   (b) 2!   (c) 5!   (d) 6!

EXAMPLES $\dfrac{7!}{3!} = \dfrac{7 \times 6 \times 5 \times 4 \times \cancel{3} \times \cancel{2} \times \cancel{1}}{\cancel{3} \times \cancel{2} \times \cancel{1}} = \boxed{840}$

Shortcut: $\dfrac{10!}{7!} = 10 \times 9 \times 8 = \boxed{720}$

> 7! cancels the last 7 numbers in 10!   *Gizmo*

2. *Evaluate:*   (a) $\dfrac{6!}{4!}$ (b) $\dfrac{12!}{9!}$ (c) $\dfrac{8!}{5!}$ (d) $\dfrac{20!}{18!}$

3. *Write using factorials:*   (a) $7 \times 6 \times 5$
   (b) $21 \times 20 \times 19 \times 18$ (c) $15 \times 14 \times 13 \times 12 \times 11 \times 10$

EXAMPLE $\dfrac{9!}{3!6!} = \dfrac{9!}{6!} \times \dfrac{1}{3!} = \dfrac{\overset{3}{\cancel{9}} \times \overset{4}{\cancel{8}} \times 7}{\cancel{3} \times \cancel{2} \times \cancel{1}} = \boxed{84}$

> Choose the largest factorial to go here.   *Optymistic*

4. *Evaluate:*   (a) $\dfrac{8!}{5!3!}$ (b) $\dfrac{7!}{2!4!}$ (c) $\dfrac{10!}{3!2!6!}$ (d) $\dfrac{13!}{9!4!}$

$\dbinom{n}{r}$ is a special notation $\dbinom{n}{r} = \dfrac{n!}{r!\,(n-r)!}$

5. *Evaluate:*   (a) $\dbinom{12}{8}$ (b) $\dbinom{7}{3}$ (c) $\dbinom{9}{2}$

6. (a) Show that $\dbinom{10}{6}$ has the same value as $\dbinom{10}{4}$

   (b) Explain, using factorials, why $\dbinom{10}{6} = \dbinom{10}{4}$

• *Check your answers.*

D7.2: Permutations of distinct items

A **permutation** is an ordered arrangement of items.

EXAMPLE In how many different ways can 4 books be arranged on a shelf ?

The number of ways of choosing a book to go in the first position = 4
The number of ways of choosing a book to go in the second position = 3
The number of ways of choosing a book to go in the third position = 2
The number of ways of choosing a book to go in the last position = 1
$\Rightarrow$ the number of ways of arranging the books = 4 x 3 x 2 x 1 = $\boxed{24}$

The number of ways of arranging n items = $n \times (n-1) \times (n-2) \times \ldots \times 2 \times 1 = n!$

EXAMPLE In how many different ways can 4 books, chosen from 6, be arranged on a shelf ?

The number of ways of choosing a book to go in the first position = 6
The number of ways of choosing a book to go in the second position = 5
The number of ways of choosing a book to go in the third position = 4
The number of ways of choosing a book to go in the last position = 3
$\Rightarrow$ the number of ways of arranging the books = 6 x 5 x 4 x 3 = $\boxed{360}$

The number of ways of arranging r items chosen from n is

$$_nP_r = \underbrace{n(n-1)(n-2) \ldots (n-r+1)}_{r\ terms} = \frac{n!}{(n-r)!}$$

Note: 0! is defined as 1.
This makes $_nP_n = \frac{n!}{0!} = n!$

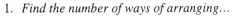

Yerwat

1. *Find the number of ways of arranging...*

    (a) ... 7 items on a shopping list.

    (b) ... 3 different coins in a row.

    (c) ... 5 different coloured electric light bulbs in 3 sockets.

    (d) ... 5 houseplants, chosen from 8, in a line on the window sill.

2. Evaluate: (a) $_5P_2$ (b) $_7P_3$ (c) $_7P_4$ (d) $_3P_3$

3. Write down expressions, in terms of n, for:

    (a) $_nP_2$ (b) $_{n-1}P_3$ (c) $_nP_{n-1}$

4. A typist has four letters and four addressed envelopes.

    (a) How many different ways are there of putting the letters in the envelopes ?

    (b) The letters are put into the envelopes at random.
    What is the probability that all the letters are in the correct envelopes ?

5. In how many ways can 10 girls be arranged in a line, if the shortest girl must be at the right hand end ?

• *Check your answers.*

D7.3: Permutations with repetitions

EXAMPLE How many arrangements are there of the letters in the words
(a) PAPER (b) PUPPY (c) PEPPER

(a) If we write PAPER as P_1AP_2ER, then the number of different arrangements is 5!
But, without the suffixes, we will have duplications.
For example P_1AP_2ER and P_2AP_1ER will appear the same.

$\Rightarrow$ the number of different arrangements $= \dfrac{5!}{2} = \boxed{60}$

(b) There are 5! different arrangements of $P_1UP_2P_3Y$ but

$P_1UP_2P_3Y$ $P_2UP_1P_3Y$ $P_3UP_1P_2Y$ $P_1UP_3P_2Y$
$P_2UP_3P_1Y$ $P_3UP_2P_1Y$ will appear the same without suffixes.

The number of repeats is equal to the number of arrangements of P_1, P_2, P_3

$\Rightarrow$ the number of different arrangements $= \dfrac{5!}{3!} = \boxed{20}$

(c) The number of different arrangements of $P_1E_1P_2P_3E_2R$ is 6!

$\Rightarrow$ the number of different arrangements $= \dfrac{6!}{3!\,2!} = \boxed{60}$

Number of arrangements of Ps $\blacktriangleright$ $\blacktriangleleft$ Number of arrangements of Es

---

Permutations with some identical items

Number of arrangements of n items of which p are alike of the first
kind, q are alike of the second kind, r are alike of the third kind ...

$$= \frac{n!}{p!\,q!\,r!\,...}$$

Find the number of ways of arranging...

1. ... the letters x y z z

2. ... 3 red balls, 1 white ball, 1 green ball in a row

3. ... the letters of the word FRENZY

4. ... the letters of the word FRENETIC

5. ... the letters of the word AARDVARK

6. (a) How many distinct arrangements can be made of the letters in the word ECSTATIC ?

   (b) How many of these arrangements start and end with T ?

   (c) What is the probability that the arrangement starts and ends with T ?

7. (a) How many different ways are there of placing 4 red, 3 green and 2 white counters in a straight line ?

   (b) How many different ways are there of placing these counters in a straight line, if the two white counters must stay together ?
   [Hint : treat the 2 white counters as one.]

• *Check answers.*

Section 8: Combinations

In this section you will:
- meet and work with combinations
- divide a group into two unequal or equal groups
- work with independent combinations

DEVELOPMENT

D8.1: Combinations

A **combination** is a selection in which the order is irrelevant.

The number of permutations of r items chosen from n is

$$_nP_r = n(n-1)(n-2) \ldots (n-r+1) = \frac{n!}{(n-r)!}$$

The number of combinations of r items chosen from n

$$= \frac{\text{number of permutations of } r \text{ from } n}{\text{number of permutations of } r}$$

$$\Rightarrow \quad _nC_r = \frac{n(n-1)(n-2) \ldots (n-r+1)}{r!} = \frac{n!}{r!\,(n-r)!} = \binom{n}{r}$$

Choosing r items from n is the same as dividing the n items into two groups, one containing r items and one containing (n–r) items.   So $^nC_r = {}^nC_{n-r}$

EXAMPLE   In how many ways can a football team be selected from a squad of 18 players, if the goalkeeper has to be included ?

This is equivalent to choosing 10 from 17 players.

Number of ways $= {}_{17}C_{10} = \dfrac{17 \times 16 \times 15}{3 \times 2 \times 1} = \boxed{680}$

Division of a group into two unequal groups

EXAMPLE   In how many ways can a group of 8 children be divided into a group of 6 and a group of 2 ?

If a group of 6 children is chosen, it will automatically leave a group of 2.

Number of ways $= {}_8C_6 = \dfrac{8!}{6!2!} = \dfrac{8 \times 7}{2 \times 1} = \boxed{28}$

Division of a group into two equal groups

EXAMPLE   In how many ways can a group of 8 children be divided into two groups of 4 ?

Number of ways of choosing 4 $= \dfrac{8 \times 7 \times 6 \times 5}{4 \times 3 \times 2 \times 1} = 70$

But, if the children are labelled ABCDEFGH, say, then the division into ABCD & EFGH is repeated later as EFGH & ABCD.

$\Rightarrow$ number of different combinations $= 70 \div 2 = \boxed{35}$

1. Evaluate: (a) $_7C_3$ (b) $_5C_1$ (c) $_4C_4$

2. Show that $_7C_3 = _7C_4$

3. In how many ways can :
    (a) 3 photographs be chosen from 8 proofs
    (b) 7 cards be dealt from 10
    (c) a team of 11 cricketers be selected from a squad of 12

4. How many different combinations of 3 letters can be chosen from the letters U V W X Y Z ?

5. In how many ways can U V W X Y Z be divided into two groups of 4 letters and 2 letters ?

6. In how many ways can U V W X Y Z be divided into two groups, each containing 3 letters ?

7. A tutor group of 24 children have been invited to send a team of 4 children to take part in a TV quiz show.
    (a) In how many ways can the team be chosen ?
    (b) The tutor group decide that Mary, who has just come out of hospital, should be in the team In how many ways can the team now be chosen ?

8. A test consists of 20 questions and each answer can only be right or wrong.
    Calculate the number of different ways in which it is possible to answer
    (a) exactly 5 questions correctly   (b) exactly 18 questions correctly

9. Your calculator should have an $_nC_r$ key.
    Work out how to use it and check your method by evaluating

       (a) $_7C_3$ (b) $_5C_1$ (c) $_4C_4$
    Check your answers against those you worked out in question 1.

10. Eight cards, four red and four black, are dealt to two players.
    (a) In how many ways could one player receive a set of the same colour cards?
    (b) How many different sets of cards could one player receive ?
    (c) What is the probability that a player receives 4 of the same colour cards?
    (d) What is the probability that a player receives at least one of each colour ?

11. There are 30 pupils in a tutor group, 17 girls and 13 boys.
    Their names are placed on pieces of paper and put into a box.
    Four names are drawn out at random to go on a trip.
    (a) In how many ways can all four tickets go to girls ?
    (b) What is the probability that all four tickets go to girls(to 3 d.p.) ?
    (c) What is the probability that at least one ticket goes to a boy (to 3 d.p.)?

    • *Check your answers.*

D8.2: The multiplication rules

If events are independent,	$P(A \text{ and } B) = P(A) \times P(B)$
$\Rightarrow$	$n(A \text{ and } B) = n(A) \times n(B)$
Similarly	$P(A \text{ and } B) = P(A) \times P(B/A)$
$\Rightarrow$	$n(A \text{ and } B) = n(A) \times n(B/A)$

EXAMPLE   In how many ways can you choose 8 apples and 3 oranges from 12 apples and 5 oranges ?

The choices of apples and oranges are independent of each other.

$\Rightarrow$ number of choices = $_{12}C_8 \times {}_5C_3 = 495 \times 10 = \boxed{4950}$

EXAMPLE   Three tables seat 3, 4, 5, people respectively. In how many ways can 12 people be allocated to the tables. The positions on each table do not matter.

number of allocations = $_{12}C_3 \times {}_9C_4 = 220 \times 126 = \boxed{27720}$

1. In how many different ways can 3 white and 1 black keys be simultaneously be pressed on a keyboard with 50 white and 35 black keys ?

2. In how many ways can a youth club committee of 4 boys and 4 girls be formed from 12 boys and 11 girls ?

3. In how many ways can a group of letters containing 1 capital letter, 3 consonants and 2 vowels be chosen from 3 capital letters, 6 consonants and 4 vowels ?

4. Tent A holds 2 people. Tent B holds 3 people. Tent C holds 4 people.
   In how many ways can 9 people be assigned to tents A, B and C ?

5. There are 3 post boxes marked A, B and C.
   Find the number of ways in which 9 different letters can be posted so that 5 of them are in box A, 2 of them are box B and 2 are in box C ?

6. It is known that one person in a gang of ten criminals is an informer, but not who it is. Three of the gang are to be chosen at random to do a job.
   (a) How many ways are there of selecting the informer and two others ?
   (b) How many ways are there of selecting three members of the gang ?
   (c) What is the probabillity that one of the three chosen is the informer ?

7. An exam paper contains 8 questions. There are 4 in Part A and 4 in Part B.
   (a) In how many ways can a candidate choose 5 questions ?
   (b) In how many ways can a candidate choose 2 questions from Part A and 3 questions from Part B ?
   (c) In how many ways can a candidate choose 3 questions from Part A and 2 questions from Part B ?
   (d) If the candidate is instructed to do at least two questions from each Part, in how many ways can this be done ?   • *Check your answers.*

Section 9: Adding complications

In this section you will:
- calculate the number of permutations with one or more restrictions
- calculate the number of selections with repetition
- combine permutations and combinations

EXTENSIONS

E9.1: Permutations with restrictions

Permutations with one restriction

EXAMPLE   How many permutations (arrangements) are there of the letters in the word TALLY where
(a) the two Ls are next to each other
(b) the two Ls are not next to each other

(a) Consider LL as one letter   T A (LL) Y
    n(all permutations) = $^4P_4$ =   4! = $\boxed{24}$

(b) n(Ls are separated) = n(all permutations) − n(with LL together)
                   = 5! − 4! = 120 − 24 = $\boxed{96}$

Permutations with one restriction

EXAMPLE   How many numbers greater than 3000 can be made from the digits 2, 3, 4, 5 if each digit can be used only once ?

Restriction: the first digit must be 3, 4 or 5

n(ways of choosing the first digit)   = 3
n(ways of choosing the second digit) = 3
n(ways of choosing the third digit)   = 2
n(ways of choosing the last digit)   = 1

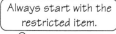
Always start with the restricted item.

⇒ number of possible numbers greater than 3000
     = 3 x 3 x 2 x 1 = $\boxed{18}$

Driller

Permutations with more than one restriction

EXAMPLE   How many **odd** numbers greater than 3000 can be made using 2, 3, 4, 5 if each digit can be used only once ?

Restrictions: the first digit must be 3, 4 or 5 and the last digit must be 3 or 5

n(ways of choosing the last digit)   = 2
n(ways of choosing the first digit)   = 2
n(ways of choosing the second digit) = 2
n(ways of choosing the third digit)   = 1

Start with the _most restricted item._

⇒ number of possible numbers greater than 3000
      = 2 x 2 x 2 x 1 = $\boxed{8}$

Sureshot

1. (a) How many distinct permutations are there of the letters in the word PARALLEL ?
   (b) How many distinct permutations are there of the letters in the word PARALLEL in which the three Ls are next to each other ?
   (c) How many distinct permutations are there of the letters in the word PARALLEL in which the two As are not next to each other ?

2. 4 digit numbers are made using the digits 2, 3, 5, 7, 8, 9 with no repetitions allowed.
   (a) How many distinct 4-digit numbers can be made ?
   (b) What is the probability that a number chosen at random from these is less than 7000 ?
   (c) What is the probability that a number chosen at random from these is odd ?
   (d) What is the probability that a number chosen at random from these is an odd number less than 7000 ?

3. Sally takes 2 pink, 2 green and 3 blue tee-shirts for her 7 day holiday. She wears one shirt each day.
   (a) What is the number of possible arrangements of colours ?
   (b) If she chooses her tee-shirt at random each day, work out the probability that she wears the two pink tee-shirts on consecutive days ?

• Check your answers.

E9.2: Permutations with repeats

EXAMPLE   5 coins are chosen from these boxes of coins.
How many different arrangements can be made ?

10p coins   20p coins

2p coins   5p coins

The number of ways of choosing each coin is 4.

$\Rightarrow$ the number of different arrangements $= 4^5$

Permutations when repeats are permitted
Number of arrangements of n unlike items taken r at a time is n^r.

1. How many three letter permutations can be made using …
   (a) … 8 letters without repetition   (b) … 8 letters with repetition

2. How many four digit numbers can be made from the digits 2, 3, 4, 5 if
   (a) no repetition is allowed
   (b) repetition is allowed
   (c) no repetition is allowed and the number must be even
   (d) no repetition is allowed and the number must be even and less than 5000

3. A coin is tossed 8 times.
   (a) How many different sequences of heads and tails are possible ?
   (b) How many different sequences of 5 heads and 3 tails are possible ?
   (c) What is the probability of getting 5 heads and 3 tails ?   *• Check answers.*

E9.3: Keeping them apart

This is a very useful 'trick of the trade'.

EXAMPLE   How many different ways can the letters of the word HEXAGONS be arranged if no two vowels come together.

There are 8 letters : 2 vowels and 5 consonants.

$$\_ \quad C \quad \_ \quad C \quad \_ \quad C \quad \_ \quad C \quad \_ \quad C \quad \_\_$$

Place the consonants so that there are gaps in between and at either end, where the vowels could be placed. In this way, no two vowels could be put next to each other.

n(arrangements of consonants) = 5!
n(arrangements of 3 vowels in 6 gaps) = $_6P_3$ = 6 x 5 x 4 = 120
⇒ n(arrangements with no two vowels together) = 5! x 120 = $\boxed{14\ 400}$

1. Four women and seven men are to be seated in a straight line.

   (a) How many possible arrangements of these people are there ?

   (b) In how many arrangements will all four women be seated together?

   (c) In how many arrangements will no two women be seated together ?

2. The letters of the word CONSTANTINOPLE are written on separate cards. The cards are shuffled and placed randomly in a straight line.

   (a) How many distinct arrangements are there ?

   (b) How many of these arrangements start with A ?

   (c) What is the probability that an arrangement starts with A (to 3 d.p.)?

   (d) What is the probability that an arrangement starts and ends with T (to 3 d.p.) ?

   (e) What is the probability that an arrangement has no two vowels next to each other (to 3 d.p.) ?

   • *Check your answers.*

E9.4: Adding permutations

1. 7-digit whole numbers are made with the digits 1, 2, 2, 3, 3, 3, 0

   (a) (i) How many distinct numbers can be made starting with 1 ?

   (ii) How many distinct numbers can be made starting with 2 ?

   (iii) How many distinct numbers can be made starting with 3 ?

   (b) The number cannot start with 0. How many distinct numbers can be made ?

   (c) How many of these numbers end in 0 ?

   (d) What is the probability that one of these numbers, chosen at random, is a multiple of 10 ?

2. 7-digit whole numbers are made with the digits 1, 2, 4, 5, 5, 5, 7.

   (a) How many distinct 7-digit numbers can be made ?

   (b) How many of these numbers are even ?

   (c) How many of these numbers are multiples of 4 ?   • *Check your answers.*

E9.5: Miscellaneous problems

1. (a) The judges in the 'Rosebud Princess' competition have to arrange 6 girls in order of photographic appeal. In how many ways could this be done ?

   (b) Two girls are to be selected from the six to be photographed by the local newspaper. In how many ways can the selection be made ?

2. Three girls and two boys are told to stand in a line. If they stand randomly, what is the probability that the two boys are not standing together ?

3. 5 people are going to a party in a 5-seater car. Only 3 of them can drive. How many different possible seating arrangements are there ?

4. Sue has 7 books on a shelf in her kitchen, five cookbooks and two books of poetry.

   (a) In how many different ways can the books be arranged if all the cookbooks are together and all the poetry books are together ?

   (b) In how many distinct ways can the books be arranged if the cookbooks are together ?

5. 3 letters are chosen at random from the letters of the word ZOOLOGY.

   (a) What is the probability that a set without any Os is chosen ?

   (a) What is the probability that a set withonly one O is chosen ?

6. There are 30 pupils in a tutor group, 17 girls and 13 boys. Their names are placed on pieces of paper and put into a box. Four names are drawn out at random to go on a trip. What is the probability that two boys and two girls get the tickets ?

7. A box contains 12 toffees, 10 peppermints and 9 sherbert lemons. Three sweets are chosen at random. What is the probability that the sweets are :

   (a) all different   (b) all toffees   (c) all the same   (d) all not peppermints ?

8. Three families go to the cinema together : Mr. and Mrs. Pahkna and their children Vladimirou, Elena, and Evros, Mr. and Mrs. Ming and their children Su and Chang, Mr. and Mrs. Andrews and their son Bruce. They are given 12 seats in one row.

   (a) In how many different ways could they be seated ?

   (b) In how many different ways could they sit down so that the members of each family all sat together ?

   (c) If they sit randomly, what is the probability that the members of each family sit together ?

   (d) In how many ways could they sit so that no two adults were sitting next to one another ?

9. A student must answer exactly 7 out of 10 questions in an exam. The student must also answer at least 3 of the frst five questions. In how many ways can the student select the 7 questions ?

• *Check your answers.*

S1: Unit 2: Probability

Facts and formulae you need to know:

P(A or B) = P(A) + P(B) − P(A and B) $_nP_r = \dfrac{n!}{(n-r)!}$ **OCR** $_nC_r = \dfrac{n!}{r!(n-r)!}$

P(A and B) = P(A) x P(B/A)

P(A') = 1 − P(A)   **only**

Competence Test S1.2

1. One girl is chosen at random from the Y7 girls football squad. For the one chosen,
   P(she plays hockey) = 0.42, P(she plays tennis) = 0.36, P(she plays hockey or tennis) =0.58
   Work out the probability that she plays tennis and hockey.   (1M,1A)

2. In this group of boys, F is the set of boys who are in the football
   squad and B is the set of boys who are in the basketball squad.
   A boy is chosen at random from this group.   (6A)
   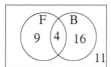
   (a) How many boys are there in the group ?
   (b) What is the probability that the boy chosen :
   (i) is in both squads   (ii) is not in either squad
   (iii) is not in the basketball squad   (iv) is in at least one of the squads
   (v) is in the football squad, given that he is in at least one of the squads ?

3. Alex and Ellen sometimes miss the bus to school.   (2M,7A)
   On any day, P(Alex will catch the bus) = 0.7   P(Ellen will catch the bus) = 0.9
   (a) Draw a tree diagram to illustrate this information.
   (b) Calculate the probability that they both miss the bus.
   (c) Calculate the probability that at least one of them misses the bus.

4. P(A) = $\frac{1}{4}$ P(B) = $\frac{2}{5}$ P(A or B) = $\frac{11}{20}$ (4M,8A)
   Work out (a) P(A and B)   (b) P(A/B)   (c) P(B')   (d) P(A/B')

5. A red and a blue dice are thrown once each. The red is fair but the probability of getting
   a 6 on the blue dice is $\frac{1}{3}$. Work out the probability that :
   (a) the red dice is a 6 and the blue dice isn't a 6   (b) at least one dice is a six
   (c) the red dice is a six, given that there is at least one six.   (3M,5A)

OCR only | **Total (AQA & Edexcel) = 37** |

6. (a) How many different arrangements are there of the letters in AWKWARD ?
   (b) What is the probability that an arrangement chosen at random has the two As
      at each end ?   (2M,2A)

7. In how many ways can 11 footballers be chosen from a squad of 15 players if:
   (a) all of them can play in goal ?
   (b) only two of them can play in goal ?   (3A)

8. Five toddlers (Bob, Barry, Frank, Delia, Donna) are to sit in a row to have their photograph
   taken. How many possible arrangments are there :   (a) altogether ?
   (b) if Frank must sit in the middle ?
   (c) if Bob and Barry must sit next to each other ?
   (d) if Donna and Delia must not sit next to each other ?   (2M,6A)

| **Total (OCR) = 52** |

AIMING HIGH
S1
Unit 3
Discrete Random Variables

CONTENTS

	OCR	AQA	Edexcel
Section 1	All	All	All
Section 2	All	All	All
Section 3	—	—	All
Section 4	All	All	—
Section 5	All	—	—
Section 6	—	All	—
Section 7	—	All	All
Section 8	—	All	—
Section 9	—	All	—

Unit 3: Discrete Random Variables
Section 1 : Probability Distributions

In this section you will:
- understand what is meant by a discrete random variable
- meet and work with probability distributions

DEVELOPMENT
D1.1 Discrete random variables

A **random variable** is a numerical variable whose value depends on chance.

EXAMPLES of random variables

Capital letters (X, Y, Z, P, H, T, ...) are used to represent random variables.

Throw two dice: T = total score
S = number of sixes
L = lower of the two scores

Toss four coins   H = number of heads

Select a potato at random from a sack :   W = weight of potato

Here, T, S, L, H are **discrete random variables**
and   W is a **continuous random variable.**
In this unit, we will consider only discrete random variables.

The **probability distribution** of a discrete random variable is a list of its possible values, with the probability that it takes each value.

EXAMPLE   A fair dice is thrown once. The random variable X is the number thrown. Tabulate the probability distribution of X.

This is always the lower case version of the letter used for the random variable.

x can only take numerical values

x	1	2	3	4	5	6
$P(X = x)$	$\frac{1}{6}$	$\frac{1}{6}$	$\frac{1}{6}$	$\frac{1}{6}$	$\frac{1}{6}$	$\frac{1}{6}$

This table is the probability distribution of X.

$P(X = x)$ is called the **probability function** [or sometimes the **probability density function**]

Headbanger

1. (a) A fair coin is thrown three times. List all the possible outcomes.
   (b) The random variable T is the number of tails.
       Make a table showing the probability distribution of T.

2. Two fair dice are thrown. The event recorded is the difference between the scores.
   (a) Display the equally likely outcomes in a sample space diagram.
   (b) The random variable X is the difference between the scores.
       Make a table showing the probability distribution of X.

3. A bag contains 5 red counters and 3 white counters.
   Two counters are drawn at random from the bag, without replacement.
   (a) Draw a tree diagram showing the outcomes and probabilities.
   (b) Make a table showing the probability distribution of the number of red counters.

4. Two fair dice are thrown.
   (a) List all 36 possible outcomes.
   (b) If X is the total score:
       (i) tabulate the probability distribution
       (ii) find the probability that X is a number greater than 8
   (c) If Y is the number of 3s:
       (i) tabulate the probability distribution
       (ii) find the probability that Y is a number greater than 0
   (d) If Z is the highest common factor of the two scores:
       (i) tabulate the probability distribution
       (ii) find the probability that Z is a number less than 4

5. Three students are selected at random from a group of 6 girls and 3 boys.
   If X is the number of boys chosen, tabulate the distribution of X.

6. A fair dice has its faces labelled 1, 2, 2, 3, 3, 3. It is thrown twice.
   If X is the product of the two scores, tabulate the distribution of X.

7. A bag contains 8 blue marbles and 4 green marbles.
   Two marbles are drawn at random from the bag, without replacement.
   The trial stops when a green marble is drawn or when 3 marbles have been drawn.
   (a) Draw a tree diagram showing the outcomes and probabilities.
   (b) If M is the total number of marbles drawn, tabulate the distribution of M.
   (c) Evaluate P(M = 1 or 2).
   • *Check your answers.*

////EXTENSION////
E1.2: Probability distribution challenge

1. A jar is full of glass balls. Each glass ball has a number inside it. If a glass ball is drawn at random, the probability of getting each number is shown in the following probability distribution table.

n	2	3	5
P(N = n)	0.5	0.3	0.2

Two balls are drawn at random, without replacement.
   (a) The random variable D is the difference between the numbers in both balls.
       Show that P(D = 3) is 0.2
   (b) Tabulate the probability distribution of D.
   • *Check your answers.*

D1.3: Probability distributions and the Σ notation

The probability distribution table contains all the probabilities for the trial. Hence, the sum of the probabilities is 1.

We write this as $\boxed{\sum P(X = x) = 1}$ $\boxed{\sum \text{ means 'the sum of'}}$

EXAMPLE   Find the value of k in this probability distribution.

x	4	5	6	8
$P(X = x)$	0.1	0.3	0.4	k

$\sum P(X = x) = 1 \implies 0.1 + 0.3 + 0.4 + k = 1 \implies \boxed{k = 0.2}$

1. Find the value of k in the following probability distribution.

h	4	5	6	7
$P(H = h)$	$1/_5$	$3/_{10}$	k	$1/_4$

2. Find the value of m in the following probability distribution.

h	1	2	3	4	5
$P(H = h)$	0.15	m	0.32	$2m$	0.23

3. An octahedral dice has the numbers 1, 2, 3, ... 8 on its faces. It is biased so that the probability of an odd number is twice the probability of an even number.
   (a) Find the probability distribution of S, the score
   (b) Find $P(S > 5)$

4. A 6-faced dice, with faces numbered from 1 to 6, is biased so that the probability of any score is inversely proportional to the score. For example, the probability of scoring 2 is $k/_2$ (k constant). Show that the probability of scoring a 2 is $10/_{49}$.

5. In the following probability distribution, show that c can only have one value and find the value.

d	1	2	3	4	5
$P(D = d)$	0.12	$1/_2 c$	0.24	c^2	0.4

• Check your answers.

D1.4: Cumulative distribution functions

The cumulative distribution function of the random variable X is

$$F(x_k) = P(X \le x_k)$$

If X is a discrete random variable (as here) then

$$F(x_k) = \sum_{x < x_k} P(X = x)$$

EXAMPLE	x	2	3	4	5	6
	$P(X = x)$	0.1	0.4	0.3	0.05	0.15

Find (a) $P(X \le 3)$ (b) F(5)   (c) F(4.3)

(a) $P(X \le 3)$ = 0.1 + 0.4 = $\boxed{0.5}$

(b)   F(5) = 0.1 + 0.4 + 0.3 + 0.05 = $\boxed{0.85}$

(c)   F(4.3) = 0.1 + 0.4 + 0.3 = $\boxed{0.8}$ [F(4.3) = F(4) since F is discrete]

1.
d	5	6	7	10	12
$P(D = d)$	0.3	0.1	0.15	0.25	0.2

Find (a) $P(D > 5)$ (b) F(7)   (c) F(10.2)

2.
x	3	4	5	6	7	8
$F(x)$	0.2	0.25	0.36	0.6	0.75	1

Tabulate the probability distribution of X.

3.
r	2	3	5	7
$P(R = r)$	a	b	c	d

Find the values of a, b, c and d, if you are given the following information:
$P(R < 5) = \frac{1}{2}$ $P(R = 7) = 2 \times P(R = 2)$ $F(5) = \frac{2}{3}$

• *Check your answers.*

D1.5: An alternative notation

$P(H = h) = \frac{1}{5}$ $h = 1, 2, 3, 4, 5$

means exactly the same as

h	1	2	3	4	5
$P(H = h)$	$\frac{1}{5}$	$\frac{1}{5}$	$\frac{1}{5}$	$\frac{1}{5}$	$\frac{1}{5}$

1. The score S on a spinner is a random variable whose distribution is given by the rule $P(S = s) = k$, where k is a constant and $s = 1, 2, 3, 4, 5$.
Find the value of k.

2. The discrete random variable has a cumulative frequency density F(x) defined by
$$F(x) = \frac{2x - 1}{7} ; \quad x = 1, 2, 3, 4$$
(a) Find F(2) and F(3)
(b) Find $P(X = 3)$
(c) Tabulate the probability distribution for X.

3. The discrete random variable Y has a probability function given by:
$$P(Y = y) = \begin{cases} (0.5)^y & \text{for } y = 1, 2, 3 \\ k & \text{for } y = 4 \end{cases}$$
where k is a constant.
(a) Calculate the value of k.
(b) Find F(2)

• *Check your answers.*

D1.6: Putting it all together

1. One spinner has the numbers 1, 2, 3 on it. A second spinner has the numbers 1, 2, 3, 4 on it. Both spinners are fair. S = the sum of the two scores.
   (a) Find P(S = 6)   (b) Find the probability distribution for S.

2. There are 5 blue socks and 3 green socks in a drawer. Socks are taken randomly, one at a time, without replacement, until two green socks are obtained or until a total of three socks have been taken out. G is the number of green socks.
   (a) Draw a tree diagram and find the probability distribution for G.
   (b) What is the probability of getting at least one green sock ?

3. Three cards are chosen at random, without replacement, from a pack of 52 cards.
   (a) Find the probability distribution of the number of court cards (K,Q,J) chosen, giving the probabilities to 5 d.p.
   (b) What is the probability of getting at least two court cards ?

• Check your answers.

E1.7: Miscellaneous challenges

1. The cumulative distribution function of a random variable X is given by:

x	0	1	2	3	4	5
F(x)	k	0.3	0.42	0.68	0.79	1

   (a) Given that P(X = 1) = 0.2, find the value of k.
   (b) Work out the probability distribution for X.
   (c) Find P(X > 3)

2. Frank has some coins in his pocket. There are two 50p coins, one 20p coin and four 10p coins. He pulls out two coins at random. The random variable A represents the amount in pence that he pulls out.
   (a) How many different ways can he choose 2 coins ?
   (b) Show that P(A = 30) = $^4/_{21}$
   (c) Find the probability distribution for A.
   (d) Find P(A ≥ 60)

3. A 6-faced dice is biased so that the probability distribution of each score is as given in the table:

s	1	2	3	4	5	6
P(S = s)	0.1	0.1	0.1	0.2	a	0.3

   (a) Work out the value of a.
   (b) Mark has two dice to choose from, this biased dice and a standard fair dice. Mark chooses one dice at random and rolls it.
   Work out the probability that Mark gets a 5 or a 6.
   (c) Work out the conditional probability that Mark chose the fair dice, given that he gets a 5 or a 6.   *• Check your answers.*

Section 2 : Expectation and Variance

In this section you will:
- calculate the expected frequency of an outcome
- understand what is meant by the expected value and variance of a random variable
- calculate the expected value and variance of a random variable

DEVELOPMENT

D2.1: Expected frequency of an outcome

Expected frequency of an outcome ≈ probability x total frequency

1. A dice is thrown 600 times. State the expected number of 5s.

2. A card is chosen at random from a standard 52 card pack. This is carried out 260 times, the card being replaced every time.

   State how many times you would expect the card to be:

   (a) a heart   (b) a King   (c) a King of Hearts   (d) a red card

   (e) a red card or a king   (f) not a red card nor a king

3. A biased dice has this probability distribution:

x	1	2	3	4	5	6
P(X = x)	0.1	0.2	0.3	0.1	0.2	0.1

   The dice is rolled 500 times.

   State how many times you would expect the score to be:

   (a) a six   (b) a three   (c) an odd number   (d) a factor of 6

4. The number of times a certain machine breaks down in one week is given by the random variable B, which has the following probability distribution.

b	0	1	2	3	4	5
P(B = b)	0.02	0.24	0.32	0.16	0.2	0.06

   The machine is working 52 weeks in every year.

   (a) State the number of weeks you would expect there to be no breakdowns.

   (b) State the number of weeks you would expect there to be 3 or more breakdowns.

5. The eggs sold in Freeway hypermarket are packed in boxes of 6.
   The probability that any egg is cracked is 0.04

   (a) What is the probability that there are no cracked eggs in a box of 6 ?

   (b) On Tuesday, 720 boxes of eggs are delivered.

   How many boxes would you expect to have no cracked eggs in them ?

• Check your answers.

D2.2: Expectation

You are now going to meet a new kind of mean.
So far, you have met $\bar{x}$ (x bar) which is the mean of a data set.
There is also a mean, μ, of a probability distribution. [Read μ as 'mew']

For a grouped data set: $\bar{x} = \dfrac{x_1 f_1 + x_2 f_2 + x_3 f_3 + \ldots + x_n f_n}{f_1 + f_2 + f_3 + \ldots + f_n} = \dfrac{\sum_{i=1}^{i=n} x_i f_i}{\sum_{i=1}^{i=n} f_i}$

where f_i is the frequency of each data value.

For a probability distribution:
the expected frequency of each outcome $= f_i \approx p_i \times N$

$\Rightarrow$ mean $= \mu = \dfrac{x_1 p_1 N + x_2 p_2 N + \ldots + x_n p_n N}{p_1 N + p_2 N + \ldots + p_n N}$

$\Rightarrow$ mean $= \dfrac{x_1 p_1 + x_2 p_2 + \ldots + x_n p_n}{p_1 + p_2 + p_3 + \ldots + p_n} = \dfrac{\sum_{i=1}^{i=n} x_i p_i}{1} = \sum_{i=1}^{i=n} x_i p_i$

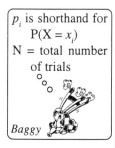

p_i is shorthand for $P(X = x_i)$
N = total number of trials

Baggy

Hence

$$\left. \begin{array}{c} \text{mean} \\ \mu \\ \text{expected value} \\ \text{expectation} \\ E[X] \end{array} \right] = \sum_{i=1}^{i=n} x_i p_i$$

Try not to use the term 'mean', as it has a different meaning for data sets and probability distributions.

Note:
- μ or $E[X]$ is the mean value you would expect to get close to, over a very large number of trials.
- From now on, use $\bar{x}$ for data sets and μ or $E[X]$ for probability distributions.

EXAMPLE   Find the expected value of the random variable X in the following probability distribution table.

x	0	1	2	4	7
$P(X = x)$	0.2	0.4	0.1	0.1	0.2

Expected value $= E[X] = 0 \times 0.2 + 1 \times 0.4 + 2 \times 0.1 + 4 \times 0.1 + 7 \times 0.2$
$= 0.4 + 0.2 + 0.4 + 1.4 = \boxed{2.4}$

1. Find the mean of the random variable Y as defined in the following table.

y	3	4	5	6
$P(Y = y)$	0.2	0.3	0.4	0.1

2. Find the expectation of the random variable H as defined in the following table.

h	1	2	4	8
$P(H = h)$	$^1/_4$	$^1/_8$	$^3/_8$	$^1/_4$

| EXAMPLE | Find μ for the probability distribution for the score when a fair dice is tossed. |

The probability distribution is

s	1	2	3	4	5	6
$P(S = s)$	$\frac{1}{6}$	$\frac{1}{6}$	$\frac{1}{6}$	$\frac{1}{6}$	$\frac{1}{6}$	$\frac{1}{6}$

Here it is simpler to use the symmetry of the distribution to find the mean.

μ is a measure of the centre of the distribution and is ∴ $\boxed{3.5}$

3. Find E[R] for the random variable R as defined in the following table.

r	3	5	7	9
$P(R = r)$	0.2	0.3	0.3	0.2

4. Find the expected number of heads when two coins are tossed.

5. The six faces of a fair 6-faced dice are numbered 1, 2, 2, 3, 3, 3
   (a) The dice is thrown once. The random variable X is the score on the top face. Find the expected score.
   (b) The dice is thrown twice and S = the total score. Find the probability distribution of S and the mean value of S.

6. The random variable H as defined in the following probability distribution.

h	2	3	4	5	6
$P(H = h)$	0.1	0.15	0.4	a	0.2

   (a) What is the value of a ?
   (b) What is the expected value of H?

7. A bag contains five red counters and 3 black counters. Two counters are drawn, one at a time and not replaced. Let R be the variable 'the number of black counters drawn. Find E[R].

8. A bag contains 8 red and 2 black snooker balls. A second bag contains 3 red and 2 black snooker balls. A ball is taken at random from the first bag and put into the second bag. A ball is then taken at random from the second bag and put into the first. What is the expected number of red balls in the first bag ?

9. A fruit machine has three windows. Fruits appear in each window with the following probabilities:

P(lemon) = 0.4	P(raspberry) = 0.1	
P(orange) = 0.2	P(banana) = 0.3	

Each go costs 20p.   3 lemons win £1.50   3 oranges win £2
                      3 raspberries win 50p

Find the expected gain or loss for one go on this fruit machine.

• *Check your answers.*

D2.3: Methods for calculating variance

For a data set:
- the mean, $\bar{x}$, is a measure of the centre of a set of data.
- the standard deviation, σ, is a measure of the spread of a set of data.
- the variance is the square of the standard deviation, σ^2.
- the standard deviation is more commonly used than the variance, as it is in the same units as the original data, whereas the variance is expressed in (units)^2.

For a probability distribution:
- the expected value, μ or E[X], is a measure of the centre of a probability distribution.
- the spread of a random variable is measured by the standard deviation, σ, or the variance, σ^2.

> σ is the lower case Greek letter s
> Σ is the upper case Greek letter s
> Both are read as 'sigma'.

- **the variance is more commonly used than the standard deviation, for probability distributions.**
- the variance of a random variable is usually denoted by Var[X]

Headbanger

For a probability distribution:	For a grouped data set:
$\mu = E[X] = \sum_{i=1}^{i=n} x_i p_i$	$x = E[X] = \dfrac{\sum_{i=1}^{i=n} x_i f_i}{\sum_{i=1}^{i=n} f_i}$
$\sigma^2 = \text{Var}[X] = \sum_{i=1}^{i=n} (x_i - \mu)^2 p_i$	$\sigma^2 = \dfrac{\sum_{i=1}^{i=n} (x_i - \bar{x})^2 f_i}{\sum_{i=1}^{i=n} f_i}$

EXAMPLE   Find E[X] and Var[X] for the following distribution:

x	1	2	3	5
P(X = x)	0.3	0.2	0.1	0.5

E[X] = 0.3 + 0.4 + 0.3 + 2 = $\boxed{3}$

Var[X] = $(1 - 3)^2 0.3 + (2 - 3)^2 0.2 + (3 - 3)^2 0.1 + (5 - 3)^2 0.1 = \boxed{3}$

Find the expected value and the variance for each distribution:

1.

x	1	2	3	6	7
P(X = x)	$3/_8$	$1/_8$	$1/_4$	$1/_8$	$1/_8$

2.

t	−2	−1	0	1	2	3
P(T = t)	0.2	0.1	0.05	0.1	0.25	0.3

3.

q	2	2.5	3	3.5
P(Q = q)	0.35	0.1	0.25	0.3

Var[X] gets more complicated to calculate when E[X] is not an integer.
However, there is a second formula for calculating variance, (just as with data sets).

For a probability distribution:	For a grouped data set:
$$\sigma^2 = \text{Var }[X] = \sum_{i=1}^{i=n} x_i^2 p_i - \mu^2$$	$$\sigma^2 = \frac{\sum_{i=1}^{i=n} x_i^2 f_i}{\sum_{i=1}^{i=n} f_i} - \bar{x}^2$$

4. In question 3, E[X] was not an integer, which made the calculation of the variance more complex than in the earlier questions. Work out the value of Var[X] for the distribution in question 3 using the second formula.

Find the expected value and the variance for each distribution, using the second formula. Give your answers to 4 s.f.

5.

y	1	2	3	4	5
$P(Y = y)$	$1/5$	$4/15$	$1/15$	$2/15$	$1/3$

6.

z	2	3	4	6	8	10
$P(Z = z)$	0.2	0.15	0.25	0.05	0.25	0.1

• *Check your answers.*

D2.4: Problems with expectation and variance

1. The sixth form committee consists of 5 girls and 4 boys.
   Two of its members are chosen at random to represent it.
   (a) Tabulate the probability distribution of the number of boys chosen.
   (b) Find the expected number of boys chosen.

2. Three letters are placed randomly in three previously addressed envelopes.
   List the ways this can be done. If C is the random variable representing the number of letters in the correct envelopes, find E[C] and Var[C].

3. A game is played with two dice. If the total score on the two dice is 6, 7 or 8, Sue pays £10. If the total score is not 6, 7 or 8, Sue wins £15.
   (a) Find Sue's expected loss or gain.
   (b) How much should she expect to win or lose if she plays the game 20 times ?
   (c) The game would be a fair game if the expected value was zero. How much should Sue pay if the total score is 6, 7 or 8, to make the game a fair game ?

4. A coin is tossed four times.
   L is the random variable representing the longest run of heads or tails.
   [eg TTTH has L = 3 and THHT has L = 2]
   Find the expectation and variance of L

5. There are just three keys on a key ring. A key is selected at random.
   If it is not the correct key to open the door, one of the other keys is chosen.
   Find the expected number of keys before the correct key is chosen.

6. Light bulbs are sent out from the Spotlight Factory in packs of 10. The number of faulty light bulbs, F, in each pack has the probability distribution given in this table:

f	0	1	2	3	4
P(F = f)	0.75	0.08	0.04	0.02	0.01

(a) Find the mean and standard deviation of F to 4 s.f.

(b) How many faulty light bulbs would you expect in an order of 1000 packs ?

(c) State the mean and standard deviation of the number of working (not faulty) light bulbs in each pack. Explain how you get each figure.

(d) Light bulbs from the Bright Light Factory are also sent out in packs of 10. The random variable representing the number of faulty light bulbs in each pack has mean = 0.21 and standard deviation = 0.782

State which factory you would order from and why ?

7. The marketing manager has to choose between two proposed advertising ideas for a new product.

The first idea, which she thinks of as 'zany', she estimates will produce a first year profit of £500 000 with a probability of 0.6, a profit of £200 000 with a probability of 0.1 and a loss of £200 000 with a probability of 0.3.

The second idea, which she thinks of as 'trad', she estimates will produce a first year profit of £400 000 with a probability of 0.5, a profit of £250 000 with a probability of 0.4 and a loss of £100 000 with a probability of 0.1.

She chooses 'zany'.

You think she should choose 'trad'.

Make a case as to why she should choose 'trad', quoting figures to back up your argument.

8. A fair game is one where the expected value is zero, that is, neither side wins in the long run.

3 coins are tossed. If there is just one head, Alan wins £1.

if there are two heads, Alan wins £2. If there are three heads, Alan wins £3.

If the game is to be fair, what should the penalty be if there are no heads ?

• *Check your answers.*

Section 3 : Expectation of a linear function of a random variable $\boxed{\text{Edexcel}}$

In this section you will find the expectation and variance of a linear function of a random variable .

DEVELOPMENT

D3.1: Linear functions of random variables

In Unit 1, Section 11, you found that :
- if each value in the data set is multiplied by a constant k, the standard deviation of the data is multiplied by k, but the mean value is unchanged.
- if a constant amount p is added to each value in a data set, the standard deviation of the data is unchanged, but the mean value is increased by p.

Similarly, if you remember that the variance is the square of the standard deviation, for a probability distribution X :
- if each value of the random variable X is multiplied by a constant a, the variance of X is multiplied by a^2, but the mean value is unchanged.
- if a constant amount b is added to each value of the random variable X, the variance of X is unchanged, but the mean value is increased by b.

You can combine the scaling a and the added constant b, to give the following formulae :

$$E(aX) = aE(X) \qquad Var(aX) = a^2 Var(X)$$
$$E(aX + b) = aE(X) + b \qquad Var(aX + b) = a^2 Var(X)$$

1. The random variable X has mean 5 and variance 9.
   Find the following:
   (a) $E(2X)$ (b) $Var(2X)$ (c) $E(X + 2)$ (d) $Var(X - 3)$
   (e) $E(5 - 2X)$ (f) $Var(3X + 1)$ (g) $Var(5 - X)$

2. Three 2p coins are tossed. The random variable Y represents the total value of the coins that land heads up.
   (a) Find $E(Y)$ and $Var(Y)$
   (b) Two new random variables are defined as: $M = 2X + 1$ and $R = \frac{1}{2}X + 2$
       Find $E(M)$, $E(R)$, $Var(M)$ and $Var(R)$.
   (c) Mary and Robert each toss three 2p coins. Mary records her score using the random variable M and Robert records his using the random variable R. After 100 throws, they each add up their scores. What are they likely to find ?
   (d) Would their scores overall be very fairly similar or not ? Explain your answer.

3. The random variable X has $E(X) = 10$ and $Var(X) = 4$.
   A random variable Z is produced using the linear transformation $Z = aX + b$
   $E(Z) = 10$ and $Var(Z) = 400$.   Find the values of a and b.

• Check your answers.

Section 4 : The Binomial Distribution

In this section you will:
- understand what is meant by a binomial distribution
- calculate probabilities, expectation and variance for a binomial distribution
- use cumulative binomial tables to calculate probabilities
- recognise when the binomial model is not suitable, and why.

OCR & AQA

DEVELOPMENT

D4.1: Introducing the binomial distribution

In a binomial distribution
- each trial has only two possible outcomes (success and failure)
- these two outcomes are mutually exclusive
- the probability of success at each trial is constant
- the outcome of each trial is independent of the outcomes of any other trial
- the number of trials, n, is fixed

EXAMPLE   A fair cubical dice is thrown four times.
The random variable X is the number of sixes thrown.
Show that the rule for the probability of X is given by
$P(X = x) = {}_4C_x \, (^1/_6)^x (^5/_6)^{4-x}$, $x = 0,1,2,3,4$

$P(X = 0)$ $= P(f_1, f_2, f_3, f_4) = (^5/_6)^4$ $= {}_4C_0 \, (^1/_6)^0 (^5/_6)^4$

$P(X = 1)$ $= P(s_1, f_2, f_3, f_4) + P(f_1, s_2, f_3, f_4) + P(f_1, f_2, s_3, f_4) + P(f_1, f_2, f_3, s_4)$
$= 4 \times (^1/_6)^1 (^5/_6)^3 = {}_4C_1 \, (^1/_6)^1 (^5/_6)^3$

$P(X = 2)$ $= P(2s, 2f)$ $= {}_4C_2 \times (^1/_6)^2 (^5/_6)^2$

$P(X = 3)$ $= P(3s, 1f)$ $= {}_4C_3 \times (^1/_6)^3 (^5/_6)^1$

$P(X = 4)$ $= P(s_1, s_2, s_3, s_4)$ $= {}_4C_4 \times (^1/_6)^4 = {}_4C_4 \times (^1/_6)^4 (^5/_6)^0$

Hence $\boxed{P(X = x) = {}_4C_x \, (^1/_6)^x (^5/_6)^{4-x}, \; x = 0,1,2,3,4}$ as required

---

1. A fair cubical dice is thrown three times.
   The random variable X is the number of sixes thrown.
   Find the rule for the probability distribution of X.

2. A fair tetrahedral dice is thrown four times. Its faces show 1, 2, 3 and 4.
   The random variable Y is the number of threes thrown.
   Find the rule for the probability distribution of Y.

3. A fair triangular spinner has one black and two white edges.
   The probability of it landing on a black edge is $^1/_3$.
   The random variable B is the number of times it lands on a black edge in six throws.
   Find the values of P(B = 2) and P(B = 5) to 4 d.p.

• Check your answers.

D4.2: The binomial distribution

In a binomial distribution, the random variable X, which represents the number of successes in the n trials of this experiment, has a probability distribution given by:

$$P(X = x) = \binom{n}{x} p^x q^{n-x} \quad \text{for } x = 0, 1, 2, \ldots n$$

or $\quad P(X = x) = {}_nC_x\, p^x q^{n-x} \quad \text{for } x = 0, 1, 2, \ldots n$

where p is the probability of a success and $q = 1 - p$ is the probability of failure.

When the random variable X has a binomial probability distribution, then

$$X \sim B(n,p)$$

where n and p are the **parameters** of the binomial distribution.

Note $\binom{n}{x} = {}_nC_x = \dfrac{n!}{x!(n-x)!}$

Most textbooks use $\binom{n}{x}$ but ${}_nC_x$ is on the calculator *and is easier to read as 'n choose x'.*

> Read $X \sim B(n,p)$ as
> 'X has a binomial
> probability
> distribution with
> parameters n and p.

1. Evaluate: (a) ${}_5C_1$ (b) ${}_4C_2$ (c) ${}_{10}C_2$

In the following questions, give probabilities to 4 decimal places.

2. The random variable X has a binomial distribution with $n = 5$ and $p = 0.4$
   Calculate: (a) $P(X = 3)$ (b) $P(X = 4)$ (c) $P(X = 5)$

3. Given that $Y \sim B(6, 0.2)$:
   calculate: (a) $P(Y = 0)$ (b) $P(Y = 2)$ (c) $P(Y = 5)$

4. The random variable S has a binomial distribution with $n = 7$ and $p = 0.1$
   Calculate: (a) $P(S = 2)$ (b) $P(S = 2 \text{ or } 3)$ (c) $P(S \le 3)$

> Hints: $P(X = a \text{ or } b) = P(X = a) + P(X = b)$
>
> $P(X \le k) = P(X = 0) + (X = 1) + \ldots + P(X = k)$
>
> $P(X \ge k) = P(X = k) + (X = k+1) + \ldots + P(X = n) \text{ or } 1 - P(X < k)$
>
> $P(X = \text{at least } c) = 1 - P(X \le c)$

5. Given that $Z \sim B(8, 0.35)$,
   calculate: (a) $P(Z = 4 \text{ or } 5)$ (b) $P(Z \ge 3)$ (c) $P(Z = \text{at least } 7)$

6. A fair dice is tossed 5 times.
   S is the random variable that represents the number of sixes.
   Calculate: (a) $P(S = 3)$ (b) $P(S \le 2)$ (c) $P(S = \text{at least } 1)$

• *Check your answers.*

D4.3: Cumulative binomial distribution tables

EXAMPLE   The random variable X has a binomial distribution with
$n = 10$ and $p = 0.3$. Use the cumulative binomial distribution
tables to calculate the values of:

(a) $P(X \leq 5)$ (b) $P(X = 5)$ (c) $P(X \geq 3)$

(a) $P(X \leq 5) = \boxed{0.9527}$ (straight from the table)

(b) $P(X = 5) = P(X \leq 5) - P(X \leq 4) = 0.9257 - 0.8497 = \boxed{0.076}$

(c) $P(X \geq 3) = 1 - P(X \leq 2) = 1 - 0.3828 = \boxed{0.6172}$

In the following questions, give probabilities to 4 decimal places.

1. The random variable X has a binomial distribution with $n = 12$ and $p = 0.65$.
    Calculate: (a) $P(X \leq 7)$ (b) $P(X = 9)$ (c) $P(X \geq 4)$

2. Given that $Y \sim B(10, 0.25)$:
    calculate: (a) $P(Y = 9)$ (b) $P(Y \leq 3)$ (c) $P(Y = 5, 6 \text{ or } 7)$

3. Given that $Q \sim B(18, 0.4)$:
    (a) calculate $P(Q < 8)$
    (b) calculate the smallest value of q such that $P(Q < q) > 0.92$

4. A fair cubical dice is tossed seven times.
    S is the random variable that represents the number of twos.
    Calculate   (a) $P(S \leq 5)$ (b) $P(S < 4)$ (c) $P(S > 3)$

• *Check your answers.*

D4.4: Binomial expectation and variance

For $X \sim B(n,p)$
$E(X) = np$ $Var(X) = npq$

1. Given that $X \sim B(10, 0.35)$, calculate:
    (a) $E(X)$ and $Var(X)$ (b) $P(X \leq E(X))$

2. At a certain driving test centre, 65% of the candidates pass the driving test. A group of 20 of those who took the test in June were chosen at random. Calculate the expectation and variance of the number who passed in this group.

3. At the Spotlight Factory the probability of a light bulb being faulty is 0.05. Bulbs are sold to shops in packs of 25. Find the expected number of faulty bulbs in a pack and the standard deviation, both correct to 4 d.p.

• *Check your answers.*

D4.5: Is a binomial model suitable ?

In a binomial distribution
- each trial has only two possible outcomes (success and failure)
- these two outcomes are mutually exclusive
- the probability of success at each trial is constant
- the outcome of each trial is independent of the outcomes of any other trial
- the number of trials, n, is fixed

In each of these situations, decide whether a binomial distribution is a suitable model for the random variable. If it is not suitable, explain why. If it is suitable, state the parameters of the random variable.

1. A fair dice is tossed 20 times; X ~ 'number of sixes recorded'
2. A fair dice is tossed until a six is obtained; X ~ 'number of tosses required'
3. The office car park has 12 parking spaces which are full 80% of the time; X ~ 'number of empty parking spaces at any particular time'
4. A box contains 6 red counters and 4 white counters. 5 counters are selected at random 5 times with replacement ; X ~ 'number of red counters obtained'
5. A box contains 6 red counters and 4 white counters. 5 counters are selected at once ; X ~ 'number of red counters obtained'
6. A particular student's school attendance record is 90%. A two week period is chosen; X ~ 'number of days absent'   • *Check your answers.*

D4.6: Putting it all together

Summary of results for the binomial distribution

$X \sim B(n,p)$ is read as 'X has a binomial distribution, with parameters n and p.'

$$P(X = x) = {_n}C_x \, p^x q^{n-x} \qquad \text{where } q = 1 - p$$

$$E(X) = np \qquad \text{Var}(X) = npq = \text{(standard deviation)}^2$$

Using cumulative binomial distribution tables

Examples $P(X \le 5) = 0.9527$ (straight from the table)
$P(X = 5) = P(X \le 5) - P(X \le 4)$
$P(X \ge 5) = 1 - P(X \le 4)$

1. In an experiment, a biased dice is thrown 25 times and the number of sixes is recorded. After the experiment has been repeated many times, the standard deviation of the number of sixes is 1.5. The probability of throwing a six is p, and it is know to be less than 0.3.
   Work out the value of p.
   Calculate, to 3 d.p., the probability that exactly 4 sixes are thrown in any one experiment.

2. At the Spotlight factory, the probability of any light bulb being defective is 0.05.
   What is the probability that, in a random sample of 10 bulbs:
   (a) there are no faulty bulbs   (b) there are less than 3 faulty bulbs
   (c) there are at least 2 faulty bulbs.   (answers to 4 s.f.)

3. Electrical switches are made on a production line. 200 samples, each of 5 switches, are tested and the number of faulty switches in each batch is recorded.

The results are :

Number faulty	0	1	2	3	4	5
Frequency	148	45	6	1	0	0

(a) The probability of any one switch being faulty is p. Estimate the value of p.

(b) By modelling the sampling as a binomial distribution, work out the expected frequencies of 0, 1, 2, 3, 4, 5 faulty switches in each batch.

(c) Are the values the model produces close enough to the actual frequencies to validate the model ?

4. (a) Six dice are thrown and the number of sixes recorded.

Work out the probability of getting 3 sixes in any one throw, to 4 s.f.

(b) If 3 sixes is a success, calculate the probability of throwing 3 sixes twice in five throws of the six dice, to 4 s.f.

5. The probability of any person chosen at random being right-handed is 0.8.
A random sample of 10 people is chosen.

(a) Find the probability that exactly 7 of the ten will be right-handed, to 4 s f.

(b) Find the probability that less than half will be right-handed, to 4 s.f.

(c) Find the mean and standard deviation of the number of right-handed people in a random sample of 25 people.

(d) Show that a random sample must contain at least 11 people, if the probability that it contains at least one left handed person is to be greater than 0.9.

6. Phil does the Times crossword six days a week. He aims to complete the crossword in under 15 minutes. He estimates that he can do this 4 times out of 5.

(a) Work out the expected value and the standard deviation of the number of times Phil is successful in any one week, to 2 d.p.

(b) Show that the probability he is successful every day in one week is 0.262.

(c) Work out the probability that he is successful at least five times in one week.

(d) On Good Friday, the Times is not published. What is the probability that he is successful on four of the five days that week that the newspaper is published.

7. If Alastair wordprocesses his own letters, the probability that any letter will contain errors is 0.4. If, however, he gets his secretary Liam to wordprocess the letter, the probability that it will contain errors drops to 0.04.

(a) Find the probability that a random sample of 10 letters wordprocessed by Alastair will include just one letter free from errors.

(b) On Friday, Alastair wordprocessed 10 letters and Liam did 70 letters. If one letter is chosen at random from these 80 letters, what is the probability that it contains errors ?   • *Check your answers.*

Section 5 : The Geometric Distribution

In this section you will:

OCR

- understand what is meant by a geometric distribution
- calculate probabilities and expectation for a geometric distribution

DEVELOPMENT

D5.1: Introducing the geometric distribution

In the **binomial distribution** the random variable represents the number of successes in a fixed number of trials

In the **geometric distribution** the random variable represents the number of attempts required to record the first success.

In a **geometric distribution - just as in the binomial distribution**

- each trial has only two possible outcomes (success and failure)
- these two outcomes are mutually exclusive
- the probability of success at each trial is constant
- the outcome of each trial is independent of the outcomes of any other trial

However, in the binomial distribution

- the number of trials, n, is fixed

Whereas, in the geometric distribution

- the trials are repeated until success is achieved.

EXAMPLE   A fair cubical dice is thrown until a six is obtained.
The random variable X is the number of throws required.
Show that the rule for the probability of X is given by
$P(X = x) = (^1/_6)(^5/_6)^{x-1}$, $x = 1,2,3 \dots$

$P(X = 1) = P(s) = ^1/_6$

$P(X = 2) = P(f,s) = (^5/_6)(^1/_6)$

$P(X = 3) = P(f,f,s) = (^5/_6)^2(^1/_6)$

$P(X = 4) = P(f,f,f,s) = (^5/_6)^3(^1/_6)$

Hence $\boxed{P(X = x) = (^1/_6)(^5/_6)^{x-1}, x = 1,2,3 \dots}$ as required

---

1. Two fair cubical dice are thrown until a double six is obtained.
The random variable X is the number of throws required.
Find the rule for the probability distribution of X.

2. A counter is selected at random from 2 green counters, 5 blue counters and 1 white counter and replaced.
(a) The random variable W is the number of throws required to get a white counter.
Find the rule for the probability distribution of W.
(a) The random variable G is the number of throws required to get a green counter.
Find the rule for the probability distribution of G.

• *Check your answers.*

D5.2: The geometric distribution

In a **geometric distribution,** the random variable X, which represents the number of attempts required to achieve the first success, has a probability distribution given by $P(X = x) = q^{x-1}p$
where p is the probability of a success and $q = 1-p$ is the probability of failure.

When the random variable X has a geometric probability distribution, then
$X \sim \textbf{Geo}(p)$ where p is the **parameter** of the geometric distribution.

$$P(X = x) = q^{x-1}p$$

$$P(X > x) = P(x \text{ failures}) = q^x$$

$$P(X \leq x) = 1 - q^x$$

Frizzbang

If X > 5, then there must have been 5 failures.

Note: $P(X \geq 8) = P(X > 7)$
Similarly, $P(X < 12) = P(X \leq 11)$

In the following questions, give probabilities to 4 decimal places.

1. The random variable X represents the number of trials up to and including a success. The probability of a success on any one trial is $p = 0.4$
   Calculate: (a) $P(X = 3)$ (b) $P(X = 4)$ (c) $P(X = 3 \text{ or } 4)$

2. The random variable Z has a geometric distribution with $p = 0.3$
   Calculate: (a) $P(Z > 3)$ (b) $P(Z \leq 3)$ (c) $P(Z \leq 4)$

3. Given that $Y \sim \text{Geo}(0.2)$:
   calculate: (a) $P(Y = 6)$ (b) $P(Y \leq 2)$ (c) $P(Y \geq 5)$

4. A card is chosen at random from an ordinary pack of 52 cards, and replaced. The process continues until an ace has been drawn. T is the total number of cards that have been drawn when an ace is obtained.
   Calculate: (a) $P(T = 5)$ (b) $P(T = 4 \text{ or } 5)$ (c) $P(T \leq 3)$

5. Adi is doing a traffic survey on the main road outside the school gates. He is testing the hypothesis that, on average, one in five vehicles on this road is a lorry. Assuming the hypothesis is true, then calculate the probability that
   (a) the first lorry he sees is the fifth vehicle that passes
   (b) the first lorry is not amongst the first ten vehicles
   (c) there is at least one lorry among the first eight vehicles.

6. A hospital researcher is testing blood samples to try and find a sample which shows evidence of sickle cell anaemia. It is known that 32% of the population of that country have sickle cell anaemia.
   (a) What is the probability that he needs to examine at least 5 blood samples before he finds what he needs ?
   (b) How many samples would he need to test to be 99% sure of finding at least one positive sample ?

• Check your answers.

D5.3: Geometric expectation

> For a geometric distribution $E(X) = \dfrac{1}{p}$

1. The random variable X has a geometric distribution and $P(X = 1) = 0.3$
   Find the expected value of X
2. The random variable Y has a geometric distribution.
   It is given that $P(Y = 2) = 0.28$.
   Calculate the expected value of Y
3. The random variable T has a geometric distribution with $P(T > 1) = 0.8$
   Find $E[T]$.
4. A pack of Supasnaks costs 50p. It is stated on the pack that one pack in 20 has a £5 voucher inside. I buy a pack every day. Calculate the expected cost of the packs that I will have bought by the time I find a voucher.
5. Erroll tosses a fair coin until he gets a head.
   Find the expected number of tosses required to get a head.

• Check your answers.

D5.4: Miscellaneous geometric problems

> For a geometric distribution, the conditional probability rule becomes
> $$P(X > a\, /\, X > b) = \frac{P(X > a)}{P(X > b)} = \frac{q^a}{q^b} = q^{a-b}$$

1. The probability that a marksman hits a bullseye is 0.6 for each shot and each shot is independent.
   (a) What is the probability that the first bullseye:
      (i) occurs on his fourth shot ?
      (ii) takes more than four shots ?
      (iii) takes at least four shots ?
      (iv) takes more than five shots, given that he misses the first two shots.
   (b) What is the mean number of shots needed to get a bullseye ?

2. Independent identical trials of an experiment are carried out until a success occurs. On average, it is found that 10 trials are required.
   (a) What is the probability of success for each trial?
   (b) What is the probability that :
      (i) 3 trials will be needed ?
      (ii) at least 5 trials will be needed ?
      (iii) fewer than 6 trials will be needed ?
      (iv) fewer than 6 trials will be needed given that at least 2 are required

3. Grannie, Luke, Joanne and Connor are playing a dice game called Beetle. They throw the dice in the order given above.
In order to start the game, a player must get a 6.

(a) What is the probability that Joanne starts with the first throw ?

(b) What is the probability that Luke takes more than 3 throws to start ?

(c) What is the probability that Connor starts in less than 6 throws ?

(d) What is the probability that Grannie takes more than 10 throws to start given that she has not started after 6 throws ?

(e) What is the probability that they each take more than 3 throws to start ?

(f) What is the probability that Grannie takes 4 throws to start, Luke takes 3 throws, Joanne takes 2 throws and Connor takes just one throw ?

(g) What is the probability that Connor starts the game first ?

(h) What is the expected overall number of throws needed before Grannie starts ?

4. A fair dice is thrown. A six is obtained on the fourth throw.

(a) Find the probability that the next six is obtained on the tenth throw.

(b) Find the probability that the next six is not obtained until at least the tenth throw.

5. Two fair dice are thrown.

(a) Find the probability that at least seven throws must be made in order to get a double 6.

(b) Find the probability of getting at least one 6 in one of the first seven throws.

6. It is given that one-eleventh of adults are left-handed. Adults are chosen, one by one, until a left-handed adult is found. The total number of adults chosen, including the left handed one is denoted by T.

State an assumption which must be made for a geometric distribution to be a suitable model for T.

Using a geometric distribution

(i)   calculate $P(T = 4)$

(ii) calculate $P(T > 10)$

(iii) obtain the mean and variance of T

(OCR)

• *Check your answers.*

Section 6 : The Poisson Distribution AQA

In this section you will:
- calculate probabilities and expectation for a Poisson distribution
- use the Poisson as an approximation to the binomial distribution

DEVELOPMENT
D6.1: The Poisson distribution

In the Poisson distribution the random variable represents the number of occurrences of a particular event in an interval of fixed length in space or time. The events occur:

- **independently** of each other
- **singly** in continuous space or time (no two events occur together)
- **at a constant rate** (the mean number in a given interval is proportional to the length of the interval)

$$P(X = x) = \frac{e^{-\lambda}\lambda^x}{x!}$$ where λ = the mean number of events in a given interval and $x = 0, 1, 2, 3, \ldots$

An important property of this distribution is that $\text{Var}(X) = \text{E}(X) = \lambda$

$e \approx 2.718$
$0! = 1$

There is no upper limit on the value of X.

When the random variable X has a Poisson probability distribution, then
$X \sim \text{Po}(\lambda)$ where λ is the **parameter** of the Poisson distribution.

Examples of such distributions are :
- the number of radioactive particles emitted by a radioactive source in fixed time intervals
- the number of white cars passing a fixed point in intervals of 1 hour
- the number of mechanical breakdowns in a large factory each day

---

EXAMPLE   In a particular cloth, the average number of flaws is 8 per 100m length. Calculate the probability that there will be :

(a) no flaws in 100m of cloth
(b) 2 flaws in 50m of cloth
(c) more than 3 flaws in 150m of cloth

The Poisson distribution is named after the French mathematician Simeon Poisson (1781-1840)

(a) interval = 100m $\lambda = 8$
    $P(F = 0)$ = $\frac{e^{-8} 8^0}{0!} = e^{-8} = \boxed{0.000335}$

(b) interval = 50 m $\lambda = 4$ the value of λ changes as the length of the interval changes
    $P(F = 2)$ = $\frac{e^{-4} 4^2}{2!} = \boxed{0.147}$

(c) interval = 150 m $\lambda = 12$
    $P(F > 3)$ = $1 - P(F \leq 3)$ using the cumulative Poisson tables at the back of the book
             = $1 - 0.0023$
             = $\boxed{0.998}$

1. The random variable X has a Poisson distribution with mean 5.
   Calculate (a) $P(X = 2)$ (b) $P(X \leq 3)$ (c) $P(X > 4)$

2. If $T \sim Po(2.3)$, calculate:
        (a) $P(T = 0)$ (b) $P(T \leq 2)$ (c) $P(T > 2)$

3. On Friday evenings, customers arrive at the check-outs of a supermarket at an average rate of 20 per minute.
   Assuming that a Poisson distribution is appropriate, calculate the probability that:
   (a) no customers arrive at the check-outs in a given 15 second interval
   (b) more than 3 customers arrive at the check-outs in a given 20 second interval.

4. The number of particles emitted by a radioactive source has a Poisson distribution with a mean of 4 particles in any one second.
   Calculate the probability that the number of emissions per second is :
        (a) 0   (b) 1   (c) less than 3   (d) 2 or more

5. The number or breakdowns of karts at a kart-racing track is, on average, 1 every 20 laps.
   Assuming that a Poisson distribution is appropriate, calculate the probability that:
   (a) no karts break down in a given 20 lap interval
   (b) 4 karts break down in a given 50 lap interval
   (c) less than 5 karts break down in a given 100 lap interval
   In a race of 40 laps, the probability that n karts, or less, break down is 0.8571
   (d) Find the value of n.

> The sum of two independent Poisson variables with parameters λ and μ is a Poisson variable with parameter $\lambda + \mu$
> $\Rightarrow$ if $X \sim Po(\lambda)$ and $Y \sim Po(\mu)$ then $X + Y \sim Po(\lambda + \mu)$

6. The number or breakdowns of karts at a kart-racing track is, on average, 1 every 20 laps. Bestever School has two Karts competing. One kart is in a 20 lap race and the other is in a 40 lap race. After any breakdown, the kart continues the race.
   What is the probability that there will be:
   (a) no breakdowns   (b) one breakdown
   (c) two breakdowns   (d) two or more breakdowns

7. During the week, the switchboard of a busy office receives, on average, one call every 30 seconds.
   Assuming that a Poisson distribution is appropriate, calculate the probability that:
   (a) no calls are received in a given 1 minute period
   (b) at least four calls are received in a given 2 minute period
   (c) Find the probability that no calls are received between 11.05 and 11.06 and that less than two calls are received between 11.06 and 11.10.

• *Check your answers.*

D6.2:The Poisson as an approximation to the binomial distribution

In order to make the calculation easier, the Poisson distribution provides a reasonable approximation to the binomial distribution provided : *a reasonable rule is that $n > 50$ and $np < 5$*
n is large and **p is small**
For large n and small p, the two values usually agree to 1 s.f., which is often accurate enough for practical problems.   Mean value $= \lambda = np$

1. (a) There are 300 students in the local primary school. Find the probability that exactly two of them have their birthdays on Christmas Day
   (i) by using $Po(^{300}/_{365})$ (ii) by using $B(300, ^1/_{365})$
   giving your answers to 4 s.f.

   (b) There are 1500 students at the local secondary school.Find the probability that exactly ten of them have their birthdays on Christmas Day by using
   (i) a Poisson distribution   (ii) a binomial distribution   (both to 4 s.f.)

2. A factory packs eggs in boxes of 500. The probability that an egg is broken is 0.005.
   (a) What are the parameters of this binomial distribution ?

   (b) Use the binomial distribution to calculate the probability of exactly two eggs in the box being broken, to 4 s.f.

   (c) What is the mean value for this distribution ?

   (d) Use this mean value as the parameter for an approximate Poisson distribution and hence calculate the probability of exactly two eggs in the box being broken, to 4 s.f.

3. 250 patients are screened for a medical condition that is present in 1.4% of the general population.
   (a) Use the binomial distribution to find the probability that they found only one person with this condition, to 4 s.f.

   (b) Use the Poisson distribution to find the probability that they found only one person with this condition, to 4 s.f.

   (c) Does the Poisson distribution give a reasonable approximation in this case ?

   (d) Find, to 1 s.f., the probability that four people were found with this condition.

4. The probability that a telephone call coming into a large office system will be wrongly connected is 0.001.
   (a) Use the Poisson distribution to estimate the probability that, in the first 10 calls of the day, exactly one of them will be wrongly connected.

   (b) Use the Poisson distribution to estimate the probability that, on a day when there are 800 incoming calls, exactly four of them will be wrongly connected.

   (c) Which of these two probability estimates is likely to be more accurate, and why ?   • *Check your answers.*

Section 7: The Normal Distribution

In this section you will:
- meet the properties of the normal distribution
- meet and use the standard normal distribution to calculate probabilities
- use the normal distribution to solve problems
- find μ and σ from given probabilities

DEVELOPMENT

D7.1: Meet the normal distribution

The distributions met so far, the uniform distribution, the binomial distribution, the geometric distribution and the Poisson distribution, have all been discrete distributions. For each of these distributions, you have met and used a formula to calculate the probabilities.

The **normal distribution** is a continuous distribution and the most important distribution in statistics, as it has been since the 17th century. It has an extremely complicated formula, as a result of which mathematicians have had to devise simpler and most effective alternative methods to calculate probabilities.

The distributions of
- the height/weight of adult males/adult females
- GCSE exam marks for a single subject
- the heights of single species of plants
- the actual weights of flour in bags labelled 1 kg
- the times taken by a garage to perform a standard task
- the lengths of sweetpea flower stems
- the life of an AA battery ...

all give bell shaped graphs.

This is the graph of a normal distribution.

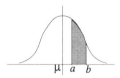

Properties of a normal distribution

The distribution is symmetrical about the mean, μ

The mode, median and mean are all equal (due to the symmetry)

The range of X is from $-\infty$ to $+\infty$

The curve approaches the x-axis as the values of x take very large positive or negative values.

The area bounded by the graph, the x-axis and the lines $x = a$ and $x = b$ is equal to $P(a < X < b)$

The total area under the curve is unity, since the sum of the probabilities = 1

The normal distribution is a two parameter distribution, the parameters being μ, its mean, and σ, its standard deviation.

$X \sim N(\mu, \sigma^2)$ means that the random variable X has a normal distribution with mean μ and standard deviation σ.

1.

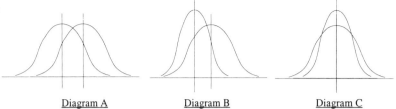

Diagram A   Diagram B   Diagram C

Each of these diagrams shows pairs of uniform distributions.
The total area under any uniform distribution is always 1.
One pair has the same mean but different standard deviations.
One pair has the same standard deviation but different means.
One pair has different means and different standard deviations.
Match the pair descriptions with the correct diagrams.

2. The uniform distributions of the two random variables
   X and Y are shown on this diagram.
   Which of the two random variables has the largest
   variance ?

• *Check your answers.*

D7.2: Normal distributions

A normal distribution has the following properties:
• the distribution is symmetrical about the mean
• approx. 68% of the data is within ±1 SD of the mean
• approx. 95% of the data is within ±2 SD of the mean
• approx. 99.5% of the data is within ±3 SD of the mean

This table records the heights of 10 000 16-19
females in the UK, measured to the nearest cm.

Heights (cm)	% of females	Heights (cm)	% of females	Heights (cm)	% of females
140.0 – 150.0	2	160.1 – 162.5	16	172.6 – 175.0	2
150.1 – 152.5	4	162.6 – 165.0	15	175.1 – 177.5	1
152.6 – 155.0	6	165.1 – 167.5	11	Over 177.5	0
155.1 – 157.5	11	167.6 – 170.0	8		
157.6 – 160.0	19	170.1 – 172.5	5		

Task 1:   Find estimates for the mean and standard deviation, to 3 d.p.

Task 2:   Plot the points for a frequency polygon for this distribution BUT, instead
              of joining the points with straight lines, join them with a smooth curve.
              This is the frequency distribution.

Task 3:   Draw a line on the distribution curve to mark the position of the mean.
              Draw two lines to mark off the values that lie within ±1SD of the mean.
              Draw two lines to mark off the values that lie within ±2SD of the mean.
              Draw two lines to mark off the values that lie within ±3SD of the mean.

D7.3: The standard normal distribution

The **standard normal distribution** is used to evaluate probabilities associated with normal distributions. It has a mean of zero and a standard deviation of 1.

The **standard normal random variable** is denoted by Z where $Z \sim N(0,1^2)$. Any normal random variable can be transformed, using a linear transformation, into the standard normal random variable.

$$Z = \frac{X - \mu}{\sigma} \qquad \text{where } X \sim N(\mu, \sigma^2) \text{ and } Z \sim N(0,1^2)$$

The **normal distribution function table** can then be used to evaluate probabilities for z, the particular values of Z.

The normal distribution function is denoted by $\Phi(z)$. (read Φ as 'fi')

$\Phi(z)$ represents the area to the left of any given z value.

Thus $\Phi(0.8) = P(Z < 0.8)$ and is equal to the area under the standard normal curve between $-\infty$ and 0.8

1. Use the normal distribution function table to evaluate:
   (a) $P(Z < 0.8)$ (b) $P(Z < 1.22)$ (c) $P(Z < 2.98)$ (d) $\Phi(2)$

2. (a) $P(Z < 0) = 0.5$ Explain why this should be so.   *The values in this table can be found on some calculators.*

The **normal distribution function table**
only gives values of $\Phi(z)$ for $0 < z < 3.5$

To find other areas under the curve, the symmetry of the distribution is used and the fact that the total area is 1.
In cases like these, it is advisable to draw a clear sketch.

EXAMPLE   For $Z \sim N(0,1^2)$, use sketches to help you find these probabilities using the normal distribution function table.

(a) $P(Z > 1)$
= $1 - \Phi(1)$
= $1 - 0.8413$
= $\boxed{0.1587}$
Here we use the fact that the total area = 1

(b) $P(Z < -1.8)$
= $\Phi(-1.8)$
= $1 - \Phi(1.8)$
= $1 - 0.9641$
= $\boxed{0.0359}$
Here we use the symmetry of the distribution

(c) $P(0.2 < Z < 2.1)$
= $\Phi(2.1) - \Phi(0.2)$
= $0.9821 - 0.5793$
= $\boxed{0.4028}$

(d) $P(-1.2 < Z < 0.7)$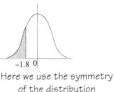
= $\Phi(0.7) - \Phi(-1.2)$
= $\Phi(0.7) - [1 - \Phi(1.2)]$
= $0.7580 - [1 - 0.8849]$
= $\boxed{0.6429}$

3. For $Z \sim N(0,1^2)$, use sketches to help you find these probabilities using the normal distribution function table.

   (a) $P(Z > 1.5)$ (b) $P(0.75 < Z < 2.25)$ (c) $P(-0.5 < Z < 1.16)$

> For negative values of z use $\Phi(-z) = 1 - \Phi(z)$

4. For the random variable $Z \sim N(0,1^2)$, find

   (a) $P(Z < -2.1)$ (b) $P(-0.5 < Z < 0)$ (c) $P(0.72 < Z < 2.74)$

   (d) $P(Z > 1.5)$ (e) $P(Z < 0.2$ or $Z > 1)$ (f) $P(Z < -0.43$ or $Z > 2.2)$

5. (a) $\Phi(z) = 0.975$ What is the value of z ?

   (b) $\Phi(z) = 0.25$ Explain how you know that z is negative.
                         What is the value of z ?

6. Find the value of z:

   (a) $\Phi(z) = 0.67$ (b) $\Phi(z) = 0.281$ (c) $\Phi(z) = 0.006$

   (d) $\Phi(-z) = 0.0244$ (e) $\Phi(-z) = 0.504$

> On the same page as the normal distribution function table, there is a table of critical values. This gives corresponding values of z for the most common values of $\Phi(z)$

                                                • *Check your answers.*

D7.4: Probabilities of non-standard distributions

> Any normal random variable can be transformed, using a linear transformation, into the standard normal random variable.
>
> $$Z = \frac{X - \mu}{\sigma} \qquad \text{where } X \sim N(\mu, \sigma^2) \text{ and } Z \sim N(0,1^2)$$
>
> The normal distribution function table can then be used to evaluate probabilities for z, and hence for x.

EXAMPLE   For $Y \sim N(24,5^2)$, transform Y to the standard normal distribution and work out these probabilities :

(a) $P(Y > 29)$

   transformation is
   $Z = \dfrac{X - 24}{5}$

$= P\left[Z > \dfrac{29 - 24}{5}\right]$

$= P(Z > 1)$

$= 1 - P(Z < 1)$

$= \boxed{0.1587}$

(b) $P(25 < Z < 28)$

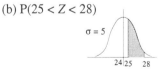

$= P\left[\dfrac{25 - 24}{5} < Z < \dfrac{28 - 24}{5}\right]$

$= P(0.2 < Z < 0.8)$

$= P(Z < 0.8) - P(Z < 0.2)$

$= 0.7881 - 0.5793 = \boxed{0.2088}$

1. For each of the following diagrams, find the transformation required to take it to the standard uniform distribution and hence find the probability represented by the shaded area:

(a)
$\sigma = 5$

30 40

(b)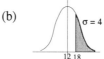
$\sigma = 4$

12 18

(c)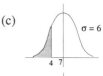
$\sigma = 6$

4 7

(d)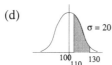
$\sigma = 20$

100 110 130

(e)
$\sigma = 6$

8 14 17

(f)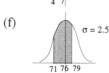
$\sigma = 2.5$

71 76 79

2. For the random variable $T \sim N(27, 3^2)$, find
   (a) $P(T < 30)$ (b) $P(T > 33)$ (c) $P(27 < T < 35)$
   (d) $P(21 < T < 33)$ (e) $P(T < 24)$ (f) $P(23.4 < T < 33)$

3. The random variable X is normally distributed with a mean of 10 and a standard deviation of 0.5. Find x, such that $P(X < x) = 0.006$

   • *Check your answers.*

D7.5: Deriving mean and SD from given probabilities

EXAMPLE   Given that for $X \sim N(\mu, \sigma^2)$, $P(X < 34.5) = 0.152$
and $P(X > 47.6) = 0.236$, find the values of μ and σ to 4 s.f.

0.152   0.236

34.5 μ 47.6

$$P(X < 34.5) = P\left[Z < \frac{34.5 - \mu}{\sigma}\right] = 0.152$$

$$\Rightarrow \Phi\left[\frac{34.5 - \mu}{\sigma}\right] = 0.152$$

$$\Rightarrow \Phi\left[-\frac{34.5 - \mu}{\sigma}\right] = 1 - 0.152 = 0.848$$

$$\Rightarrow -\left[\frac{34.5 - \mu}{\sigma}\right] = 1.028$$

Similarly

$$P(X > 47.6) = P\left[Z > \frac{47.6 - \mu}{\sigma}\right] = 0.236$$

$$\Rightarrow \Phi\left[\frac{47.6 - \mu}{\sigma}\right] = 1 - 0.236 = 0.764$$

$$\Rightarrow \frac{47.6 - \mu}{\sigma} = 0.762$$

Hence $-34.5 + \mu = 1.028\sigma$
and $47.6 - \mu = 0.762\sigma$

Solving these simultaneously $\Rightarrow$ $\boxed{\mu = 42.28 \ \& \ \sigma = 7.765}$

Give all answers to 4 s.f.

1. For the random variable $X \sim N(\mu, 0.8^2)$ and $P(X < 2.8) = 0.06$
   Work out the value of μ.

2. For the random variable $Y \sim N(\mu, 5^2)$ and $P(X > 42) = 0.25$
   Work out the value of μ.

3. For the random variable $T \sim N(\mu, 1.25^2)$ and $P(\mu < X < 2.8) = 0.3686$
   Work out the value of μ.

4. For the random variable $Q \sim N(10, \sigma^2)$ and $P(Q < 12.5) = 0.6554$
   Work out the value of σ.

5. For the random variable $V \sim N(120, \sigma^2)$ and $P(V > 135) = 0.23$
   Work out the value of σ.

6. Given that for $X \sim N(\mu, \sigma^2)$, $P(X > 57) = 0.236$
   and $P(X < 52) = 0.6915$, find the values of μ and σ to 4 s.f.

7. Given that for $X \sim N(\mu, \sigma^2)$, $P(X > 3.25) = 0.0681$
   and $P(X < 2.75) = 0.4$, find the values of μ and σ to 4 s.f.

• *Check your answers.*

D7.6: Normal distribution problems

1. A new car model, just launched on the market, is advertised to have a mean petrol consumption of 36.8 miles per gallon with a standard deviation of 1.6 miles per gallon, when travelling at 56 miles per hour. Assuming the distribution of the new cars is normal, calculate the probability that a car chosen at random from this model will have a petrol consumption greater than 37 miles per gallon when travelling at 56 miles per hour.

2. The weights of cereal in each box have a mean of 510 gm and a standard deviation of 10 gm. Boxes with less than 485 gm of cereal are rejected. What percentage of the boxes are rejected ?

3. The time required to travel by car from home to Grannie's house has been found, from experience, to have a mean of 1 hour 40 minutes with a standard deviation of 15 minutes. Assuming the distribution of times to be normal, calculate the probability that tomorrow we should complete the journey between 1 hour 30 minutes and 1 hour 45 minutes.

4. The weights of steel sheets produced by a certain rolling mill are known to be normally distributed with a mean weight of 35.6 kg. The probability that any sheet chosen at random will weigh less than 32 kg is 0.2981. Calculate the standard deviation of the distribution to 4 s.f.

• *Check your answers.*

Section 8: Random Sampling [AQA]

In this section you will:
- understand the distinction between a population and a sample
- meet various ways of taking random samples from a population
- use random numbers from tables and calculators

DEVELOPMENT

D8.1: Random samples of a population

The collection of items you wish to study is called **the population**. It may be a collection of people, but it is more likely to be a collection of numerical data. The population is generally large and, in order to study it, we usually take **a sample** of the population.

The sample should represent the population. When a sampling method over-represents or under-represents a feature of the population, it is said to be **biased**. For example, if you were trying to determine the average amount of homework done each night by students in a school, if you only asked Y11 students, the sample would be biased. A good selection method should try to reduce any bias as far as possible. The most common approach is to select **a random sample**.

> A **random sample** is one where every member of the
> target population is equally likely to be chosen for the sample.

> The question to be put to students is
> "How many minutes homework did you do last night ?"
> Lucy and Zoe want a random sample of 50.
> Lucy's first thought is to give everyone in the school a number, put each number onto a piece of paper and put all the pieces of paper in a box.
> Then she would mix them all up and draw one out, 50 times.

1. Would this give a random sample ?

2. Lucy decided that this was not a good idea. Why is it not ?

> Zoe used the school registers to give everyone a number.
> To make things easier, she just wrote down
> 7AB: 1 – 28, 7MC: 29 – 55, 7BJ: 56 – ... ... 13 PJ: 736 – 759
> She used the random number generator on her calculator to generate the fifty members of her random sample. (RAND or RND on most calculators)

3. The first number her calculator gave her was 0.036

    Zoe just wrote down 036   036 would be the 7th person in 7MC

    The next two numbers her calculator gave were 0.058 and 0.737

    Where will she find the two people corresponding to these numbers?

4. Zoe wrote down: 036   058   737   671   490   ~~943~~   033   ~~761~~   ~~938~~   (671) ...
    (a) Why did she cross out   943   761   and   938 ?
    (b) She did not count the number with a circle round it. Why not ?

> Lucy thought of another way of getting a random sample. She would choose the first number at random from the first register (either with a pin or just asking someone to choose a number between 1 and 28). Then she would take every 15th number after that – and, if possible, before that.
>
> This is **a systematic random sample**

5. Why did she choose every fifteenth number to get a sample of around 50 ?

6. This is a random sample because the random choice of the first number means that all numbers in the target population are equally likely to be selected. Why could she not toss a dice to give the first number ?

7. You are now going to select a random sample from a list of students numbered 1 – 350.
   (a) Find out how to get random numbers on your calculator.
   (b) Use the random number function to get a sample of 12 students.
      Make two lists : one of the numbers of the students selected for the sample
      one of the numbers that you could not use
   (c) Explain why there were so many numbers that you could not use.

8. You are now going to streamline the process used in question 7. Each student will have two numbers. 1 & 2 will be the first student, 3 & 4 will be the second student, …
   (a) Use the random number function to get a sample of 12 students.
      Make two lists : one of the numbers of the students selected for the sample
      one of the numbers that you could not use
   (b) Explain why you could *not* allocate three numbers to each student in this case.
   (c) What would be the maximum student population size in order to be able to allocate three numbers to each student ?

> **Random number tables** are produced by computer. There is no significance whatsoever in how the digits are arranged. Some tables may place them in pairs, some in threes, some in blocks of five … You choose your own starting point at random on the table and move left, or right, or up, or down, or diagonally, or … to the next digit. Your starting point does not have to be at the beginning of a block of digits. It is usual to continue moving in the same way as you started.

9. Use the random number table below to get a sample of 12 students from a population of 350.

Random number table																	
470	974	976	476	125	505	761	885	675	199	938	851	293	574	392	146	212
772	131	970	879	643	925	536	227	865	868	330	052	224	820	739	715	597
383	847	008	444	448	616	084	136	342	385	861	888	532	085	812	791	656
920	744	348	671	270	780	929	208	763	935	588	726	029	192	418	473	896
165	058	334	701	544	399	054	489	731	992	120	979	867	968	194	870	299
506	549	083	556	744	907	254	548	881	682	264	604	165	977	019	109	679
141	160	746	324	045	030	174	746	493	740	028	084	308	031	547	679	094
598	923	254	137	653	505	429	526	116	840	763	917	661	796	096	048	460
785	819	896	317	600	515	071	307	605	282	462	473	160	025	385	320	897
138	629	490	328	465	759	214	148	037	636	649	578	829	072	658	138	185

Section 9: Distribution of the Sample Mean

In this section you will:
- understand the distinction between a simple sample and an unrestricted sample
- meet and use the sample mean
- calculate the mean of the sample means
- work with the distribution of the sample means from a normal distribution
- meet and use the Central Limit Theorem

DEVELOPMENT

D9.1: Sampling and sample means

Simple sampling (without replacement)

If $X_1, X_2, X_3, X_4 \ldots \ldots X_n$ is a random sample of size n, <u>taken without replacement from a finite population</u>, then this is a simple sample of size n.

The mean of each sample, $\overline{X}$, is called **the sample mean**.

EXAMPLE Samples of size 2 are taken, without replacement, from the population 1, 5, 9

$\overline{X}$ is the random variable representing the mean of each possible sample. Draw up a frequency distribution table for $\overline{X}$ and calculate the value of $E(\overline{X})$.

Sample	(1,5)	(1,9)	(5,1)	(5,9)	(9,1)	(9,5)
Sample mean ($\overline{X}$)	3	5	3	7	5	7

$$E(\overline{X}) = \text{mean of sample means}$$
$$= \frac{3 + 5 + 3 + 7 + 5 + 7}{6} = \frac{30}{6} = \boxed{5}$$

Unrestricted sampling

If $X_1, X_2, X_3, X_4 \ldots \ldots X_n$ is a random sample of size n, <u>taken with replacement from a finite population</u> *or* <u>taken from an infinite population</u>, then this is an unrestricted sample of size n.

EXAMPLE Samples of size 2 are taken, with replacement, from the population 1, 5, 9

$\overline{X}$ is the random variable representing the mean of each possible sample. Draw up a frequency distribution table for $\overline{X}$ and calculate the mean of the sample means.

Sample	(1,1)	(1,5)	(1,9)	(5,1)	(5,5)	(5,9)	(9,1)	(9,5)	(9,9)
Sample mean	1	3	5	3	5	7	5	7	9

Mean of sample means
$$= \frac{1 + 3 + 5 + 3 + 5 + 7 + 5 + 7 + 9}{9} = \frac{45}{9} = \boxed{5}$$

1. Samples of size 2 are taken, without replacement, from 1, 4, 7, 8.
   Draw up a frequency distribution table for $\overline{X}$ and calculate the value of $E(\overline{X})$.

2. Samples of size 3 are taken, without replacement, from 3, 4, 6, 11
   (a) Draw up a frequency distribution table for $\overline{X}$
   (b) Calculate the mean of the sample means.
   (c) Calculate the mean of the population.

3. Samples of size 2 are taken, with replacement, from 10, 15, 17
   (a) Draw up a frequency distribution table for $\overline{X}$
   (b) Calculate the mean of the sample means.
   (c) Calculate the mean of the population.

4. Samples of size 3 are taken, with replacement, from 1, 5, 9
   (a) Complete this frequency table:

Numbers in sample	Sample mean	Frequency
1, 1, 1	1	1
5, 5, 5	5	1
9, 9, 9	9	1
1, 1, 5	$^7/_3$	3
1, 1, 9	...	
...		

   There are three possible arrangements of 1,1,5

   Big Edd

   (b) Calculate the value of $E(\overline{X})$.

5. A discrete random variable Y has the distribution:

y	-2	-1	0	1	2
$P(Y = y)$	$^1/_{12}$	$^1/_4$	$^1/_3$	$^1/_4$	$^1/_{12}$

   (a) Find the mean and variance of the distribution of Y.
   (b) The population of Y is large enough so that the selection of a sample is unrestricted. Random samples of 2 are taken from this distribution.
   Copy and complete this table of probabilities of the samples.
   (c) On the same table, but using a different colour, put the mean of each sample.
   (d) Obtain the probability distribution of the mean of these samples.
   (e) Use symmetry, or otherwise, to show that $E(\overline{Y}) = 0$

	-2	-1	0	1	2
-2	$^1/_{144}$	$^1/_{48}$			
-1					
0					
1					
2					

   Note:
   $P(a,b) = P(a) \times P(b)$

   • *Check your answers.*

Summary
$E(\overline{X})$ = mean of sample means = population mean

D9.2: Distribution of the sample mean from a normal population

If a random sample of size n is taken from a normal distribution $X \sim N(\mu, \sigma^2)$ then the distribution of the sample mean, $\overline{X}$, is also normal and $\overline{X} \sim N(\mu, \sigma^2/n)$
This is one of the reasons why the normal distribution is so powerful a tool.
The distribution of the sample mean, $\overline{X}$,
is known as the **sampling distribution of means**
and the standard deviation of this distribution, $\sigma/\sqrt{n}$
is known as the **standard error of the mean**

EXAMPLE   A random sample of size 15 is taken from a normal distribution with mean 50 and standard deviation 4. Find the probability that the mean of the sample is greater than 52.

$$X \sim N(50,16)$$

$\Rightarrow$ for a sample of size 15, $\overline{X} \sim N(50,{}^{16}/_{15})$

We need $P(\overline{X} > 52)$ $\sigma = \sqrt{({}^{16}/_{15})}$

$$= P\left[Z > \frac{52-50}{\sqrt{({}^{16}/_{15})}}\right]$$

transformation is
$$Z = \frac{\overline{X} - 50}{\sqrt{({}^{16}/_{15})}}$$

$= P(Z > 1.936)$

$= 1 - P(Z < 1.936)$

$= 1 - 0.9738$ $= \boxed{0.0262}$

1. A random sample of size 20 is taken from a noraal distribution with mean 35 and standard deviation 5.
   (a) Find the parameters of the distribution of the sample mean.
   (b) Find the probability that the mean of the sample is less than (i) 38 (ii) 34

2. If $X \sim N(400,100)$ and a random sample of size 10 is taken from the distribution, find the probability that the sample mean lies within the range 395 to 405.

3. Random samples of size n are taken from a distribution of X, where $X \sim N(94, 36)$. If the probability that the sample mean is greater than 92 is 0.8784, find the least value of n.

4. The masses of 1 kilogram bags of sugar bought to sell in the corner shop have a normal distribution with mean 1.005 kg and standard deviation 0.0082 kg.
   (a) Show that the probability that a randomly chosen bag has a mass less than 1 kilogram is 0.2709.
   (b) 20 of these bags are placed on a shelf. Find the probability that the mean mass of the 20 bags is less than 1 kilogram.
   (c) A notice on the shelf says "Maximum load 40.25kg".
   What is the probability that the 40 bags of sugar exceed this maximum ?

5. The marks on a particular GCSE paper have a normal distribution with mean 62 and variance 100. For a randomly chosen sample of 50 scripts, find the probability that the total marks on all the scripts is less than 3 000.

6. If X ~ N(65,15) and a random sample of size 200 has mean X. Find the value of a for which $P(\overline{X} < a) = 0.25$.

7. A conveyor belt has a load limit of 2000 kg. It carries boxes whose masses are normally distributed with a mean of 49.2 kg and standard deviation 5.5 kg.
   (a) Find the probability that the conveyor belt can carry 40 randomly selected boxes without breaching the load limit.
   (b) Show that 43 randomly selected boxes are highly likely to breach the load limit.

   • *Check your answers.*

D9.3: The Central Limit Theorem

If a random sample of size n is taken from *any* distribution with mean μ and variance σ^2, then the distribution of the sample mean is approximately a normal distribution with mean μ and variance $\sigma^2/_n$, provided n is sufficiently large.

This is one of the reasons why the normal distribution is so powerful a tool.

The size of n required varies with the distribution, but a good rule of thumb is to apply the theorem when $n > 30$.

1. A random sample of size 50 is taken from each of the following distributions. Find, for each case, the probability that the sample mean is greater than 5.
   (a) X ~ Po(4.8)   (b) X ~ B(9, 0.5)

2. An unbiased dice is thrown once. The score is given by the random variable X.
   (a) Make a table for the probability distribution of X
   (b) Find the value of E(X)
   (c) Show that $Var(X) = {}^{35}/_{12}$
   This dice is thrown 80 times.
   (d) Find the probability that the mean score is less than 3.2
   (e) Find the probability that the total score is greater than 300

3. Samples of size n, are taken from Po(2.9). Approximately 2% of the sample means are greater than 3.45. Estimate the value of n.   • *Check answers.*

S1: Unit 3: Discrete Random Variables

Facts and formulae you need to know:

$E(x) = \Sigma xp$ $\qquad \sigma^2 = Var(x) = \Sigma x^2 p - \mu^2$

$X \sim B(n,p)$ (n = no. of trials and p = prob. of success) $E(X) = np$ $Var(X) = npq$

$X \sim Geo(p)$ (p = prob. of success) $\qquad P(X = x) = q^{x-1}p$ $\qquad E(X) = \frac{1}{p}$ **(OCR)**

$X \sim Po(\lambda) = \dfrac{e^{-\lambda}\lambda^x}{x!}$ $\qquad E(X) = Var(X) = \lambda$ $\hfill$ **(AQA)**

$X \sim N(\mu,\sigma^2)$ $\qquad Z \sim N(0,1^2)$ where $Z = \dfrac{X - \mu}{\sigma}$ $\hfill$ **(Edexcel, AQA)**

Central Limit Theorem: The distribution of the sample mean of a sample of size n from <u>any</u> distribution is approximately equal to $X \sim N(\mu,\sigma^2/_n)$, <u>provided n is large.</u>

Competence Test S1.3

1. A spinner is labelled with the values of 0, 1, 2, 3 only in such a way that
   $P(X = r) = \dfrac{k}{(r + 1)}$ where X is the value obtained on an individual spin.

   Show that $k = {}^{12}/_{25}$ and find E(X) and Var(X).

   In a game between two contestants A and B, A wins if the value of the variable X is 0 or 3 and B wins if it 1 or 2. State with justification whether or not the game is fair one. (4M, 4A)

2. A box of chocolates contains 4 with hard centres and 6 with soft centres. If 4 chocolates are chosen at random, show that the probability that they consist of 2 hard and 2 soft centred chocolates is $^3/_7$.

   If X is the number of soft centred ones chosen, complete the probability distribution table given and find E(X), E(X^2) and Var(X)

x	0	1	2	3	4
P(X = x)			$^3/_7$		

   $\hfill$ (4M,6A)

3. Oranges are packed in boxes of 20. The probability that any individual orange selected froma box is damaged is 0.5.
   (a) Find the probability that a box picked at random contains:
   (i) less than 3 damaged oranges $\qquad$ (ii) more than 5 damaged oranges
   (iii) exactly 4 damaged oranges
   (b) An inspector tests 30 boxes of oranges, rejecting any that contain more
   $\qquad$ than one damaged orange. $\hfill$ (2M, 5A)
   $\qquad$ State the condition for the Binomial model to be valid in both parts (a) and (b).

[Edexcel & AQA] $\hfill$ | **Total (OCR) = 25** |

4. The manufacturers of new model of car state that, when travelling at 56 mph, the petrol consumption has a mean value of 34.6 miles per gallon with standard deviation 1.3 miles per gallon. Assuming a normal distribution, calculate the probability that a randomly chosen car of that model will have a petrol consumption greater than 30mpg at 56 mph. $\hfill$ (2M,3A)

$\hfill$ | **Total (Edexcel, AQA) = 30** |

AIMING HIGH

Unit 4
Correlation and Regression

CONTENTS
Section 1: Correlation
Section 2: Regression
Section 3: Dependent/Independent variables
Section 4: Spearman Rank Correlation   [OCR]

	OCR	AQA	Edexcel
Section 1	All	All	All
Section 2	All	All	All
Section 3	All	All	All
Section 4	All	—	—

S1.4: Correlation & Regression
Section 1 : Correlation

In this section you will:
- understand what is meant by bivariate data
- relate correlation to scatter diagrams
- meet and use ways of measuring correlation

DEVELOPMENT
D1.1: Scatter graphs and correlation

So far we have worked with data sets of values of a single variable for each member of a group. In this unit we are going to work with values of TWO variables for each member of a group. This kind of data is called **bivariate data**.

 Graph A Graph B Graph C

Set P: noon temperature and sales of icecream

Set Q: scores on two fair dice

Set R: GCSE maths mark and A-Level test mark

1. Here are three sets of bivariate data and three scatter diagrams which illustrate the data. Which set of bivariate data is illustrated by which scatter diagram ?

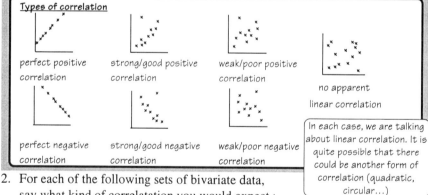

Types of correlation

perfect positive correlation

strong/good positive correlation

weak/poor positive correlation

no apparent linear correlation

perfect negative correlation

strong/good negative correlation

weak/poor negative correlation

In each case, we are talking about linear correlation. It is quite possible that there could be another form of correlation (quadratic, circular...)

2. For each of the following sets of bivariate data, say what kind of correlatation you would expect :

(a) GCSE maths mock mark and GCSE maths exam mark
(b) French GCSE mark and Science GCSE mark
(c) noon temperature and number of icecreams sold
(d) noon temperature and number of hot drinks sold
(e) scores on two dice
(f) length of Y12 student's leg and time for student to run 100m
(g) length of journey and cost of taxi fare
(h) height and weight of Y12 student

Plektra

• *Check your answers.*

D1.2: Measuring correlation

The closer a set of points are to a straight, the stronger the (linear) correlation.
We need a way of measuring the strength of the correlation.

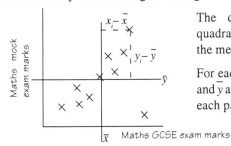

The diagram is split into four quadrants with two lines representing the mean of each set of values.

For each point, the deviations from $\bar{x}$ and $\bar{y}$ are measured, and the product of each pair of deviations calculated.

1.

Mock mark x_i	GCSE mark y_i	$x_i - \bar{x}$	$y_i - \bar{y}$	$(x_i - \bar{x})(y_i - \bar{y})$
65	67			
56	56			
86	63			
87	80			
74	51			
33	80			
31	29			
44	33			
66	48			
36	42			
72	58			
46	41			

$\Sigma x = \ldots\ldots$ $\Sigma y = \ldots\ldots$ $n = \ldots\ldots$ $\bar{x} = \ldots\ldots$ $\bar{y} = \ldots\ldots$

The covariance $= \dfrac{1}{n} \Sigma (x_i - x)(y_i - y) = \ldots\ldots\ldots$

Copy and complete this table and work out the calculations below it.

The sum of the product of the deviations is divided by n in order to make it independent of the size of the sample.

Icee

The disadvantager of using covariance as a measure of correlation is that it is dependent on the scales used on the axes of the scatter diagram. For example, if the exam marks had been halved (expressed out of 50 instead of 100), then the covariance would have been quartered. If the exam marks had been out of 300 instead of 100, the covariance would have been nine times as big.

However, if the covariance is divided by the product of the standard deviations of x and y, the resulting measurement would be independent of the scales used.

> The ratio of covariance to the product of the standard deviations of x and y
>
> $$= r = \dfrac{\frac{1}{n}\Sigma(x_i-\bar{x})(y_i-\bar{y})}{\sqrt{\dfrac{\Sigma(x_i-\bar{x})^2}{n}} \times \sqrt{\dfrac{\Sigma(y_i-\bar{y})^2}{n}}} = \dfrac{\Sigma(x_i-\bar{x})(y_i-\bar{y})}{\sqrt{\Sigma(x_i-\bar{x})^2 \times \Sigma(y_i-\bar{y})^2}}$$

2. You have already worked out the covariance for the data in Question 1.
Use the same data to copy and work out the values under the following headings and hence calculate the value of r.

x_i	y_i	$x_i-\bar{x}$	$y_i-\bar{y}$	$(x_i-\bar{x})^2$	$(y_i-\bar{y})^2$
65	67				
:	:				
:	:				
$\Sigma x = \ldots$	$\Sigma y = \ldots$			$\Sigma(x_i-\bar{x})^2 = \ldots$	$\Sigma(y_i-\bar{y})^2 = \ldots$

$$r = \dfrac{\Sigma(x_i-\bar{x})(y_i-\bar{y})}{\sqrt{\Sigma(x_i-\bar{x})^2 \times \Sigma(y_i-\bar{y})^2}} =$$

3. Now you are going to show that the value of r is unchanged when each x_i and y_i is doubled.

Make a table with the following headings.

x_i	y_i	$x_i-\bar{x}$	$y_i-\bar{y}$	$(x_i-\bar{x})(y_i-\bar{y})$	$(x_i-\bar{x})^2$	$(y_i-\bar{y})^2$

For x_i and y_i use the values of x_i and y_i from questions 1 and 2, doubled.

Show clearly how you work out the value of r.

The value of r should be the same as in question 2.

4. Note that there is no point in working out the values of $\Sigma(x_i-\bar{y})$ and $\Sigma(y_i-\bar{y})$ as they will always both be zero. Explain why.

• *Check your answers.*

D1.3: The product moment correlation coefficient

The **product moment correlation coefficent** is given by

$$r = \frac{\Sigma (x_i - \overline{x})(y_i - \overline{y})}{\sqrt{\Sigma (x_i - \overline{x})^2 \times \Sigma (y_i - \overline{y})^2}}$$

It measures how close the points on a scatter diagram are to a straight line.

The largest value r can take is $+1$.
This happens when the points on the graph lie in a straight line with a positive slope (perfect positive correlation).

The smallest value r can take is -1.
This happens when the points on the graph lie in a straight line with a negative slope (perfect negative correlation).

If r is close to zero, there is very little linear correlation.

Calculating r involves working out three sums:

$$\left. \begin{array}{l} S_{xx} = \Sigma (x_i - \overline{x})^2 \\ S_{yy} = \Sigma (y_i - \overline{y})^2 \\ S_{xy} = \Sigma (x_i - \overline{x})(y_i - \overline{y}) \end{array} \right\} \Rightarrow \quad r = \frac{S_{xy}}{\sqrt{S_{xx} \times S_{yy}}}$$

For each of the following sets of data:
- *describe the linear correlation as strong positive correlation/strong negative correlation/weak positive correlation, weak negative correlation or no linear correlation (from the scatter graph)*
- *calculate S_{xx}, S_{yy}, S_{xy}*
- *calculate r.*

1.

x	1	2	3	4	5
y	1	5	9	13	17

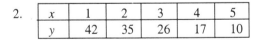

2.

x	1	2	3	4	5
y	42	35	26	17	10

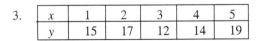

3.

x	1	2	3	4	5
y	15	17	12	14	19

4.

x	1	1	4	6	6
y	5	1	3	1	5

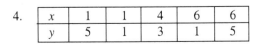

- *Check your answers.*

D1.4: Calculation methods

> The **product moment correlation coefficent** = $\dfrac{S_{xy}}{\sqrt{S_{xx}\,S_{yy}}}$
>
> where $\quad S_{xx} = \Sigma\,(x_i - \bar{x})^2 \qquad S_{yy} = \Sigma\,(y_i - \bar{y})^2 \qquad S_{xy} = \Sigma\,(x_i - \bar{x})(y_i - \bar{y})$

1. Work out the value of r.

   $(2, 17) \qquad (5,19) \qquad (3,12) \qquad (1,15) \qquad (4,12)$

   Show all working clearly.

> Just as with standard deviation, there are alternative formulae for S_{xx}, S_{yy} and S_{xy} which make the calculations easier.
>
> $S_{xx} = \Sigma\,(x_i - \bar{x})^2 \qquad \Rightarrow \qquad S_{xx} = \Sigma x^2 - \frac{1}{n}(\Sigma x)^2$
>
> $S_{yy} = \Sigma\,(y_i - \bar{y})^2 \qquad \Rightarrow \qquad S_{yy} = \Sigma y^2 - \frac{1}{n}(\Sigma y)^2$
>
> $S_{xy} = \Sigma\,(x_i - \bar{x})(y_i - \bar{y}) \qquad \Rightarrow \qquad S_{xy} = \Sigma xy - \frac{1}{n}(\Sigma x)(\Sigma y)$

2. Use these new formulae to calculate r for :

x	2	2.5	4	3.5	7
y	8	4	6	3	5

   Use a table with these headings:

   $x_i \qquad y_i \qquad x_i^2 \qquad y_i^2 \qquad x_i y_i \qquad$ Show all working.

3. Calculate r for :

t	15	16	20	14	18	15
v	3	7	2	5	4	2

4. $n = 9 \qquad \Sigma x = 12 \qquad \Sigma y = 20 \qquad \Sigma x^2 = 24 \qquad \Sigma y^2 = 50 \qquad \Sigma xy = 27$

   Calculate r.

5. $n = 9 \qquad \Sigma p = 12 \qquad \Sigma q = 20 \qquad \Sigma p^2 = 24 \qquad \Sigma q^2 = 50 \qquad \Sigma pq = 27$

   However, one extra set of values is to be added to this set : $(3,5)$

   Calculate r.

6. (a) $n = 7 \qquad \Sigma x = 39 \qquad \Sigma y = 126 \qquad \Sigma x^2 = 281 \qquad \Sigma y^2 = 2806 \qquad \Sigma xy = 887$

   Calculate r.

   (b) From this set of bivariate data, two data pairs $(1,7)$ and $(4,10)$ are added. Calculate the new value of r.

   (c) What does this tell you about the final set of data ?

   • *Check your answers.*

D1.5: Using calculator functions

1. Find out how to put your calculator into 2 variable statistical mode (usually it is 2ndF MODE 2).

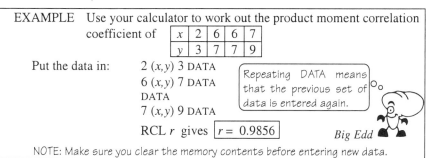

EXAMPLE   Use your calculator to work out the product moment correlation coefficient of

x	2	6	6	7
y	3	7	7	9

Put the data in: 2 (x,y) 3 DATA
6 (x,y) 7 DATA
DATA
7 (x,y) 9 DATA

Repeating DATA means that the previous set of data is entered again.

RCL r gives $r = 0.9856$ *Big Edd*

NOTE: Make sure you clear the memory contents before entering new data.

Find the product moment correlation coefficient for each set of data values (to 4 d.p.)

2.

x	2	3	4	7	8
y	8	4	6	8	12

3.

t	25	16	16	12	18	15
w	3	7	2	5	4	2

• *Check your answers.*

D1.6: Working with real data

Find the product moment correlation coefficient for each set of data values (to 3 d.p.)

Case 1: Average number of eggs and incubation time for birds

Bird	No. of eggs	Incubation time	Bird	No. of eggs	Incubation time
Blackbird	4.5	15	Goose	5	28
Falcon	3.5	30	Flamingo	2	32
Jackdaw	5	18	Lark	3.5	12
Mallard	10.5	26	Oyster catcher	3	27
Puffin	1.5	42	Longeared owl	14.5	28
Vulture	1	51	Kingfisher	7	21
Blue tit	10	15	Cuckoo	12	12

Case 2: Goals for and goals against

Team	Goal difference	Points	Team	Goal difference	Points
Man Utd	52	80	Arsenal	25	66
Ipswich	15	62	Leeds	15	62
Liverpool	23	59	Chelsea	21	4
Sunderland	4	53	Aston Villa	5	51
Charlton	−3	49	Newcastle	−6	46
Tottenham	−7	46	Southampton	−7	45
Leicester	−12	45	Everton	−13	41

D1.7: Scaling data

Replacing either data set by a linearly transformed set of data values of the form
$u = \dfrac{x - A}{B}$ does not affect the value of r.

Subtracting a constant from x does not alter the deviations $(x - \bar{x})$ because $\bar{x}$ is also decreased by A.
Dividing x by B does not alter r. In D1.2, you found that multiplying or dividing x by a constant, which is the same as altering the scale, had no effect on r.

1. (a) Calculate r:

height of Y11 boys in mm (h)	1800	1720	1690	1750	1820	1660	1900
weight of Y11 boys in kg (w)	70	68	68	70	58	69	73

(b) Transform (h) using the transformation $\frac{1}{10}(h - 1700)$ and w using the transformation $w - 60$. Show that the value of r obtained remains the same.

Transformations like these used to be applied to simplify calculations of r, but, with the advent of modern efficient calculators, the technique is rarely used now.

Important note: A correlation between two variables does not imply that one thing **CAUSES** the other. High marks in a mock exam and the real exam do tend to go together, but this is because both marks depend on a third variable – the ability and amount of work put in by the student.

Section 2 : Regression

In this section you will:
- look at ways of finding the line of best fit for a scatter diagram
- calculate equations for least squares regression lines
- use regression lines to predict values

DEVELOPMENT

D2.1: Finding a line of best fit

If the points on a scatter diagram are close to a straight line (r is near to 1 or –1),
it is easy to draw a fairly accurate line of best fit through the points 'by eye'.
If there is no correlation (r ≈ 0), then there is no such thing as a line of best fit.
If the points do not fit either of these cases, then it is difficult to find an
accurate line line of best fit 'by eye'.

The method of least squares is commonly used to find the line of best fit.
The aim is to minimise the sum of the squares of the deviations
in the y-direction of each point from the line of best fit.
The line of best fit must pass through the mean values of the two sets of data.

GCSE	'A' test mark
234	92
205	85
231	86
191	67
197	79
208	66
206	81
200	70
219	88
205	82
220	83
219	84
202	79
212	93
202	92
194	88
221	88
202	84
212	90
219	80
$\bar{x} = 210$	$\bar{y} = 83$

1. The table on the left shows the GCSE maths marks of students now taking A-Level maths and also their marks in the first A-Level unit test. The scatter diagram shows the same bivariate data.

This line of best fit has been drawn 'by eye'. This line passes through the point whose coordinates are the mean values of the data (marked with a cross). The distances e_1, e_2, ... are the deviations in the y-direction from the line of best fit.

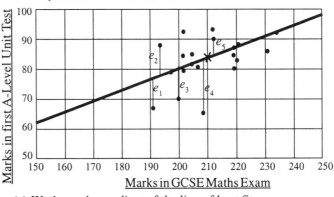

(a) Work out the gradient of the line of best fit.

(b) Use the fact that the line of best fit passes through the point whose coordinates are the two mean values to find the equation of the line of best fit.

(c) Make a table with the headings:

x_i	y_i	predicted y_i	e_i	e_i^2

Complete the table with the data for each point on the scatter diagram. and evaluate Σe_i^2 (the sum of the deviations).

You could try drawing several lines of 'best fit' by eye and seeing which give the least value for Σe_i^2 – but there is a way of working out the equation of the line of best fit that uses calculations that you have already met.

> The line for which Σe_i^2 is least is given by the equation
> $$y = a + bx$$
> where $\quad b = \dfrac{S_{xy}}{S_{xx}} = $ **the regression coefficient of y on x**
>
> This line passes through the point $(\bar{x}, \bar{y})$ and we can use this fact to work out the value of a. $\qquad a = \bar{y} - b\bar{x}$
>
> This line is called the **least-squares regression line of y on x.**

2. (a) Calculate the equation of the least-squares regression line of y on x for the data in question 1.

  (b) A student scored 225 in the GCSE maths exam but was in hospital and missed the first unit test. Use the equation of the regression line to calculate an estimate for her score in the unit test.

> Σe_i^2 (the sum of the deviations) would be less than the value found in question 1, as this method gives the least possible value of Σe_i^2

Calculate the equation of the least-squares regression line of y on x for the data given in each of the following questions. Show your working clearly.

3. $(x,y) = $ (7.2, 185) (7.9, 165) (8, 135) (8.1,150) (8.4, 140) (8.8, 135) (8.9, 120)

4. $n = 10 \qquad \Sigma x = 12 \qquad \Sigma y = 20 \qquad \Sigma x^2 = 24 \qquad \Sigma y^2 = 50 \qquad \Sigma xy = 27$

5. $n = 20 \qquad \Sigma x = 24 \qquad \Sigma y = 25 \qquad \Sigma x^2 = 43 \qquad \Sigma y^2 = 160 \qquad \Sigma xy = 82$

6. (a) An experiment to find the time to dissolve a solid in water is repeated three times at each of four different temperatures. The results are given below.

Temperature ($x°$)	Time taken (y minutes)		
10	6.7	5.9	7.2
30	3.3	4.5	5.1
50	4.4	3.6	2.9
70	2.6	3.1	1.9

Calculate the equation of the least-squares regression line of y on x.

  (b) Use the regression line to estimate the time taken at $40°$.

  (c) Why might an estimate produced in the same way for the time taken at $100°$ not be very accurate ?

• Check your answers.

D2.2: Using calculator functions

> If you enter the bivariate data on your calculator as usual, then it should give you the regression coefficient b and the constant a directly.

The closer the set of points on the scatter diagram are to a straight line, the more accurate any estimates produced using the regression line are likely to be. So, if the product moment correlation coefficient r is near to +1 or –1, the estimates should be good, but if r is near zero, the regression line will not produce accurate estimates.

If the value of r indicates that good estimates could be obtained, then INTERPOLATION (calculating values of points within the values on the scatter diagram) will give reasonable estimates. However EXTRAPOLATION (calculating values by extending the line outside the given points) may not be accurate as the correlation may not be the same at extrapolated points.

1. In an experiment, the temperature of a metal rod is raised from 400°. The extensions of the metal rod in mm at certain temperatures during the experiment are given here.

Temperature (T)	400°	450°	500°	550°	650°	700°	800°
Extension (E)	0.9	1.34	1.69	2.1	2.84	3.25	3.98

(a) Draw a scatter graph with temperature along the horizontal axis.

(b) Calculate the equation of the least-squares regression line of E on T and estimate the extension of the rod at 600°.

(c) Find the product moment correlation coefficent and say how accurate you think the estimate of the extension at 600° will be.

(d) Obtain an estimate of the likely extension at 900°.

(e) Give a reason why the estimate of the extension at 900° might not be as accurate.

2.

Team	Man Utd	Arsenal	Ipswich	Leeds	Liverpool
Goal difference	52	25	15	15	23
Points	80	66	62	62	59

Team	Chelsea	Sunderland	Aston Villa	Charlton	Newcastle
Goal difference	21	4	5	–3	–6
Points	54	53	51	49	46

Team	Tottenham	So'ton	Leicester	Everton	West Ham
Goal difference	–7	–7	–12	–13	–7
Points	46	45	45	41	39

(a) Calculate the product moment correlation coefficient.

(b) Calculate the equation of the least-squares regression line of P (points) on G (goal difference).

(c) At the same point in the season, Man City had a goal difference of –22. Use the regression line to estimate the number of points Man City had.

(d) Man City actually had 34 points. Explain the discrepancy. • *Check answers*

D2.3: The two regression lines

The story so far:

- There is no point in finding a regression line if there is no correlation ($r \approx 0$).
- The regression of y on x is the line for which Σe_i^2 is a minimum, where e_i is the deviation of y_i from the regression line.
- The regression line of y on x predicts the <u>average</u> value of y for a given value of x.
- If r is near 1 or –1 then predicted values of y are likely to be reasonably accurate. However, all predictions are prone to error.
- The regression line of y on x <u>cannot</u> be used to predict values of x from values of y.
- Interpolated values are likely to be more accurate than extrapolated values.

In order to predict values of x from values of y we need to find
the least squares regression line of x on y.
This line predicts the average value of x for any given value of y.
The regression of y on x is the line for which Σd_i^2 is a minimum,
where d_i is the deviation of x_i from the regression line.

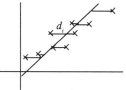

The least squares regression line of x on y
is given by $x = a' + b'y$

where $b' = \dfrac{S_{xy}}{S_{yy}}$ = the regression coefficent of x on y

and $a' = \bar{x} - b'\bar{y}$

Reminder

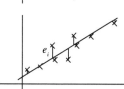

The least squares regression line of y on x
is given by $y = a + bx$

where $b = \dfrac{S_{xy}}{S_{xx}}$ = the regression coefficent of y on x

and $a = \bar{y} - b\bar{x}$

If $r = \pm1$, the two regression lines coincide.

Calculator shortcuts:

- If you enter the bivariate data onto your calculator then the calculator should give you the values of b, the regression coefficient of y on x, and a.

However, b' and a' are not among the calculator functions. In order to calculate the values of b' and a' using a calculator, you could use one of the following methods:

- You could enter the data again, with y before x. The values of b and a thus obtained will then be the values of b' and a'. If your original data has been entered as two lists, as on graphical calculators, specify the lists in reverse..

- Using the statistical functions on the calculator, evaluate b' as $\dfrac{S_{xy}}{S_{yy}}$

- $r^2 = \dfrac{S_{xy}^2}{S_{xx} \times S_{yy}} = \dfrac{S_{xy}}{S_{xx}} \times \dfrac{S_{xy}}{S_{yy}} \Rightarrow r^2 = b\,b' \Rightarrow \boxed{b' = \dfrac{r^2}{b}}$

For Q 1-2, calculate the equations of the regression lines of y on x and of x on y.
Give the equations in the form $y = a + bx$ and $x = a' + b'y$

1. $(x,y) = (6, 58)$ $(6, 65)$ $(7, 72)$ $(8,85)$ $(8, 88)$ $(9, 92)$ $(10, 98)$

2. $n = 10$ $\Sigma x = 15$ $\Sigma y = 25$ $\Sigma x^2 = 80$ $\Sigma y^2 = 90$ $\Sigma xy = 120$

For Q 3-4, calculate the equations of the two regression lines.

3.

t	9	9.2	10	10.5	11.1	11.3	11.5
V	185	165	135	150	140	135	120

4. $n = 40$ $\Sigma m = 120$ $\Sigma p = 55$ $\Sigma m^2 = 632$ $\Sigma p^2 = 168$ $\Sigma mp = 580$

• *Check your answers.*

D2.4: Making predictions

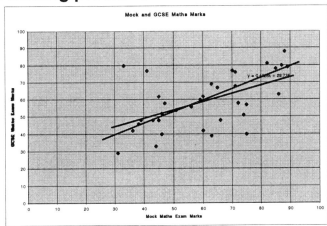

1. The head of maths wants to use the above data for last year's Higher Level GCSE maths students to predict the marks for this year's Higher Level students.
   The equations of the two regression lines are
   $$y = 29.375 + 0.4828x \text{ and } x = 19.933 + 0.6615y$$

   (a) Molly got 68% in this year's mock exam.
   (i) Which regression line should you use to predict Molly's GCSE mark ?
   (ii) Work out her predicted mark.

   (b) Last year the boundary between A and B in this GCSE exam was 72%.The head of maths wants to work out what mark the A-B boundary should be on the mock exam.
   (i) Which regression line should you use to work out the A-B boundary on the mock exam?
   (ii) Work out the A-B boundary mark.

2. A survey was made of the heights of 100 twenty-five year old men and their fathers. x represents the height of each son in cm and y represents the height of each father in cm. The data is summarised here. $n = 100$ $\Sigma x = 18030$ $\Sigma y = 17510$
$$\Sigma x^2 = 3\,275\,150 \qquad \Sigma y^2 = 2\,118\,180 \qquad \Sigma xy = 2\,144\,500$$

(a) Calculate the mean and standard deviation of
   (i) the sons' heights (ii) the fathers' heights.

(b) Calculate the product moment correlation coefficient of the heights. Use it to assess the reliability of any estimates made using the regression lines.

(c) Calculate the equations of the two regression lines for this data.

(d) Calculate an estimate for the height of the father whose son is 190 cm tall.

(e) Calculate an estimate for the height of the son whose father is 175 cm tall.

3. Some years ago, I used to drive to work in Warrington. To get there I had to drive across the Thelwall Viaduct on the M6. At that time, there were always serious traffic jams on the viaduct between 08.30 and 09.00. For a period of 12 days, I kept a record of the time I left home and the time I arrived at work each morning.

x = the number of minutes after 7.30 that I left home
y = the number of minutes after 7.30 that I arrived at work.

Left home	7.40	8.00	7.50	8.23	7.52	8.00	7.48	8.12	8.30	7.33	8.15	8.21
x	10	30	20	53	22	30	18	42	60	03	45	51
y	60	76	74	104	71	74	65	95	105	52	92	99

(a) $n = 12$ $\Sigma x = ??$ $\Sigma y = ??$ $\Sigma x^2 = ??$ $\Sigma y^2 = ??$ $\Sigma xy = ??$ $\overline{x} = ??$ $\overline{y} = ??$
   Enter the data on your calculator and fill in the missing figures in the data above.

(b) Find the equation of the regression line of y on x in the form $y = a + bx$, giving a and b to 4 significant figures.

(c) Predict the time I should arrive if I leave home at 8.05.

(d) Find the value of the product moment correlation coefficient.

(e) The equation of the regression line of x on y has the form $x = a' + b'y$
   where $b' = \dfrac{r^2}{b}$ and $a' = \overline{y} - b\,\overline{x}$
   Find the equation of the regression line of x on y.

(f) Calculate the time I should leave home if I am to arrive at work at 9.00.

(g) Use the equation of the regression line of y on x to calculate the time I should leave home if I am to arrive at work at 9.00.

(h) Why are the estimates obtained in (f) and (g) so close together ?

• *Check your answers.*

If $r = 1$ or -1, then the two regression lines are the same line.
If $r \approx 1$ or -1, the two regression lines are very close together and using each of the two lines to predict a particular value gives approximately the same result.

Section 3 : Dependent/Independent Variables

In this section you will:
* understand what is meant by dependent and independent variables
* understand what is meant by a controlled variable

DEVELOPMENT

D3.1: Dependent and independent variables

In certain cases, one of the variables being considered is dependent on the other variable. Examples of this include:

* an experiment where the temperature of a metal rod is raised in steady steps and the extension of the rod measured at each step
* an experiment where the length of a spring is measured for various loads hung from the end of the spring
* the number of coats of varnish applied to a yacht hull and the hull's resistance to weathering
* the time I leave home to go to work and the time I get to work

Terminology

The **independent variable** is sometimes called **the explanatory variable** or **the controlled variable**. It's values are chosen (or controlled). It is NOT a random variable.

The dependent variable is sometimes called **the response variable**. It IS a random variable.

In a scatter diagram, the independent variable is always along the bottom of the diagram.

If the values of x are controlled (ie are not random), then only the regression line of y on x has meaning. This line is used to estimate values of y from values of x <u>and</u> values of x from values of y.

1. In the following data, x is a controlled variable.

x	10	20	30	40	50	60
y	31	59	90	122	153	179

(a) Work out out the equation of the line of regression and use it to estimate:
(i) the value of y when $x = 35$ (ii) the value of x when $y = 140$

(b) Work out an estimate for the value of y when $x = 100$

(c) Explain why the estimated value of y when $x = 100$ not as reliable as the estimated value of y when $x = 35$?

2. A vertical spring is compressed by a load placed on top of the spring. Its compression is measured for each load.
What is the explanatory variable and what is the response variable ?

3. A rock is dropped from the top of a tall tower.
The distance it has fallen after 1, 2, 3, ... seconds is measured.

t (in s)	1	2	3	4	5	6
d (in m)	4.8	19.8	44	80.5	125	178

(a) What is the independent variable ?

(b) What is the dependent variable ?

(c) Calculate how long it would take to fall 100 m.

(d) Calculate how far it would fall in 2.5 s.

4. The life in hours, h, of a high powered drill depends on the running speed of the drill, r revs/min.
In a series of quality control experiments, the following data is obtained.

$n = 20$ $\Sigma r = 280$ $\Sigma h = 465$

$\Sigma r^2 = 3\,458$ $\Sigma h^2 = 12\,684$ $\Sigma rh = 5680$

(a) Find the regr ession line of h on r.

(b) Estimate the life of a drill which runs at 40 rev/min.

• Check your answers.

Section 4 : Spearman's Rank Correlation

In this section you will: OCR
- understand what is meant by rank correlation
- meet Spearman's rank correlation and relate it to the product moment correlation

DEVELOPMENT

D4.1: Rank correlation

A set of items is **ranked** when it is put into order of preference.

1. Eight divers are taking part in a competition. Each dive is being marked by two judges. At the end of the competition, each judge places the divers in order, starting with the one that he thought was the best.

Judge 1:	H	E	F	B	D	A	C	G
Judge 2:	E	F	D	H	B	C	G	A

(a) *Copy and complete this table of rankings:*

Diver	Rank for Judge 1 (x_i)	Rank for Judge 2 (y_i)
A	6	8
B	4	5
C		
D		
E		
F		
G		
H		

(b) Draw a scatter diagram of the two sets of ranks.

(c) From the scatter diagram, you can see that there is a degree of positive correlation between the two rankings. Work out the **product moment correlation coefficient** of the two sets of ranks.

Note that x and y are ranks, not random variables. This correlation coefficient is called **Spearman's rank correlation coefficient** and the label r_s is used, rather than r.

The British psychologist, Charles Spearman, studied this coefficient and gave his name to it.

Icee

2. Imagine that, in the case of the eight divers in question 1, that a third judge also ranked the divers. The ranking of the first and third judges is compared.

What can you say about the ranking for the third judge if the Spearman's rank correlation coefficient is :   (a) 1   (b) –1   (c) 0

• *Check your answers.*

D4.2: Spearman's rank correlation coefficient

An alternative formula for calculating Spearman's rank correlation coefficient

Since r_s is calculated from the ranks of n items,
x and y always take the values $1, 2, 3, \ldots n$.
In this case, there is an alternative formula for r_s, which is easier to calculate.

$$r_s = 1 - \frac{6\Sigma d_i^2}{n(n^2 - 1)} \quad \text{where} \quad d_i = x_i - y_i$$

1. Calculate Spearman's rank correlation coefficient for the following ranked data:

Rank A:	1	2	3	4	5	6
Rank B:	6	3	2	4	1	5

   (a) using calculator functions
   (b) using the above formula

2. (a) What do you think the value of r_s would be if Rank B was reversed ?
   (b) Reverse rank B and calculate r_s. Were you correct ?

3. These marks were given to iceskaters by two judges.

Skater	A	B	C	D	E	F
Judge 1	5.5	5.8	5.2	5.7	5.9	5.2
Judge 2	5.5	6.0	5.3	5.6	5.8	5.4

   (a) Rank each set of marks, with the highest mark being given rank 1.

   (b) Calculate Spearman's rank correlation coefficient for the two rankings.

   (c) How much agreement was there between the two judges as to rank order ?

4. A Y9 student was asked to estimate the age of each of his teachers.

Actual age	27	34	28	45	58	42	37
Estimated age	22	37	31	42	65	43	36

   (a) Work out the product moment correlation coefficient of the two sets of ages.

   (b) Calculate Spearman's rank correlation coefficient for the actual and estimated ages.

   (d) How good was he at estimating his teachers' ages ?

   (e) How good was he at estimating the relative ages of his teachers ?

5. Two newspapers did a survey of five schools in the same area. The Gazette and The Leader awarded marks to each school for a variety of reasons.

School	P	Q	R	S	T
The Gazette	345	356	362	348	369
The Leader	682	675	684	680	688

   (a) Work out the product moment correlation coefficient of the two sets of scores.

   (b) Calculate Spearman's rank correlation coefficient for the two sets of scores.

   (c) Is there much to choose between the five schools ? Explain your answer.

• Check your answers.

D4.3: Ranking methods

EXAMPLE   Rank each of these sets of values:

(a)
x	73	76	72	77	71	78
Rank	3	4	2	5	1	6

In (b) the 2nd and 3rd values are equal, so both are assigned the rank 2.5. The sum of the rankings must remain the same.

(b)
x	63	66	63	68	64	61
Rank	2.5	5	2.5	6	4	1

(c)
x	35	36	36	39	37	34	35	36
Rank	2.5	5	5	8	7	1	2.5	5

In (c) the 2nd and 3rd values are equal, so both are assigned the rank 2.5.
The 4th, 5th and 6th values are the same, so all three are ranked 5th

1. The marks of 10 students in tests for History and Geography are as follows:

History	9	12	16	12	10	7	12	16	8	12
Geography	10	10	13	8	6	4	7	7	5	6

Copy and complete the table that follows and use it to calculate Spearman's coefficient of rank correlation, to 2 d.p.

History (x)	Geography (y)	Rank(x)	Rank(y)	$|d|$	d^2
9	10	3	...	...	...
12	10				
:					

2. The mean rainfall per day and the mean hours of sunshine per day observed at a Lancashire weather station are as follows:

Month	Rainfall (mm)	Sunshine (hours)
January	1.3	1.4
February	1.3	2.6
March	0.7	4.6
April	2.1	5.2
May	2.5	5.9
June	2.2	7.7
July	2.8	5.9
August	1.8	5.6
September	2.5	4.6
October	1.7	4.6
November	1.5	2.9
December	1.8	1.5

Calculate the Spearman's coefficient of rank correlation to 2 d.p.

• *Check your answers.*

D4.4: Ranking without data

EXAMPLE   A set of bivariate data is shown on the scattergraph below.
List the pairs of rankings.

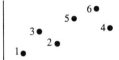

The x-rankings have been written underneath the graph.
The y-rankings have been written next to each point.

Rank x	1	2	3	4	5	6
Rank y	1	3	2	5	6	4

Taz

1. A set of bivariate data is shown on the scattergraph.
   (a) List the pairs of rankings.

   (b) Calculate the Spearman's rank correlation
   coefficient, to 3 d.p.

2. A set of bivariate data is shown on the scattergraph.
   (a) List the pairs of rankings.

   (b) Calculate the Spearman's rank correlation
   coefficient, to 3 d.p.

3. For each of these two scattergraphs, state the Spearman's rank correlation
   coefficient.

   (a)

   (b)

4. In an iceskating competition, Judge A ranks the seven competitors in this
   order: 5   4   2   1   7   3   6

   Judge B ranks the same competitors.

   The Spearman's rank correlation between the two rankings is –1.

   Find the ranking given by Judge B.

   • *Check your answers.*

S1: Unit 4: Correlation and Regression

Facts and formulae you need to know:

The **product moment correlation coefficient** $= r = \dfrac{S_{xy}}{\sqrt{S_{xx} \times S_{yy}}}$

where $S_{xx} = \Sigma x^2 - \frac{1}{n}(\Sigma x)^2$ $S_{yy} = \Sigma y^2 - \frac{1}{n}(\Sigma y)^2$ $S_{xy} = \Sigma xy - \frac{1}{n}(\Sigma x)(\Sigma y)$

The least squares regression line of y on x : $y = a + bx$

where $b = S_{xy} \div S_{xx}$ and the fact that the line passes through $(\bar{x}, \bar{y})$ gives a.

Spearman's rank correlation coefficient is the product moment coefficient of the two sets of ranks.   **[OCR]**

Competence Test S1.4

1. The resistive force y newtons acting on a motor-cyclist depends on his speed x kph. The following table shows the appropriate data.

x	10	20	40	50	60	70
y	70	85	115	130	168	214

(5M,7A)

   (i) Plot a scatter diagram to illustrate the data.

   (ii) Find the value of the product moment correlation coefficent and the equation of the regression line of y on x.

   (iii) Estimate values of y corresponding to $x = 30$ and $x = 80$, indicating how you have made the estimates and comment on the reliability of the answers.

2. Obtain the product moment correlation coefficient for the bivariate dàta summarised by:

   $[n = 8$ $\Sigma x = 22.4$ $\Sigma x^2 = 69.44$ $\Sigma y = 52.0$ $\Sigma y^2 = 452.24$ $\Sigma xy = 138.88]$

   It is known that there is a very strong relationship between x and y.

   State, with a reason, whether the relationship is linear of non-linear. (3M,3A)

3. A statistician discovers part of an old incomplete research paper containing data that he wishes to research again. He can see that $\bar{x} = 21$ and that the line of regression of y on x can be written as $y = -\frac{1}{7}x + ??$ and that the line of regression of x on y can be written as $y = -7x + 163$.

   (i) Show that $\bar{y} = 16$

   (ii) Calculate the missing term in the line of regression of y on x.

   (iii) Use the appropriate regression line to estimate x when $y = 128$ (4M,4A)

Total (AQA & Edexcel) = 26

[OCR]

4. In a fashion competition, judges gave marks to 7 contestants as follows:

Contestant	A	B	C	D	E	F	G
Judge X	64	65	67	78	79	80	96
Judge Y	70	63	61	81	81	78	98

Calculate Spearman's rank correlation coefficient. (3M,4A)

Total (OCR) = 33

AIMING HIGH
AS/A-Level Questions
Revision for S1 Exam

| Students should do all questions, regardless of board, unless specifically told not to. |

Unit 1: Representation of Data

1. The salaries, £x a year, of 63 employees of a bank are summarised below.

Salary (£x)	Frequency
$5\,000 < x \leq 10\,000$	5
$10\,000 < x \leq 15\,000$	21
$15\,000 < x \leq 20\,000$	20
$20\,000 < x \leq 30\,000$	10
$30\,000 < x \leq 40\,000$	6
$40\,000 < x \leq 80\,000$	1

(a) Represent this data by a cumulative frequency polygon.

(b) Use your cumulative frequency polygon to estimate
   (i) the median salary of the employees
   (ii) the proportion of the employees whose salary is less than £12 000 a year

Two employees are to be chosen at random.

(c) Calculate the probability that both of the employees chosen will earn more than £20 000 a year. *(Edexcel)*

2. Summarised below is the data relating to the number of minutes, to the nearest minute, that a random sample of 65 trains from Darlington were late arriving at a main line station.

Minutes late (0|2 means 2)   Totals

0	2 3 3 3 4 4 4 4 5 5 5 5 5 5	(14)
0	6 6 6 7 7 8 8 8 9	(9)
1	0 0 0 2 2 3 3 4 4 4 5	(11)
1	6 6 7 7 8 8 8 9 9	(...)
2	1 2 2 3 3 3 3 4	(...)
2	6	(...)
3	3 4 4 5	(4)
3	6 8	(2)
4	1 3	(2)
4	7 7 9	(3)
5	2 4	(2)

(a) Write down the values needed to complete the stem and leaf diagram.

(b) Find the median and quartiles of these times.

(c) Find the 67th percentile.

(d) On graph paper construct a box plot for these data, showing clearly your scale.

(e) Comment on the skewness of the distribution.

A random sample of trains arriving at the same main line station from Shefton had a minimum value of 15 minutes late and a maximum value of 30 minutes. The quartiles were 18, 22 and 27 minutes.

(f) On the same graph paper and using the same scale, construct a box plot for these data.

(g) Compare and contrast the train journeys from darlington and Shefton based on these data. *(Edexcel)*

3. The weight of luggage belonging to each of the 135 passengers on an aeroplane is summarised in the frequency distribution shown.

Weight (kg)	Number of pasengers
0 –	23
20 –	28
30 –	31
35 –	4
40 –	33
60 – 90	16

(a) Illustrate these data using a histogram.

(b) Comment on the distribution of luggage weight given the fact that on this flight any passenger taking more than 35 kg of luggage had to pay an excess baggage charge.

(c) Draw a box-and-whisker plot of the data above using the following additional information.

Lightest luggage	Lower quartile	Median	Upper quartile	Heaviest luggage
4 kg	25 kg	32 kg	53 kg	87 kg

There are no outliers.

(d) Discuss which of your two diagrams better illustrates the distribution of luggage weight. *(AQA)*

4. Given that the mean and standard deviation of the numbers
$$2, 3, 4, 5, 6, 7, 8$$
are 5 and 2 respectively, write down the mean and standard deviation of

(a) 12, 13, 14, 15, 16, 17, 18

(b) 20, 30, 40, 50, 60, 70, 80

(c) $2x + y, 3x + y, 4x + y, 5x + y, 6x + y, 7x + y, 8x + y$

(Edexcel)

5. The following table shows data about the time taken, in seconds to the nearest second, for completing each one of a series of 75 similar chemical experiments.

Time (s)	50 – 60	61 – 65	66 – 70	71 – 75	76 – 86
Number of experiments	4	13	26	22	10

(i)   State the type of diagram appropriate for illustrating the data.

(ii) Calculations using the data in the table give estimates as follows:
      Mean time of the experiments   69.64 s
      standard deviation   6.37 s
    explain why these are estimates rather than precise values.

(iii) Estimate the median and the interquartile range of the times taken for completing the experiments.

(iv) It was subsequently revealed that the four experiments in the 50 – 60 class had actually taken 57, 59, 59, 60 seconds respectively. State, without further calculation, what effect (if any) there would be on the estimate of the median, interquartile range and mean if this information were taken into account. *(OCR)*

6. Examinations in English, Mathematics and Science were taken by 400 students. Each examination was marked out 100 and the cumulative frequency graphs illustrating the results are shown below.

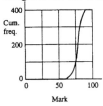 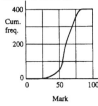 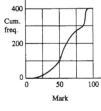

(i)   In which subject was the median mark the highest ?
(ii) In which subject was the interquartile range of the marks the greatest ?
(iii) In which subject did approximately 75% of the students score 50 marks or over ? *(OCR)*

Unit 2: Probability

1. A coin is biased so that, on each toss, the probability of obtaining a head is 0.4. The coin is tossed twice.

(i) Calculate the probability that at least one head is obtained.

(ii) Calculate the conditional probability that exactly one head is obtained, given that at least one head is obtained. *(OCR)*

2. Each time a tennis player serves, the probability that she wins the point is 0.6, independently of the result of any preceding serves. At the start of a particular game, she serves for each of the first five points.

Calculate the probability that, for the first two points of this game,
   (i)   she wins both points
   (ii) she wins exactly one of these points

Calculate the probability that, for the first five points of this game,
   (iii) she loses all five points
   (iv) she wins at least one of these five points   *(OCR)*

3. A penalty shoot out in a game of hockey requires each of two players to take a penalty hit to try to score a goal. In a simple model, each player has a probability of 0.8 of scoring a goal, and independence is assumed. Calculate the probability that exactly one goal is scored from the two hits.

In an alternative model, the probability of the second player scoring is reduced to 0.7 if the first player does not score. Calculate the probability that the second player has scored, given that only one goal is scored.   *(OCR)*

4. A bus serving a number of outlying villages is due to arrive in a particular village at 10 o'clock. Past experience tells the people waiting in the village for the bus tht the probability of the service being cancelled on any day is 0.05, and that, when it runs, the probability of the bus being more than 10 minutes late is 0.1.

Using a tree diagram, or otherwise, find the conditional probability tha the service has been cancelled, given that at 10 minutes past 10 the bus has not arrived in the village.   *(OCR)*

5. The probability that an A-Level candidate will be absent at the start of an examination is 0.01, independently of whether or not other candidates are absent. Find the probability that, of 50 A-Level candidates, three or more will be absent at the start of the examination.   *(AQA)*

6. The events A and B are such that

   $P(A/B) = 0.4$ $P(B/A) = 0.25$ $P(A \cap B) = 0.12$

   (i)   Calculate the value of $P(B)$.

   (ii) Give a reason why A and B are not independent.

   (iii) Calculate the value of $P(A \cap B')$

                    (Edexcel)

For OCR students only

7. The letters of the word MATHEMATICS are written, one on each of 11 separate cards. The cards are lais out in a line.

   (i) Calculate the number of different arrangements of these letters.

   (ii) Determine the probability that the vowels are all placed together.

   (Edexcel)

Unit 3: Discrete Random Variables

1. A die is numbered and weighted so that when it is thrown once the score X has the following probability distribution

x	1	2	3
$P(X = x)$	0.2	0.3	0.5

   Find the expectation and variance of X.

   The die is thrown twice and Y is the result of multiplying the two scores together. Tabulate all the possible values of Y and their corresponding probabilities.

   (OCR)

2. The random variable V has the probability distribution given in the following table.

v	1	2	3	4
$P(V = v)$	$1/3$	k	$1/6$	k

   (i) Find the value of the constant k.

   (ii) Calculate the expectation and the variance of V, giving your answers as exact fractions. *(OCR)*

3. The discrete random variable X has the probability distribution given by the following table.

x	1	2	3	4
$P(X = x)$	0.4	0.3	0.1	0.2

   Two independent observations of X are made. The value of the random variable Y is found by subtracting the smaller of the two values of X from the larger. If the two values of X are equal, Y is zero. Show that $P(Y = 1) = 0.34$ and tabulate the complete probability distribution of Y.

   Find   (i) E(Y)   (ii) Var(Y)   (iii) $P(Y \geq E(Y))$ *(OCR)*

Questions 4 - 6 for OCR and AQA students only

4. Of the sweets made by a manufacturer, 30% are green. The contents of a packet of sweets may be assumed to be a random sample of the manufacturer's output. I pick seven sweets out of a packet with my eyes closed. Find the probability that

   (i) exactly two of the seven are green

   (ii) fewer than three are green   *(OCR)*

5. The random variable X is such that $X \sim B(3, p)$. Given that $P(X = 0) = 0.512$, find the value of p and hence find $P(X = 2)$. *(OCR)*

6. (a) A pack of 52 playing cards consists of 4 suits: hearts, clubs, diamonds and spades. Each suit contains 13 cards.

   A card is drawn at random from the pack and its suit noted. The card is then replaced and the pack of cards shuffled. This procedure is carried out 8 times.

   Find the probability that
   (i)   at most one of the eight cards drawn is a diamond.
   (ii) exactly two of the eight cards drawn are diamonds.

   (b) Indicate why the probability model that you used in part (a) would not be appropriate if, at each drawing, the card was not replaced. *(AQA)*

7. A multiple choice test consists of 20 questions. There are 5 choices for each question and only one choice is correct. A certain candidate made a random guess for each question.

   (a) Suggest a suitable model to describe the number of questions the candidate guessed correctly and give suitable values for any parameters required.

   Find the probability that the candidate obtained
   (b) no correct answers
   (c) more than 7 correct answers *(Edexcel)*

Questions 8 - 9 for OCR students only

8. Before starting to play the game 'Snakes and Ladders' each player throws an ordinary unbiased die until a six is obtained. The number of throws before a player starts is the random variable Y, where Y takes the values 1, 2, 3, ...
   (i)   Name the probability distribution of Y, stating a necessary assumption
   (ii) Find Var(Y)
   (iii) Two people play Snakes and Ladders. Calculate the probability that they will each need at least 5 throws before starting. *(OCR)*

9. It is given that one-eleventh of adults are left-handed. Adults are chosen, one by one, until a left-handed adult is found. The total number of adults chosen, including the left-handed one, is denoted by T. State an assumption which must be made for a geometric distribution to be a suitable model for T.

   Using a geometric distribution
   (i)   calculate $P(T = 4)$
   (ii) calculate $P(T > 10)$
   (iii) obtain the mean and variance of T *(OCR)*

Questions 10-11 for AQA students only

10. A small shop stocks expensive boxes of chocolates whose sales may be modelled by a Poisson distribution with mean 1.8 per day. Find the probability that on a particular day the shop will sell
    (a) no boxes
    (b) three or more boxes of these chocolates   *(AQA)*

11. An insurance company employs agents who use their cars to travel a large number of miles each year. The company observes that the number of accidents involving each agent can be modelled by a Poisson distribution with mean 0.2 per year.
    (a) What is the probability that a particular agent is involved in
        (i) two or fewer accidents in a particular year
        (ii) exactly three accidents in a particular year
    Recently 20 agents were issued with mobile phones. The company observe that, for the six of these 20 agents who used mobile phones whilst driving, the number of accidents can be modelled by a Poisson distribution with mean 0.7 per year. The accident rate for the other 14 agents has a Poisson distribution with mean 0.2 per year.
    (b) Deduce that for these 20 agents their total number of accidents in a particular year may be modelled by a Poisson distribution with mean 7
    (c) Determine the probability that these 20 agents are involved in a total of more than 6 accidents in a particular year.   *(AQA)*

Questions 12-14 for AQA and Edexcel students only

12. Squash balls, dropped onto a concrete floor from a given point, revound to heights which can be modelled by a normal distribution with mean 0.8 m and standard deviation 0.2 m. The balls are classified by height of rebound, in order of decreasing height, into these categories: Fast, Medium, Slow, Super-Slow and Rejected.
    (i) Balls which rebound to heights between 0.65 m and 0.9 m are classified as Slow. Calculate the percentage of balls classified as Slow.
    (ii) Given that 9% of balls are classified as Rejected, calculate the maximum height of rebound of these balls.
    (iii) The percentages of balls classified as Fast and Medium are equal. Calculate the minimum height of rebound of a ball classified as Fast, giving your answer correct to 2 decimal places.   *(OCR)*

13. The random variable X is normally distributed with mean μ and variance σ^2. It is given that $P(X > 81.89) = 0.010$ and $P(X < 27.27) = 0.100$. Calculate the values of μ and σ.   *(OCR)*

14. A machine is used to fill tubes, of nominal content 100 ml, with toothpaste. The amount of toothpaste delivered by the machine is normally distributed and may be set to any required mean value. Immediately after the machine has been overhauled, the standard deviation of the amount delivered is 2 ml. As time passes, the standard deviation increases until the machine is again overhauled.

The following three conditions are necessary for a batch of tubes of toohpaste to comply with current legislation:

   (I)   the average content of the tubes must be at least 100 ml

   (II) not more than 2.5% of the tubes may contain less than 95.5 ml

   (III) not more than 0.1% of the tubes may contain less than 91 ml

(a) For a batch of tubes with mean content 98.8 ml and standard deviation 2 ml, find the proportion of tubes which contain

   (i)   less than 95.5 ml

   (ii) less than 91 ml

Hence state which, if any, of the three conditions above are **not** satisfied.

(b) If the standard deviation is 5 ml, find the mean in each of the following cases:

   (i)   exactly 2.5% of tubes contain less tha 95.5 ml

   (ii) exactly 0.1% of tubes contain less than 91 ml

Hence state the smallest value of the mean which would enable all three conditions to be met when the standard deviation is 5 ml.

(c) Currently exactly 0.1% of the tubes contain less than 91 ml and exactly 2.5% contain less than 95.5 ml.

   (i)   Find the current values of the mean and standard deviation

   (ii) State, giving a reason, whether you would recommend that the machine be overhauled immediately.   *(AQA)*

Question 15 for AQA students only

15. A tour operator organises a visit for cricket enthusiasts to the Carribean in March. The package includes a ticket for a one-day international in Jamaica. Places on the tour must be booked three months in advance. From past experience, the tour operator knows that the probability of a person who has booked a place subsequently withdrawing is 0.08 and is independent of other withdrawals.

(a) Twenty people book places. Find the probability that   *(AQA)*

   (i) none withdraw   (ii) two or more withdraw

(b) The tour operator accepts 22 bookings but has only 20 tickets available for the one-day international. What is the probability that he will be able to provide everyone who goes on the tour with a ticket ?

(c) An organiser of a similar but larger tour accepts 220 bookings but has only 200 tickets for the one-day international. Find, using a suitable approximation, the probability that this organiser will be able to provide everyone on the tour with a ticket. (Assume the probability of a person withdrawing remains at 0.08)

Unit 4: Correlation and Regression

1. (i) The product moment correlation coefficient for the data illustrated in Fig 1 is known to take one of the values –0.9, –0.5, 0, 0.5, 0.9. State which value is correct.

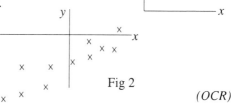

(ii) Describe the nature of the correlation between the variables x and y shown in Fig 2.

Fig 2

(OCR)

2. A set of bivariate data can be summarised as follows.

$n = 6$ $\Sigma x = 21$ $\Sigma y = 43$ $\Sigma x^2 = 91$ $\Sigma y^2 = 91$ $\Sigma xy = 171$

(i) Calculate the equation of the regression line of y on x. Give your answer in the form $y = a = bx$, where the values of a and b should be stated correct t 3 s.f.

(ii) It is required to estimate the value of y for a given value of x. State circumstances under which the regression line of x on y should be used, rather than the regression line of y on x.

(OCR)

3. (a) A road haulage contractor owns four lorries of the same age and specification, She employs four drivers: Ahmed (A), Beryl (B), Chris (C) and Danny (D). She collects data for a number of long journeys, on the driver, load carried and the diesel consumption.

Driver	A	B	D	A	D	C	C	A	D	B
Load (x kg)	5650	10 100	7800	8450	5500	6950	7600	8300	6250	6600
Diesel cons. y km/l	6.22	5.18	5.25	5.49	6.01	5.00	5.89	5.42	5.77	6.11

(i) Draw a scatter diagram of y against x.

(ii) Calculate the equation of the regression line of y on x and draw it on your scatter diagram.

(iii) Give an interpretation of the slope and of the intercept of the regression line.

(iv) Why would it be unwise to use the regression equation to predict the diesel consumption if the load was 30 000 kg ?

(v) Comment on the diesel consumption of lorries driven by Danny.

(vi) Why was the regression line of y on x used rather than the regression line of x on y ?

(AQA)

Questions 4 - 5 for OCR students only

4. The rules for a flower competition in a village fete are as follows.

Three judges each give a score out of 100 to each entry. The two judges whose rankings are in closest agreement are identified and their scores for each entry are added. The three prizewinners are those whose total scores from these two judges are the highest. The scores of the third judge are ignored.

The judges awarded marks as shown in the table below.

Contestant	A	B	C	D	E	F	G
Judge X	89	83	80	72	69	54	41
Judge Y	77	84	85	65	79	72	69
Judge Z	73	83	89	80	67	75	69

The value of Spearman's rank correlation coefficient between X and Y is 0.5, and between X and Z is 0.46, correct to 2 d.p. Calcualte the value of Spearman's rank correlation coefficient between judges Y and Z, and hence establish which were the three prizewinners. *(OCR)*

5. Two students, Arif and Beth, collected the following data relating the mean diversity d of a plant species with the distance s metres up an irregular cliff face.

s	0	1.25	2.5	3.85	5.2	6.5	7.8	9.1
d	8.17	8.65	7.47	7.77	6.80	7.21	6.23	6.77

$[n = 8 \quad \Sigma s = 36.2 \quad \Sigma d = 59.07 \quad \Sigma s^2 = 235.575 \quad \Sigma d^2 = 440.6151 \quad \Sigma sd = 251.828]$

(i) Arif finds the product moment correlation coefficient between s and d. Calculate the answer he should get.

(ii) Beth finds Spearman's rank correlation coefficient between s and d. Calculate the answer she should get.

(iii)

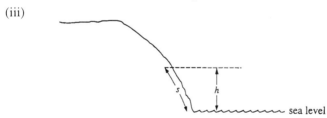

Subsequently, the vertical heights, h metres, above sea level were measured (see diagram). The students now find their respective correlation coefficient between h and d. State, with a reason in each case, whether

(a) Arif   (b) Beth

should obtain the same answer as before. *(OCR)*

CUMULATIVE BINOMIAL PROBABILITIES for $n = 5, 6, 7, 8$

$n = 5$

p	0.05	0.1	0.15	1/6	0.2	0.25	0.3	1/3	0.35	0.4	0.45	0.5	0.55	0.6	0.65	2/3	0.7	0.75	0.8	5/6	0.85	0.9	0.95
$x = 0$	0.7738	0.5905	0.4437	0.4019	0.3277	0.2373	0.1681	0.1317	0.1160	0.0778	0.0503	0.0313	0.0185	0.0102	0.0053	0.0041	0.0024	0.0010	0.0003	0.0001	0.0001	0.0000	0.0000
1	0.9774	0.9185	0.8352	0.8038	0.7373	0.6328	0.5282	0.4609	0.4284	0.3370	0.2562	0.1875	0.1312	0.0870	0.0540	0.0453	0.0308	0.0156	0.0067	0.0033	0.0022	0.0005	0.0000
2	0.9988	0.9914	0.9734	0.9645	0.9421	0.8965	0.8369	0.7901	0.7648	0.6826	0.5931	0.5000	0.4069	0.3174	0.2352	0.2099	0.1631	0.1035	0.0579	0.0355	0.0266	0.0086	0.0012
3	1.0000	0.9995	0.9978	0.9967	0.9933	0.9844	0.9692	0.9547	0.9460	0.9130	0.8688	0.8125	0.7438	0.6630	0.5716	0.5391	0.4718	0.3672	0.2627	0.1962	0.1648	0.0815	0.0226
4	1.0000	1.0000	0.9999	0.9999	0.9997	0.9990	0.9976	0.9959	0.9947	0.9898	0.9815	0.9688	0.9497	0.9222	0.8840	0.8683	0.8319	0.7627	0.6723	0.5981	0.5563	0.4095	0.2262
5	1.0000	1.0000	1.0000	1.0000	1.0000	1.0000	1.0000	1.0000	1.0000	1.0000	1.0000	1.0000	1.0000	1.0000	1.0000	1.0000	1.0000	1.0000	1.0000	1.0000	1.0000	1.0000	1.0000

$n = 6$

p	0.05	0.1	0.15	1/6	0.2	0.25	0.3	1/3	0.35	0.4	0.45	0.5	0.55	0.6	0.65	2/3	0.7	0.75	0.8	5/6	0.85	0.9	0.95
$x = 0$	0.7351	0.5314	0.3771	0.3349	0.2621	0.1780	0.1176	0.0878	0.0754	0.0467	0.0277	0.0156	0.0083	0.0041	0.0018	0.0014	0.0007	0.0002	0.0001	0.0000	0.0000	0.0000	0.0000
1	0.9672	0.8857	0.7765	0.7368	0.6554	0.5339	0.4202	0.3512	0.3191	0.2333	0.1636	0.1094	0.0692	0.0410	0.0223	0.0178	0.0109	0.0046	0.0016	0.0007	0.0004	0.0001	0.0000
2	0.9978	0.9842	0.9527	0.9377	0.9011	0.8306	0.7443	0.6804	0.6471	0.5443	0.4415	0.3438	0.2553	0.1792	0.1174	0.1001	0.0705	0.0376	0.0170	0.0087	0.0059	0.0013	0.0001
3	0.9999	0.9987	0.9941	0.9913	0.9830	0.9624	0.9295	0.8999	0.8826	0.8208	0.7447	0.6563	0.5585	0.4557	0.3529	0.3196	0.2557	0.1694	0.0989	0.0623	0.0473	0.0159	0.0022
4	1.0000	0.9999	0.9996	0.9993	0.9984	0.9954	0.9891	0.9822	0.9777	0.9590	0.9308	0.8906	0.8364	0.7667	0.6809	0.6488	0.5798	0.4661	0.3446	0.2632	0.2235	0.1143	0.0328
5	1.0000	1.0000	1.0000	1.0000	0.9999	0.9998	0.9993	0.9986	0.9982	0.9959	0.9917	0.9844	0.9723	0.9533	0.9246	0.9122	0.8824	0.8220	0.7379	0.6651	0.6229	0.4686	0.2649
6	1.0000	1.0000	1.0000	1.0000	1.0000	1.0000	1.0000	1.0000	1.0000	1.0000	1.0000	1.0000	1.0000	1.0000	1.0000	1.0000	1.0000	1.0000	1.0000	1.0000	1.0000	1.0000	1.0000

$n = 7$

p	0.05	0.1	0.15	1/6	0.2	0.25	0.3	1/3	0.35	0.4	0.45	0.5	0.55	0.6	0.65	2/3	0.7	0.75	0.8	5/6	0.85	0.9	0.95
$x = 0$	0.6983	0.4783	0.3206	0.2791	0.2097	0.1335	0.0824	0.0585	0.0490	0.0280	0.0152	0.0078	0.0037	0.0016	0.0006	0.0005	0.0002	0.0001	0.0000	0.0000	0.0000	0.0000	0.0000
1	0.9556	0.8503	0.7166	0.6698	0.5767	0.4449	0.3294	0.2634	0.2338	0.1586	0.1024	0.0625	0.0357	0.0188	0.0090	0.0069	0.0038	0.0013	0.0004	0.0001	0.0001	0.0000	0.0000
2	0.9962	0.9743	0.9262	0.9042	0.8520	0.7564	0.6471	0.5706	0.5323	0.4199	0.3164	0.2266	0.1529	0.0963	0.0556	0.0453	0.0288	0.0129	0.0047	0.0020	0.0012	0.0002	0.0000
3	0.9998	0.9973	0.9879	0.9824	0.9667	0.9294	0.8740	0.8267	0.8002	0.7102	0.6083	0.5000	0.3917	0.2898	0.1998	0.1733	0.1260	0.0706	0.0333	0.0176	0.0121	0.0027	0.0002
4	1.0000	0.9998	0.9988	0.9980	0.9953	0.9871	0.9712	0.9547	0.9444	0.9037	0.8471	0.7734	0.6836	0.5801	0.4677	0.4294	0.3529	0.2436	0.1480	0.0958	0.0738	0.0257	0.0038
5	1.0000	1.0000	0.9999	0.9999	0.9996	0.9987	0.9962	0.9931	0.9910	0.9812	0.9643	0.9375	0.8976	0.8414	0.7662	0.7366	0.6706	0.5551	0.4233	0.3302	0.2834	0.1497	0.0444
6	1.0000	1.0000	1.0000	1.0000	1.0000	0.9999	0.9998	0.9995	0.9994	0.9984	0.9963	0.9922	0.9848	0.9720	0.9510	0.9415	0.9176	0.8665	0.7903	0.7209	0.6794	0.5217	0.3017
7	1.0000	1.0000	1.0000	1.0000	1.0000	1.0000	1.0000	1.0000	1.0000	1.0000	1.0000	1.0000	1.0000	1.0000	1.0000	1.0000	1.0000	1.0000	1.0000	1.0000	1.0000	1.0000	1.0000

$n = 8$

p	0.05	0.1	0.15	1/6	0.2	0.25	0.3	1/3	0.35	0.4	0.45	0.5	0.55	0.6	0.65	2/3	0.7	0.75	0.8	5/6	0.85	0.9	0.95
$x = 0$	0.6634	0.4305	0.2725	0.2326	0.1678	0.1001	0.0576	0.0390	0.0319	0.0168	0.0084	0.0039	0.0017	0.0007	0.0002	0.0002	0.0001	0.0000	0.0000	0.0000	0.0000	0.0000	0.0000
1	0.9428	0.8131	0.6572	0.6047	0.5033	0.3671	0.2553	0.1951	0.1691	0.1064	0.0632	0.0352	0.0181	0.0085	0.0036	0.0026	0.0013	0.0004	0.0001	0.0000	0.0000	0.0000	0.0000
2	0.9942	0.9619	0.8948	0.8652	0.7969	0.6785	0.5518	0.4682	0.4278	0.3154	0.2201	0.1445	0.0885	0.0498	0.0253	0.0197	0.0113	0.0042	0.0012	0.0004	0.0002	0.0000	0.0000
3	0.9996	0.9950	0.9786	0.9693	0.9437	0.8862	0.8059	0.7414	0.7064	0.5941	0.4770	0.3633	0.2604	0.1737	0.1061	0.0879	0.0580	0.0273	0.0104	0.0046	0.0029	0.0004	0.0000
4	1.0000	0.9996	0.9971	0.9954	0.9896	0.9727	0.9420	0.9121	0.8939	0.8263	0.7396	0.6367	0.5230	0.4059	0.2936	0.2586	0.1941	0.1138	0.0563	0.0307	0.0214	0.0050	0.0004
5	1.0000	1.0000	0.9998	0.9996	0.9988	0.9958	0.9887	0.9803	0.9747	0.9502	0.9115	0.8555	0.7799	0.6846	0.5722	0.5318	0.4482	0.3215	0.2031	0.1348	0.1052	0.0381	0.0058
6	1.0000	1.0000	1.0000	1.0000	0.9999	0.9996	0.9987	0.9974	0.9964	0.9915	0.9819	0.9648	0.9368	0.8936	0.8309	0.8049	0.7447	0.6329	0.4967	0.3953	0.3428	0.1869	0.0572
7	1.0000	1.0000	1.0000	1.0000	1.0000	1.0000	0.9999	0.9998	0.9998	0.9993	0.9983	0.9961	0.9916	0.9832	0.9681	0.9610	0.9424	0.8999	0.8322	0.7674	0.7275	0.5695	0.3366
8	1.0000	1.0000	1.0000	1.0000	1.0000	1.0000	1.0000	1.0000	1.0000	1.0000	1.0000	1.0000	1.0000	1.0000	1.0000	1.0000	1.0000	1.0000	1.0000	1.0000	1.0000	1.0000	1.0000

CUMULATIVE BINOMIAL PROBABILITIES for $n = 9, 10, 12$

$n = 9$

p \ x	0.05	0.1	0.15	1/6	0.2	0.25	0.3	1/3	0.35	0.4	0.45	0.5	0.55	0.6	0.65	2/3	0.7	0.75	0.8	5/6	0.85	0.9	0.95
0	0.6302	0.3874	0.2316	0.1938	0.1342	0.0751	0.0404	0.0260	0.0207	0.0101	0.0046	0.0020	0.0008	0.0003	0.0001	0.0001	0.0000	0.0000	0.0000	0.0000	0.0000	0.0000	0.0000
1	0.9288	0.7748	0.5995	0.5427	0.4362	0.3003	0.1960	0.1431	0.1211	0.0705	0.0385	0.0195	0.0091	0.0038	0.0014	0.0010	0.0004	0.0001	0.0000	0.0000	0.0000	0.0000	0.0000
2	0.9916	0.9470	0.8591	0.8217	0.7382	0.6007	0.4628	0.3772	0.3373	0.2318	0.1495	0.0898	0.0498	0.0250	0.0112	0.0083	0.0043	0.0013	0.0003	0.0001	0.0001	0.0000	0.0000
3	0.9994	0.9917	0.9661	0.9520	0.9144	0.8343	0.7297	0.6503	0.6089	0.4826	0.3614	0.2539	0.1658	0.0994	0.0536	0.0424	0.0253	0.0100	0.0031	0.0011	0.0006	0.0001	0.0000
4	1.0000	0.9991	0.9944	0.9910	0.9804	0.9511	0.9012	0.8552	0.8283	0.7334	0.6214	0.5000	0.3786	0.2666	0.1717	0.1448	0.0988	0.0489	0.0196	0.0090	0.0056	0.0009	0.0000
5	1.0000	0.9999	0.9994	0.9989	0.9969	0.9900	0.9747	0.9576	0.9464	0.9006	0.8342	0.7461	0.6386	0.5174	0.3911	0.3497	0.2703	0.1657	0.0856	0.0480	0.0339	0.0083	0.0006
6	1.0000	1.0000	0.9999	0.9999	0.9997	0.9987	0.9957	0.9917	0.9888	0.9750	0.9502	0.9102	0.8505	0.7682	0.6627	0.6228	0.5372	0.3993	0.2618	0.1783	0.1409	0.0530	0.0084
7	1.0000	1.0000	1.0000	1.0000	1.0000	0.9999	0.9996	0.9990	0.9986	0.9962	0.9909	0.9805	0.9615	0.9295	0.8789	0.8569	0.8040	0.6997	0.5638	0.4573	0.4005	0.2252	0.0712
8	1.0000	1.0000	1.0000	1.0000	1.0000	1.0000	1.0000	0.9999	0.9999	0.9997	0.9992	0.9980	0.9954	0.9899	0.9793	0.9740	0.9596	0.9249	0.8658	0.8062	0.7684	0.6126	0.3698
9	1.0000	1.0000	1.0000	1.0000	1.0000	1.0000	1.0000	1.0000	1.0000	1.0000	1.0000	1.0000	1.0000	1.0000	1.0000	1.0000	1.0000	1.0000	1.0000	1.0000	1.0000	1.0000	1.0000

$n = 10$

p \ x	0.05	0.1	0.15	1/6	0.2	0.25	0.3	1/3	0.35	0.4	0.45	0.5	0.55	0.6	0.65	2/3	0.7	0.75	0.8	5/6	0.85	0.9	0.95
0	0.5987	0.3487	0.1969	0.1615	0.1074	0.0563	0.0282	0.0173	0.0135	0.0060	0.0025	0.0010	0.0003	0.0001	0.0000	0.0000	0.0000	0.0000	0.0000	0.0000	0.0000	0.0000	0.0000
1	0.9139	0.7361	0.5443	0.4845	0.3758	0.2440	0.1493	0.1040	0.0860	0.0464	0.0233	0.0107	0.0045	0.0017	0.0005	0.0004	0.0001	0.0000	0.0000	0.0000	0.0000	0.0000	0.0000
2	0.9885	0.9298	0.8202	0.7752	0.6778	0.5256	0.3828	0.2991	0.2616	0.1673	0.0996	0.0547	0.0274	0.0123	0.0048	0.0034	0.0016	0.0004	0.0001	0.0000	0.0000	0.0000	0.0000
3	0.9990	0.9872	0.9500	0.9303	0.8791	0.7759	0.6496	0.5593	0.5138	0.3823	0.2660	0.1719	0.1020	0.0548	0.0260	0.0197	0.0106	0.0035	0.0009	0.0003	0.0001	0.0000	0.0000
4	0.9999	0.9984	0.9901	0.9845	0.9672	0.9219	0.8497	0.7869	0.7515	0.6331	0.5044	0.3770	0.2616	0.1662	0.0949	0.0766	0.0473	0.0197	0.0064	0.0024	0.0014	0.0001	0.0000
5	1.0000	0.9999	0.9986	0.9976	0.9936	0.9803	0.9527	0.9234	0.9051	0.8338	0.7384	0.6230	0.4956	0.3669	0.2485	0.2131	0.1503	0.0781	0.0328	0.0155	0.0099	0.0016	0.0001
6	1.0000	1.0000	0.9999	0.9997	0.9991	0.9965	0.9894	0.9803	0.9740	0.9452	0.8980	0.8281	0.7340	0.6177	0.4862	0.4407	0.3504	0.2241	0.1209	0.0697	0.0500	0.0128	0.0010
7	1.0000	1.0000	1.0000	1.0000	0.9999	0.9996	0.9984	0.9966	0.9952	0.9877	0.9726	0.9453	0.9004	0.8327	0.7384	0.7009	0.6172	0.4744	0.3222	0.2248	0.1798	0.0702	0.0115
8	1.0000	1.0000	1.0000	1.0000	1.0000	1.0000	0.9999	0.9996	0.9995	0.9983	0.9955	0.9893	0.9767	0.9536	0.9140	0.8960	0.8507	0.7560	0.6242	0.5155	0.4557	0.2639	0.0861
9	1.0000	1.0000	1.0000	1.0000	1.0000	1.0000	1.0000	1.0000	1.0000	0.9999	0.9997	0.9990	0.9975	0.9940	0.9865	0.9827	0.9718	0.9437	0.8926	0.8385	0.8031	0.6513	0.4013
10	1.0000	1.0000	1.0000	1.0000	1.0000	1.0000	1.0000	1.0000	1.0000	1.0000	1.0000	1.0000	1.0000	1.0000	1.0000	1.0000	1.0000	1.0000	1.0000	1.0000	1.0000	1.0000	1.0000

$n = 12$

p \ x	0.05	0.1	0.15	1/6	0.2	0.25	0.3	1/3	0.35	0.4	0.45	0.5	0.55	0.6	0.65	2/3	0.7	0.75	0.8	5/6	0.85	0.9	0.95
0	0.5404	0.2824	0.1422	0.1122	0.0687	0.0317	0.0138	0.0077	0.0057	0.0022	0.0008	0.0002	0.0001	0.0000	0.0000	0.0000	0.0000	0.0000	0.0000	0.0000	0.0000	0.0000	0.0000
1	0.8816	0.6590	0.4435	0.3813	0.2749	0.1584	0.0850	0.0540	0.0424	0.0196	0.0083	0.0032	0.0011	0.0003	0.0001	0.0000	0.0000	0.0000	0.0000	0.0000	0.0000	0.0000	0.0000
2	0.9804	0.8891	0.7358	0.6774	0.5583	0.3907	0.2528	0.1811	0.1513	0.0834	0.0421	0.0193	0.0079	0.0028	0.0008	0.0005	0.0002	0.0000	0.0000	0.0000	0.0000	0.0000	0.0000
3	0.9978	0.9744	0.9078	0.8748	0.7946	0.6488	0.4925	0.3931	0.3467	0.2253	0.1345	0.0730	0.0356	0.0153	0.0056	0.0039	0.0017	0.0004	0.0001	0.0000	0.0000	0.0000	0.0000
4	0.9998	0.9957	0.9761	0.9636	0.9274	0.8424	0.7237	0.6315	0.5833	0.4382	0.3044	0.1938	0.1117	0.0573	0.0255	0.0188	0.0095	0.0028	0.0006	0.0002	0.0001	0.0000	0.0000
5	1.0000	0.9995	0.9954	0.9921	0.9806	0.9456	0.8822	0.8223	0.7873	0.6652	0.5269	0.3872	0.2607	0.1582	0.0846	0.0664	0.0386	0.0143	0.0039	0.0013	0.0007	0.0001	0.0000
6	1.0000	0.9999	0.9993	0.9987	0.9961	0.9857	0.9614	0.9336	0.9154	0.8418	0.7393	0.6128	0.4731	0.3348	0.2127	0.1777	0.1178	0.0544	0.0194	0.0079	0.0046	0.0005	0.0000
7	1.0000	1.0000	0.9999	0.9998	0.9994	0.9972	0.9905	0.9812	0.9745	0.9427	0.8883	0.8062	0.6956	0.5618	0.4167	0.3685	0.2763	0.1576	0.0726	0.0363	0.0239	0.0043	0.0002
8	1.0000	1.0000	1.0000	1.0000	0.9999	0.9996	0.9983	0.9961	0.9944	0.9847	0.9644	0.9270	0.8655	0.7747	0.6533	0.6069	0.5075	0.3512	0.2054	0.1252	0.0922	0.0256	0.0022
9	1.0000	1.0000	1.0000	1.0000	1.0000	1.0000	0.9998	0.9995	0.9992	0.9972	0.9921	0.9807	0.9579	0.9166	0.8487	0.8189	0.7472	0.6093	0.4417	0.3226	0.2642	0.1109	0.0196
10	1.0000	1.0000	1.0000	1.0000	1.0000	1.0000	1.0000	1.0000	0.9999	0.9997	0.9989	0.9968	0.9917	0.9804	0.9576	0.9460	0.9150	0.8416	0.7251	0.6187	0.5565	0.3410	0.1184
11	1.0000	1.0000	1.0000	1.0000	1.0000	1.0000	1.0000	1.0000	1.0000	1.0000	0.9999	0.9998	0.9992	0.9978	0.9943	0.9923	0.9862	0.9683	0.9313	0.8878	0.8578	0.7176	0.4596
12	1.0000	1.0000	1.0000	1.0000	1.0000	1.0000	1.0000	1.0000	1.0000	1.0000	1.0000	1.0000	1.0000	1.0000	1.0000	1.0000	1.0000	1.0000	1.0000	1.0000	1.0000	1.0000	1.0000

CUMULATIVE BINOMIAL PROBABILITIES for $n = 14, 16$

n = 14

x	0.05	0.1	0.15	1/6	0.2	0.25	0.3	1/3	0.35	0.4	0.45	0.5	0.55	0.6	0.65	2/3	0.7	0.75	0.8	5/6	0.85	0.9	0.95
0	0.4877	0.2288	0.1028	0.0779	0.0440	0.0178	0.0068	0.0034	0.0024	0.0008	0.0002	0.0001	0.0000	0.0000	0.0000	0.0000	0.0000	0.0000	0.0000	0.0000	0.0000	0.0000	0.0000
1	0.8470	0.5846	0.3567	0.2960	0.1979	0.1010	0.0475	0.0274	0.0205	0.0081	0.0029	0.0009	0.0003	0.0001	0.0000	0.0000	0.0000	0.0000	0.0000	0.0000	0.0000	0.0000	0.0000
2	0.9699	0.8416	0.6479	0.5795	0.4481	0.2811	0.1608	0.1053	0.0839	0.0398	0.0170	0.0065	0.0022	0.0006	0.0001	0.0001	0.0000	0.0000	0.0000	0.0000	0.0000	0.0000	0.0000
3	0.9958	0.9559	0.8535	0.8063	0.6982	0.5213	0.3552	0.2612	0.2205	0.1243	0.0632	0.0287	0.0114	0.0039	0.0011	0.0007	0.0002	0.0000	0.0000	0.0000	0.0000	0.0000	0.0000
4	0.9996	0.9908	0.9533	0.9310	0.8702	0.7415	0.5842	0.4755	0.4227	0.2793	0.1672	0.0898	0.0426	0.0175	0.0060	0.0040	0.0017	0.0003	0.0000	0.0000	0.0000	0.0000	0.0000
5	1.0000	0.9985	0.9885	0.9809	0.9561	0.8883	0.7805	0.6898	0.6405	0.4859	0.3373	0.2120	0.1189	0.0583	0.0243	0.0174	0.0083	0.0022	0.0004	0.0001	0.0000	0.0000	0.0000
6	1.0000	0.9998	0.9978	0.9959	0.9884	0.9617	0.9067	0.8505	0.8164	0.6925	0.5461	0.3953	0.2586	0.1501	0.0753	0.0576	0.0315	0.0103	0.0024	0.0007	0.0003	0.0000	0.0000
7	1.0000	1.0000	0.9997	0.9993	0.9976	0.9897	0.9685	0.9424	0.9247	0.8499	0.7414	0.6047	0.4539	0.3075	0.1836	0.1495	0.0933	0.0383	0.0116	0.0041	0.0022	0.0002	0.0000
8	1.0000	1.0000	1.0000	0.9999	0.9996	0.9978	0.9917	0.9826	0.9757	0.9417	0.8811	0.7880	0.6627	0.5141	0.3595	0.3102	0.2195	0.1117	0.0439	0.0191	0.0115	0.0015	0.0000
9	1.0000	1.0000	1.0000	1.0000	1.0000	0.9997	0.9983	0.9960	0.9940	0.9825	0.9574	0.9102	0.8328	0.7207	0.5773	0.5245	0.4158	0.2585	0.1298	0.0690	0.0467	0.0092	0.0004
10	1.0000	1.0000	1.0000	1.0000	1.0000	1.0000	0.9998	0.9993	0.9989	0.9961	0.9886	0.9713	0.9368	0.8757	0.7795	0.7388	0.6448	0.4787	0.3018	0.1937	0.1465	0.0441	0.0042
11	1.0000	1.0000	1.0000	1.0000	1.0000	1.0000	1.0000	0.9999	0.9999	0.9994	0.9978	0.9935	0.9830	0.9602	0.9161	0.8947	0.8392	0.7189	0.5519	0.4205	0.3521	0.1584	0.0301
12	1.0000	1.0000	1.0000	1.0000	1.0000	1.0000	1.0000	1.0000	1.0000	0.9999	0.9997	0.9991	0.9971	0.9919	0.9795	0.9726	0.9525	0.8990	0.8021	0.7040	0.6433	0.4154	0.1530
13	1.0000	1.0000	1.0000	1.0000	1.0000	1.0000	1.0000	1.0000	1.0000	1.0000	1.0000	0.9999	0.9998	0.9992	0.9976	0.9966	0.9932	0.9822	0.9560	0.9221	0.8972	0.7712	0.5123
14	1.0000	1.0000	1.0000	1.0000	1.0000	1.0000	1.0000	1.0000	1.0000	1.0000	1.0000	1.0000	1.0000	1.0000	1.0000	1.0000	1.0000	1.0000	1.0000	1.0000	1.0000	1.0000	1.0000

n = 16

x	0.05	0.1	0.15	1/6	0.2	0.25	0.3	1/3	0.35	0.4	0.45	0.5	0.55	0.6	0.65	2/3	0.7	0.75	0.8	5/6	0.85	0.9	0.95
0	0.4401	0.1853	0.0743	0.0541	0.0281	0.0100	0.0033	0.0015	0.0010	0.0003	0.0001	0.0000	0.0000	0.0000	0.0000	0.0000	0.0000	0.0000	0.0000	0.0000	0.0000	0.0000	0.0000
1	0.8108	0.5147	0.2839	0.2272	0.1407	0.0635	0.0261	0.0137	0.0098	0.0033	0.0010	0.0003	0.0001	0.0000	0.0000	0.0000	0.0000	0.0000	0.0000	0.0000	0.0000	0.0000	0.0000
2	0.9571	0.7892	0.5614	0.4868	0.3518	0.1971	0.0994	0.0594	0.0451	0.0183	0.0066	0.0021	0.0006	0.0001	0.0000	0.0000	0.0000	0.0000	0.0000	0.0000	0.0000	0.0000	0.0000
3	0.9930	0.9316	0.7899	0.7291	0.5981	0.4050	0.2459	0.1659	0.1339	0.0651	0.0281	0.0106	0.0035	0.0009	0.0002	0.0001	0.0000	0.0000	0.0000	0.0000	0.0000	0.0000	0.0000
4	0.9991	0.9830	0.9209	0.8866	0.7982	0.6302	0.4499	0.3391	0.2892	0.1666	0.0853	0.0384	0.0149	0.0049	0.0013	0.0008	0.0003	0.0000	0.0000	0.0000	0.0000	0.0000	0.0000
5	0.9999	0.9967	0.9765	0.9622	0.9183	0.8103	0.6598	0.5469	0.4900	0.3288	0.1976	0.1051	0.0486	0.0191	0.0062	0.0040	0.0016	0.0003	0.0000	0.0000	0.0000	0.0000	0.0000
6	1.0000	0.9995	0.9944	0.9899	0.9733	0.9204	0.8247	0.7374	0.6881	0.5272	0.3660	0.2272	0.1241	0.0583	0.0229	0.0159	0.0071	0.0016	0.0002	0.0000	0.0000	0.0000	0.0000
7	1.0000	0.9999	0.9989	0.9979	0.9930	0.9729	0.9256	0.8735	0.8406	0.7161	0.5629	0.4018	0.2559	0.1423	0.0671	0.0500	0.0257	0.0075	0.0015	0.0004	0.0002	0.0000	0.0000
8	1.0000	1.0000	0.9998	0.9996	0.9985	0.9925	0.9743	0.9500	0.9329	0.8577	0.7441	0.5982	0.4371	0.2839	0.1594	0.1265	0.0744	0.0271	0.0070	0.0021	0.0011	0.0001	0.0000
9	1.0000	1.0000	1.0000	1.0000	0.9998	0.9984	0.9929	0.9841	0.9771	0.9417	0.8759	0.7728	0.6340	0.4728	0.3119	0.2626	0.1753	0.0796	0.0267	0.0101	0.0056	0.0005	0.0000
10	1.0000	1.0000	1.0000	1.0000	1.0000	0.9997	0.9984	0.9960	0.9938	0.9809	0.9514	0.8949	0.8024	0.6712	0.5100	0.4531	0.3402	0.1897	0.0817	0.0378	0.0235	0.0033	0.0001
11	1.0000	1.0000	1.0000	1.0000	1.0000	1.0000	0.9997	0.9992	0.9987	0.9951	0.9851	0.9616	0.9147	0.8334	0.7108	0.6609	0.5501	0.3698	0.2018	0.1134	0.0791	0.0170	0.0009
12	1.0000	1.0000	1.0000	1.0000	1.0000	1.0000	1.0000	0.9999	0.9998	0.9991	0.9965	0.9894	0.9719	0.9349	0.8661	0.8341	0.7541	0.5950	0.4019	0.2709	0.2101	0.0684	0.0070
13	1.0000	1.0000	1.0000	1.0000	1.0000	1.0000	1.0000	1.0000	1.0000	0.9999	0.9994	0.9979	0.9934	0.9817	0.9549	0.9406	0.9006	0.8029	0.6482	0.5132	0.4386	0.2108	0.0429
14	1.0000	1.0000	1.0000	1.0000	1.0000	1.0000	1.0000	1.0000	1.0000	1.0000	0.9999	0.9997	0.9990	0.9967	0.9902	0.9863	0.9739	0.9365	0.8593	0.7728	0.7161	0.4853	0.1892
15	1.0000	1.0000	1.0000	1.0000	1.0000	1.0000	1.0000	1.0000	1.0000	1.0000	1.0000	1.0000	0.9999	0.9997	0.9990	0.9985	0.9967	0.9900	0.9719	0.9459	0.9257	0.8147	0.5599
16	1.0000	1.0000	1.0000	1.0000	1.0000	1.0000	1.0000	1.0000	1.0000	1.0000	1.0000	1.0000	1.0000	1.0000	1.0000	1.0000	1.0000	1.0000	1.0000	1.0000	1.0000	1.0000	1.0000

CUMULATIVE BINOMIAL PROBABILITIES for $n = 18, 20$

$n = 18$

p \ x	0.05	0.1	0.15	1/6	0.2	0.25	0.3	1/3	0.35	0.4	0.45	0.5	0.55	0.6	0.65	2/3	0.7	0.75	0.8	5/6	0.85	0.9	0.95
0	0.3972	0.1501	0.0536	0.0376	0.0180	0.0056	0.0016	0.0007	0.0004	0.0001	0.0000	0.0000	0.0000	0.0000	0.0000	0.0000	0.0000	0.0000	0.0000	0.0000	0.0000	0.0000	0.0000
1	0.7735	0.4503	0.2241	0.1728	0.0991	0.0395	0.0142	0.0068	0.0046	0.0013	0.0003	0.0001	0.0000	0.0000	0.0000	0.0000	0.0000	0.0000	0.0000	0.0000	0.0000	0.0000	0.0000
2	0.9419	0.7338	0.4797	0.4027	0.2713	0.1353	0.0600	0.0326	0.0236	0.0082	0.0025	0.0007	0.0001	0.0000	0.0000	0.0000	0.0000	0.0000	0.0000	0.0000	0.0000	0.0000	0.0000
3	0.9891	0.9018	0.7202	0.6479	0.5010	0.3057	0.1646	0.1017	0.0783	0.0328	0.0120	0.0038	0.0010	0.0002	0.0000	0.0000	0.0000	0.0000	0.0000	0.0000	0.0000	0.0000	0.0000
4	0.9985	0.9718	0.8794	0.8318	0.7164	0.5187	0.3327	0.2311	0.1886	0.0942	0.0411	0.0154	0.0049	0.0013	0.0003	0.0001	0.0000	0.0000	0.0000	0.0000	0.0000	0.0000	0.0000
5	0.9998	0.9936	0.9581	0.9347	0.8671	0.7175	0.5344	0.4122	0.3550	0.2088	0.1077	0.0481	0.0183	0.0058	0.0014	0.0009	0.0003	0.0000	0.0000	0.0000	0.0000	0.0000	0.0000
6	1.0000	0.9988	0.9882	0.9794	0.9487	0.8610	0.7217	0.6085	0.5491	0.3743	0.2258	0.1189	0.0537	0.0203	0.0062	0.0039	0.0014	0.0002	0.0000	0.0000	0.0000	0.0000	0.0000
7	1.0000	0.9998	0.9973	0.9947	0.9837	0.9431	0.8593	0.7767	0.7283	0.5634	0.3915	0.2403	0.1280	0.0576	0.0212	0.0144	0.0061	0.0012	0.0002	0.0000	0.0000	0.0000	0.0000
8	1.0000	1.0000	0.9995	0.9989	0.9957	0.9807	0.9404	0.8924	0.8609	0.7368	0.5778	0.4073	0.2527	0.1347	0.0597	0.0433	0.0210	0.0054	0.0009	0.0002	0.0001	0.0000	0.0000
9	1.0000	1.0000	0.9999	0.9998	0.9991	0.9946	0.9790	0.9567	0.9403	0.8653	0.7473	0.5927	0.4222	0.2632	0.1391	0.1076	0.0596	0.0193	0.0043	0.0011	0.0005	0.0000	0.0000
10	1.0000	1.0000	1.0000	1.0000	0.9998	0.9988	0.9939	0.9856	0.9788	0.9424	0.8720	0.7597	0.6085	0.4366	0.2717	0.2233	0.1407	0.0569	0.0163	0.0053	0.0027	0.0002	0.0000
11	1.0000	1.0000	1.0000	1.0000	1.0000	0.9998	0.9986	0.9961	0.9938	0.9797	0.9463	0.8811	0.7742	0.6257	0.4509	0.3915	0.2783	0.1390	0.0513	0.0206	0.0118	0.0012	0.0000
12	1.0000	1.0000	1.0000	1.0000	1.0000	1.0000	0.9997	0.9991	0.9986	0.9942	0.9817	0.9519	0.8923	0.7912	0.6450	0.5878	0.4656	0.2825	0.1329	0.0653	0.0419	0.0064	0.0002
13	1.0000	1.0000	1.0000	1.0000	1.0000	1.0000	1.0000	0.9999	0.9997	0.9987	0.9951	0.9846	0.9589	0.9058	0.8114	0.7689	0.6673	0.4813	0.2836	0.1682	0.1206	0.0282	0.0015
14	1.0000	1.0000	1.0000	1.0000	1.0000	1.0000	1.0000	1.0000	1.0000	0.9998	0.9990	0.9962	0.9880	0.9672	0.9217	0.8983	0.8354	0.6943	0.4990	0.3521	0.2798	0.0982	0.0109
15	1.0000	1.0000	1.0000	1.0000	1.0000	1.0000	1.0000	1.0000	1.0000	1.0000	0.9999	0.9993	0.9975	0.9918	0.9764	0.9674	0.9400	0.8647	0.7287	0.5973	0.5203	0.2662	0.0581
16	1.0000	1.0000	1.0000	1.0000	1.0000	1.0000	1.0000	1.0000	1.0000	1.0000	1.0000	0.9999	0.9997	0.9987	0.9954	0.9932	0.9858	0.9605	0.9009	0.8272	0.7759	0.5497	0.2265
17	1.0000	1.0000	1.0000	1.0000	1.0000	1.0000	1.0000	1.0000	1.0000	1.0000	1.0000	1.0000	1.0000	0.9999	0.9996	0.9993	0.9984	0.9944	0.9820	0.9624	0.9464	0.8499	0.6028
18	1.0000	1.0000	1.0000	1.0000	1.0000	1.0000	1.0000	1.0000	1.0000	1.0000	1.0000	1.0000	1.0000	1.0000	1.0000	1.0000	1.0000	1.0000	1.0000	1.0000	1.0000	1.0000	1.0000

$n = 20$

p \ x	0.05	0.1	0.15	1/6	0.2	0.25	0.3	1/3	0.35	0.4	0.45	0.5	0.55	0.6	0.65	2/3	0.7	0.75	0.8	5/6	0.85	0.9	0.95
0	0.3585	0.1216	0.0388	0.0261	0.0115	0.0032	0.0008	0.0003	0.0002	0.0000	0.0000	0.0000	0.0000	0.0000	0.0000	0.0000	0.0000	0.0000	0.0000	0.0000	0.0000	0.0000	0.0000
1	0.7358	0.3917	0.1756	0.1304	0.0692	0.0243	0.0076	0.0033	0.0021	0.0005	0.0001	0.0000	0.0000	0.0000	0.0000	0.0000	0.0000	0.0000	0.0000	0.0000	0.0000	0.0000	0.0000
2	0.9245	0.6769	0.4049	0.3287	0.2061	0.0913	0.0355	0.0176	0.0121	0.0036	0.0009	0.0002	0.0000	0.0000	0.0000	0.0000	0.0000	0.0000	0.0000	0.0000	0.0000	0.0000	0.0000
3	0.9841	0.8670	0.6477	0.5665	0.4114	0.2252	0.1071	0.0604	0.0444	0.0160	0.0049	0.0013	0.0003	0.0000	0.0000	0.0000	0.0000	0.0000	0.0000	0.0000	0.0000	0.0000	0.0000
4	0.9974	0.9568	0.8298	0.7687	0.6296	0.4148	0.2375	0.1515	0.1182	0.0510	0.0189	0.0059	0.0015	0.0003	0.0000	0.0000	0.0000	0.0000	0.0000	0.0000	0.0000	0.0000	0.0000
5	0.9997	0.9887	0.9327	0.8982	0.8042	0.6172	0.4164	0.2972	0.2454	0.1256	0.0553	0.0207	0.0064	0.0016	0.0003	0.0002	0.0000	0.0000	0.0000	0.0000	0.0000	0.0000	0.0000
6	1.0000	0.9976	0.9781	0.9629	0.9133	0.7858	0.6080	0.4793	0.4166	0.2500	0.1299	0.0577	0.0214	0.0065	0.0015	0.0009	0.0003	0.0000	0.0000	0.0000	0.0000	0.0000	0.0000
7	1.0000	0.9996	0.9941	0.9887	0.9679	0.8982	0.7723	0.6615	0.6010	0.4159	0.2520	0.1316	0.0580	0.0210	0.0060	0.0037	0.0013	0.0002	0.0000	0.0000	0.0000	0.0000	0.0000
8	1.0000	0.9999	0.9987	0.9972	0.9900	0.9591	0.8867	0.8095	0.7624	0.5956	0.4143	0.2517	0.1308	0.0565	0.0196	0.0130	0.0051	0.0009	0.0001	0.0000	0.0000	0.0000	0.0000
9	1.0000	1.0000	0.9998	0.9994	0.9974	0.9861	0.9520	0.9081	0.8782	0.7553	0.5914	0.4119	0.2493	0.1275	0.0532	0.0376	0.0171	0.0039	0.0006	0.0001	0.0000	0.0000	0.0000
10	1.0000	1.0000	1.0000	0.9999	0.9994	0.9961	0.9829	0.9624	0.9468	0.8725	0.7507	0.5881	0.4086	0.2447	0.1218	0.0919	0.0480	0.0139	0.0026	0.0006	0.0002	0.0000	0.0000
11	1.0000	1.0000	1.0000	1.0000	0.9999	0.9991	0.9949	0.9870	0.9804	0.9435	0.8692	0.7483	0.5857	0.4044	0.2376	0.1905	0.1133	0.0409	0.0100	0.0028	0.0013	0.0001	0.0000
12	1.0000	1.0000	1.0000	1.0000	1.0000	0.9998	0.9987	0.9963	0.9940	0.9790	0.9420	0.8684	0.7480	0.5841	0.3990	0.3385	0.2277	0.1018	0.0321	0.0113	0.0059	0.0004	0.0000
13	1.0000	1.0000	1.0000	1.0000	1.0000	1.0000	0.9997	0.9991	0.9985	0.9935	0.9786	0.9423	0.8701	0.7500	0.5834	0.5207	0.3920	0.2142	0.0867	0.0371	0.0219	0.0024	0.0000
14	1.0000	1.0000	1.0000	1.0000	1.0000	1.0000	1.0000	0.9998	0.9997	0.9984	0.9936	0.9793	0.9447	0.8744	0.7546	0.7028	0.5836	0.3828	0.1958	0.1018	0.0673	0.0113	0.0003
15	1.0000	1.0000	1.0000	1.0000	1.0000	1.0000	1.0000	1.0000	1.0000	0.9997	0.9985	0.9941	0.9811	0.9490	0.8818	0.8485	0.7625	0.5852	0.3704	0.2313	0.1702	0.0432	0.0026
16	1.0000	1.0000	1.0000	1.0000	1.0000	1.0000	1.0000	1.0000	1.0000	1.0000	0.9997	0.9987	0.9951	0.9840	0.9556	0.9396	0.8929	0.7748	0.5886	0.4335	0.3523	0.1330	0.0159
17	1.0000	1.0000	1.0000	1.0000	1.0000	1.0000	1.0000	1.0000	1.0000	1.0000	1.0000	0.9998	0.9991	0.9964	0.9879	0.9824	0.9645	0.9087	0.7939	0.6713	0.5951	0.3231	0.0755
18	1.0000	1.0000	1.0000	1.0000	1.0000	1.0000	1.0000	1.0000	1.0000	1.0000	1.0000	1.0000	0.9999	0.9995	0.9979	0.9967	0.9924	0.9757	0.9308	0.8696	0.8244	0.6083	0.2642
19	1.0000	1.0000	1.0000	1.0000	1.0000	1.0000	1.0000	1.0000	1.0000	1.0000	1.0000	1.0000	1.0000	1.0000	0.9998	0.9997	0.9992	0.9968	0.9885	0.9739	0.9612	0.8784	0.6415
20	1.0000	1.0000	1.0000	1.0000	1.0000	1.0000	1.0000	1.0000	1.0000	1.0000	1.0000	1.0000	1.0000	1.0000	1.0000	1.0000	1.0000	1.0000	1.0000	1.0000	1.0000	1.0000	1.0000

CUMULATIVE BINOMIAL PROBABILITIES for n = 25

n = 25 p	0.05	0.1	0.15	1/6	0.2	0.25	0.3	1/3	0.35	0.4	0.45	0.5	0.55	0.6	0.65	2/3	0.7	0.75	0.8	5/6	0.85	0.9	0.95
x = 0	0.2774	0.0718	0.0172	0.0105	0.0038	0.0008	0.0001	0.0000	0.0000	0.0000	0.0000	0.0000	0.0000	0.0000	0.0000	0.0000	0.0000	0.0000	0.0000	0.0000	0.0000	0.0000	0.0000
1	0.6424	0.2712	0.0931	0.0629	0.0274	0.0070	0.0016	0.0005	0.0003	0.0001	0.0000	0.0000	0.0000	0.0000	0.0000	0.0000	0.0000	0.0000	0.0000	0.0000	0.0000	0.0000	0.0000
2	0.8729	0.5371	0.2537	0.1887	0.0982	0.0321	0.0090	0.0035	0.0021	0.0004	0.0001	0.0000	0.0000	0.0000	0.0000	0.0000	0.0000	0.0000	0.0000	0.0000	0.0000	0.0000	0.0000
3	0.9659	0.7636	0.4711	0.3816	0.2340	0.0962	0.0332	0.0149	0.0097	0.0024	0.0005	0.0001	0.0000	0.0000	0.0000	0.0000	0.0000	0.0000	0.0000	0.0000	0.0000	0.0000	0.0000
4	0.9928	0.9020	0.6821	0.5937	0.4207	0.2137	0.0905	0.0462	0.0320	0.0095	0.0023	0.0005	0.0001	0.0000	0.0000	0.0000	0.0000	0.0000	0.0000	0.0000	0.0000	0.0000	0.0000
5	0.9988	0.9666	0.8385	0.7720	0.6167	0.3783	0.1935	0.1120	0.0826	0.0294	0.0086	0.0020	0.0004	0.0001	0.0000	0.0000	0.0000	0.0000	0.0000	0.0000	0.0000	0.0000	0.0000
6	0.9998	0.9905	0.9305	0.8908	0.7800	0.5611	0.3407	0.2215	0.1734	0.0736	0.0258	0.0073	0.0016	0.0003	0.0000	0.0000	0.0000	0.0000	0.0000	0.0000	0.0000	0.0000	0.0000
7	1.0000	0.9977	0.9745	0.9553	0.8909	0.7265	0.5118	0.3703	0.3061	0.1536	0.0639	0.0216	0.0058	0.0012	0.0002	0.0001	0.0000	0.0000	0.0000	0.0000	0.0000	0.0000	0.0000
8	1.0000	0.9995	0.9920	0.9843	0.9532	0.8506	0.6769	0.5376	0.4668	0.2735	0.1340	0.0539	0.0174	0.0043	0.0008	0.0004	0.0001	0.0000	0.0000	0.0000	0.0000	0.0000	0.0000
9	1.0000	0.9999	0.9979	0.9953	0.9827	0.9287	0.8106	0.6956	0.6303	0.4246	0.2424	0.1148	0.0440	0.0132	0.0029	0.0016	0.0005	0.0000	0.0000	0.0000	0.0000	0.0000	0.0000
10	1.0000	1.0000	0.9995	0.9988	0.9944	0.9703	0.9022	0.8220	0.7712	0.5858	0.3843	0.2122	0.0960	0.0344	0.0093	0.0056	0.0018	0.0002	0.0000	0.0000	0.0000	0.0000	0.0000
11	1.0000	1.0000	0.9999	0.9997	0.9985	0.9893	0.9558	0.9082	0.8746	0.7323	0.5426	0.3450	0.1827	0.0778	0.0255	0.0164	0.0060	0.0009	0.0001	0.0000	0.0000	0.0000	0.0000
12	1.0000	1.0000	1.0000	0.9999	0.9996	0.9966	0.9825	0.9585	0.9396	0.8462	0.6937	0.5000	0.3063	0.1538	0.0604	0.0415	0.0175	0.0034	0.0004	0.0001	0.0000	0.0000	0.0000
13	1.0000	1.0000	1.0000	1.0000	0.9999	0.9991	0.9940	0.9836	0.9745	0.9222	0.8173	0.6550	0.4574	0.2677	0.1254	0.0918	0.0442	0.0107	0.0015	0.0003	0.0001	0.0000	0.0000
14	1.0000	1.0000	1.0000	1.0000	1.0000	0.9998	0.9982	0.9944	0.9907	0.9656	0.9040	0.7878	0.6157	0.4142	0.2288	0.1780	0.0978	0.0297	0.0056	0.0012	0.0005	0.0000	0.0000
15	1.0000	1.0000	1.0000	1.0000	1.0000	1.0000	0.9995	0.9984	0.9971	0.9868	0.9560	0.8852	0.7576	0.5754	0.3697	0.3044	0.1894	0.0713	0.0173	0.0047	0.0021	0.0001	0.0000
16	1.0000	1.0000	1.0000	1.0000	1.0000	1.0000	0.9999	0.9996	0.9992	0.9957	0.9826	0.9461	0.8660	0.7265	0.5332	0.4624	0.3231	0.1494	0.0468	0.0157	0.0080	0.0005	0.0000
17	1.0000	1.0000	1.0000	1.0000	1.0000	1.0000	1.0000	0.9999	0.9998	0.9988	0.9942	0.9784	0.9361	0.8464	0.6939	0.6297	0.4882	0.2735	0.1091	0.0447	0.0255	0.0023	0.0000
18	1.0000	1.0000	1.0000	1.0000	1.0000	1.0000	1.0000	1.0000	1.0000	0.9997	0.9984	0.9927	0.9742	0.9264	0.8266	0.7785	0.6593	0.4389	0.2200	0.1092	0.0695	0.0095	0.0002
19	1.0000	1.0000	1.0000	1.0000	1.0000	1.0000	1.0000	1.0000	1.0000	0.9999	0.9996	0.9980	0.9914	0.9706	0.9174	0.8880	0.8065	0.6217	0.3833	0.2280	0.1615	0.0334	0.0012
20	1.0000	1.0000	1.0000	1.0000	1.0000	1.0000	1.0000	1.0000	1.0000	1.0000	0.9999	0.9995	0.9977	0.9905	0.9680	0.9538	0.9095	0.7863	0.5793	0.4063	0.3179	0.0980	0.0072
21	1.0000	1.0000	1.0000	1.0000	1.0000	1.0000	1.0000	1.0000	1.0000	1.0000	1.0000	0.9999	0.9995	0.9976	0.9903	0.9851	0.9668	0.9038	0.7660	0.6184	0.5289	0.2364	0.0341
22	1.0000	1.0000	1.0000	1.0000	1.0000	1.0000	1.0000	1.0000	1.0000	1.0000	1.0000	1.0000	0.9999	0.9996	0.9979	0.9965	0.9910	0.9679	0.9018	0.8113	0.7463	0.4629	0.1271
23	1.0000	1.0000	1.0000	1.0000	1.0000	1.0000	1.0000	1.0000	1.0000	1.0000	1.0000	1.0000	1.0000	0.9999	0.9997	0.9995	0.9984	0.9930	0.9726	0.9371	0.9069	0.7288	0.3576
24	1.0000	1.0000	1.0000	1.0000	1.0000	1.0000	1.0000	1.0000	1.0000	1.0000	1.0000	1.0000	1.0000	1.0000	1.0000	1.0000	0.9999	0.9992	0.9962	0.9895	0.9828	0.9282	0.7226
25	1.0000	1.0000	1.0000	1.0000	1.0000	1.0000	1.0000	1.0000	1.0000	1.0000	1.0000	1.0000	1.0000	1.0000	1.0000	1.0000	1.0000	1.0000	1.0000	1.0000	1.0000	1.0000	1.0000

CUMULATIVE POISSON PROBABILITIES for λ = 0.01 – 2.90

λ	0.01	0.02	0.03	0.04	0.05	0.06	0.07	0.08	0.09
x = 0	0.9900	0.9802	0.9704	0.9608	0.9512	0.9418	0.9324	0.9231	0.9139
1	1.0000	0.9998	0.9996	0.9992	0.9988	0.9983	0.9977	0.9970	0.9962
2	1.0000	1.0000	1.0000	1.0000	1.0000	1.0000	0.9999	0.9999	0.9999
3	1.0000	1.0000	1.0000	1.0000	1.0000	1.0000	1.0000	1.0000	1.0000

λ	0.10	0.20	0.30	0.40	0.50	0.60	0.70	0.80	0.90
x = 0	0.9048	0.8187	0.7408	0.6703	0.6065	0.5488	0.4966	0.4493	0.4066
1	0.9953	0.9825	0.9631	0.9384	0.9098	0.8781	0.8442	0.8088	0.7725
2	0.9998	0.9989	0.9964	0.9921	0.9856	0.9769	0.9659	0.9526	0.9371
3	1.0000	0.9999	0.9997	0.9992	0.9982	0.9966	0.9942	0.9909	0.9865
4	1.0000	1.0000	1.0000	0.9999	0.9998	0.9996	0.9992	0.9986	0.9977
5	1.0000	1.0000	1.0000	1.0000	1.0000	1.0000	0.9999	0.9998	0.9997
6	1.0000	1.0000	1.0000	1.0000	1.0000	1.0000	1.0000	1.0000	1.0000

λ	1.00	1.10	1.20	1.30	1.40	1.50	1.60	1.70	1.80	1.90
x = 0	0.3679	0.3329	0.3012	0.2725	0.2466	0.2231	0.2019	0.1827	0.1653	0.1496
1	0.7358	0.6990	0.6626	0.6268	0.5918	0.5578	0.5249	0.4932	0.4628	0.4337
2	0.9197	0.9004	0.8795	0.8571	0.8335	0.8088	0.7834	0.7572	0.7306	0.7037
3	0.9810	0.9743	0.9662	0.9569	0.9463	0.9344	0.9212	0.9068	0.8913	0.8747
4	0.9963	0.9946	0.9923	0.9893	0.9857	0.9814	0.9763	0.9704	0.9636	0.9559
5	0.9994	0.9990	0.9985	0.9978	0.9968	0.9955	0.9940	0.9920	0.9896	0.9868
6	0.9999	0.9999	0.9997	0.9996	0.9994	0.9991	0.9987	0.9981	0.9974	0.9966
7	1.0000	1.0000	1.0000	0.9999	0.9999	0.9998	0.9997	0.9996	0.9994	0.9992
8	1.0000	1.0000	1.0000	1.0000	1.0000	1.0000	1.0000	0.9999	0.9999	0.9998
9	1.0000	1.0000	1.0000	1.0000	1.0000	1.0000	1.0000	1.0000	1.0000	1.0000

λ	2.00	2.10	2.20	2.30	2.40	2.50	2.60	2.70	2.80	2.90
x = 0	0.1353	0.1225	0.1108	0.1003	0.0907	0.0821	0.0743	0.0672	0.0608	0.0550
1	0.4060	0.3796	0.3546	0.3309	0.3084	0.2873	0.2674	0.2487	0.2311	0.2146
2	0.6767	0.6496	0.6227	0.5960	0.5697	0.5438	0.5184	0.4936	0.4695	0.4460
3	0.8571	0.8386	0.8194	0.7993	0.7787	0.7576	0.7360	0.7141	0.6919	0.6696
4	0.9473	0.9379	0.9275	0.9162	0.9041	0.8912	0.8774	0.8629	0.8477	0.8318
5	0.9834	0.9796	0.9751	0.9700	0.9643	0.9580	0.9510	0.9433	0.9349	0.9258
6	0.9955	0.9941	0.9925	0.9906	0.9884	0.9858	0.9828	0.9794	0.9756	0.9713
7	0.9989	0.9985	0.9980	0.9974	0.9967	0.9958	0.9947	0.9934	0.9919	0.9901
8	0.9998	0.9997	0.9995	0.9994	0.9991	0.9989	0.9985	0.9981	0.9976	0.9969
9	1.0000	0.9999	0.9999	0.9999	0.9998	0.9997	0.9996	0.9995	0.9993	0.9991
10	1.0000	1.0000	1.0000	1.0000	1.0000	0.9999	0.9999	0.9999	0.9998	0.9998
11	1.0000	1.0000	1.0000	1.0000	1.0000	1.0000	1.0000	1.0000	1.0000	0.9999
12	1.0000	1.0000	1.0000	1.0000	1.0000	1.0000	1.0000	1.0000	1.0000	1.0000

CUMULATIVE POISSON PROBABILITIES for λ = 3.00 – 4.90

λ	3.00	3.10	3.20	3.30	3.40	3.50	3.60	3.70	3.80	3.90
x = 0	0.0498	0.0450	0.0408	0.0369	0.0334	0.0302	0.0273	0.0247	0.0224	0.0202
1	0.1991	0.1847	0.1712	0.1586	0.1468	0.1359	0.1257	0.1162	0.1074	0.0992
2	0.4232	0.4012	0.3799	0.3594	0.3397	0.3208	0.3027	0.2854	0.2689	0.2531
3	0.6472	0.6248	0.6025	0.5803	0.5584	0.5366	0.5152	0.4942	0.4735	0.4532
4	0.8153	0.7982	0.7806	0.7626	0.7442	0.7254	0.7064	0.6872	0.6678	0.6484
5	0.9161	0.9057	0.8946	0.8829	0.8705	0.8576	0.8441	0.8301	0.8156	0.8006
6	0.9665	0.9612	0.9554	0.9490	0.9421	0.9347	0.9267	0.9182	0.9091	0.8995
7	0.9881	0.9858	0.9832	0.9802	0.9769	0.9733	0.9692	0.9648	0.9599	0.9546
8	0.9962	0.9953	0.9943	0.9931	0.9917	0.9901	0.9883	0.9863	0.9840	0.9815
9	0.9989	0.9986	0.9982	0.9978	0.9973	0.9967	0.9960	0.9952	0.9942	0.9931
10	0.9997	0.9996	0.9995	0.9994	0.9992	0.9990	0.9987	0.9984	0.9981	0.9977
11	0.9999	0.9999	0.9999	0.9998	0.9998	0.9997	0.9996	0.9995	0.9994	0.9993
12	1.0000	1.0000	1.0000	1.0000	0.9999	0.9999	0.9999	0.9999	0.9998	0.9998
13	1.0000	1.0000	1.0000	1.0000	1.0000	1.0000	1.0000	1.0000	1.0000	0.9999
14	1.0000	1.0000	1.0000	1.0000	1.0000	1.0000	1.0000	1.0000	1.0000	1.0000

λ	4.00	4.10	4.20	4.30	4.40	4.50	4.60	4.70	4.80	4.90
x = 0	0.0183	0.0166	0.0150	0.0136	0.0123	0.0111	0.0101	0.0091	0.0082	0.0074
1	0.0916	0.0845	0.0780	0.0719	0.0663	0.0611	0.0563	0.0518	0.0477	0.0439
2	0.2381	0.2238	0.2102	0.1974	0.1851	0.1736	0.1626	0.1523	0.1425	0.1333
3	0.4335	0.4142	0.3954	0.3772	0.3594	0.3423	0.3257	0.3097	0.2942	0.2793
4	0.6288	0.6093	0.5898	0.5704	0.5512	0.5321	0.5132	0.4946	0.4763	0.4582
5	0.7851	0.7693	0.7531	0.7367	0.7199	0.7029	0.6858	0.6684	0.6510	0.6335
6	0.8893	0.8786	0.8675	0.8558	0.8436	0.8311	0.8180	0.8046	0.7908	0.7767
7	0.9489	0.9427	0.9361	0.9290	0.9214	0.9134	0.9049	0.8960	0.8867	0.8769
8	0.9786	0.9755	0.9721	0.9683	0.9642	0.9597	0.9549	0.9497	0.9442	0.9382
9	0.9919	0.9905	0.9889	0.9871	0.9851	0.9829	0.9805	0.9778	0.9749	0.9717
10	0.9972	0.9966	0.9959	0.9952	0.9943	0.9933	0.9922	0.9910	0.9896	0.9880
11	0.9991	0.9989	0.9986	0.9983	0.9980	0.9976	0.9971	0.9966	0.9960	0.9953
12	0.9997	0.9997	0.9996	0.9995	0.9993	0.9992	0.9990	0.9988	0.9986	0.9983
13	0.9999	0.9999	0.9999	0.9998	0.9998	0.9997	0.9997	0.9996	0.9995	0.9994
14	1.0000	1.0000	1.0000	1.0000	0.9999	0.9999	0.9999	0.9999	0.9999	0.9998
15	1.0000	1.0000	1.0000	1.0000	1.0000	1.0000	1.0000	1.0000	1.0000	0.9999
16	1.0000	1.0000	1.0000	1.0000	1.0000	1.0000	1.0000	1.0000	1.0000	1.0000

CUMULATIVE POISSON PROBABILITIES for λ = 5.00 – 9.50

λ	5.00	5.50	6.00	6.50	7.00	7.50	8.00	8.50	9.00	9.50
x = 0	0.0067	0.0041	0.0025	0.0015	0.0009	0.0006	0.0003	0.0002	0.0001	0.0001
1	0.0404	0.0266	0.0174	0.0113	0.0073	0.0047	0.0030	0.0019	0.0012	0.0008
2	0.1247	0.0884	0.0620	0.0430	0.0296	0.0203	0.0138	0.0093	0.0062	0.0042
3	0.2650	0.2017	0.1512	0.1118	0.0818	0.0591	0.0424	0.0301	0.0212	0.0149
4	0.4405	0.3575	0.2851	0.2237	0.1730	0.1321	0.0996	0.0744	0.0550	0.0403
5	0.6160	0.5289	0.4457	0.3690	0.3007	0.2414	0.1912	0.1496	0.1157	0.0885
6	0.7622	0.6860	0.6063	0.5265	0.4497	0.3782	0.3134	0.2562	0.2068	0.1649
7	0.8666	0.8095	0.7440	0.6728	0.5987	0.5246	0.4530	0.3856	0.3239	0.2687
8	0.9319	0.8944	0.8472	0.7916	0.7291	0.6620	0.5925	0.5231	0.4557	0.3918
9	0.9682	0.9462	0.9161	0.8774	0.8305	0.7764	0.7166	0.6530	0.5874	0.5218
10	0.9863	0.9747	0.9574	0.9332	0.9015	0.8622	0.8159	0.7634	0.7060	0.6453
11	0.9945	0.9890	0.9799	0.9661	0.9467	0.9208	0.8881	0.8487	0.8030	0.7520
12	0.9980	0.9955	0.9912	0.9840	0.9730	0.9573	0.9362	0.9091	0.8758	0.8364
13	0.9993	0.9983	0.9964	0.9929	0.9872	0.9784	0.9658	0.9486	0.9261	0.8981
14	0.9998	0.9994	0.9986	0.9970	0.9943	0.9897	0.9827	0.9726	0.9585	0.9400
15	0.9999	0.9998	0.9995	0.9988	0.9976	0.9954	0.9918	0.9862	0.9780	0.9665
16	1.0000	0.9999	0.9998	0.9996	0.9990	0.9980	0.9963	0.9934	0.9889	0.9823
17	1.0000	1.0000	0.9999	0.9998	0.9996	0.9992	0.9984	0.9970	0.9947	0.9911
18	1.0000	1.0000	1.0000	0.9999	0.9999	0.9997	0.9993	0.9987	0.9976	0.9957
19	1.0000	1.0000	1.0000	1.0000	1.0000	0.9999	0.9997	0.9995	0.9989	0.9980
20	1.0000	1.0000	1.0000	1.0000	1.0000	1.0000	0.9999	0.9998	0.9996	0.9991
21	1.0000	1.0000	1.0000	1.0000	1.0000	1.0000	1.0000	0.9999	0.9998	0.9996
22	1.0000	1.0000	1.0000	1.0000	1.0000	1.0000	1.0000	1.0000	0.9999	0.9999
23	1.0000	1.0000	1.0000	1.0000	1.0000	1.0000	1.0000	1.0000	1.0000	0.9999
24	1.0000	1.0000	1.0000	1.0000	1.0000	1.0000	1.0000	1.0000	1.0000	1.0000

CUMULATIVE POISSON PROBABILITIES for λ = 10.00 – 19.00

λ	10.00	11.00	12.00	13.00	14.00	15.00	16.00	17.00	18.00	19.00
x = 0	0.0000	0.0000	0.0000	0.0000	0.0000	0.0000	0.0000	0.0000	0.0000	0.0000
1	0.0005	0.0002	0.0001	0.0000	0.0000	0.0000	0.0000	0.0000	0.0000	0.0000
2	0.0028	0.0012	0.0005	0.0002	0.0001	0.0000	0.0000	0.0000	0.0000	0.0000
3	0.0103	0.0049	0.0023	0.0011	0.0005	0.0002	0.0001	0.0000	0.0000	0.0000
4	0.0293	0.0151	0.0076	0.0037	0.0018	0.0009	0.0004	0.0002	0.0001	0.0000
5	0.0671	0.0375	0.0203	0.0107	0.0055	0.0028	0.0014	0.0007	0.0003	0.0002
6	0.1301	0.0786	0.0458	0.0259	0.0142	0.0076	0.0040	0.0021	0.0010	0.0005
7	0.2202	0.1432	0.0895	0.0540	0.0316	0.0180	0.0100	0.0054	0.0029	0.0015
8	0.3328	0.2320	0.1550	0.0998	0.0621	0.0374	0.0220	0.0126	0.0071	0.0039
9	0.4579	0.3405	0.2424	0.1658	0.1094	0.0699	0.0433	0.0261	0.0154	0.0089
10	0.5830	0.4599	0.3472	0.2517	0.1757	0.1185	0.0774	0.0491	0.0304	0.0183
11	0.6968	0.5793	0.4616	0.3532	0.2600	0.1848	0.1270	0.0847	0.0549	0.0347
12	0.7916	0.6887	0.5760	0.4631	0.3585	0.2676	0.1931	0.1350	0.0917	0.0606
13	0.8645	0.7813	0.6815	0.5730	0.4644	0.3632	0.2745	0.2009	0.1426	0.0984
14	0.9165	0.8540	0.7720	0.6751	0.5704	0.4657	0.3675	0.2808	0.2081	0.1497
15	0.9513	0.9074	0.8444	0.7636	0.6694	0.5681	0.4667	0.3715	0.2867	0.2148
16	0.9730	0.9441	0.8987	0.8355	0.7559	0.6641	0.5660	0.4677	0.3751	0.2920
17	0.9857	0.9678	0.9370	0.8905	0.8272	0.7489	0.6593	0.5640	0.4686	0.3784
18	0.9928	0.9823	0.9626	0.9302	0.8826	0.8195	0.7423	0.6550	0.5622	0.4695
19	0.9965	0.9907	0.9787	0.9573	0.9235	0.8752	0.8122	0.7363	0.6509	0.5606
20	0.9984	0.9953	0.9884	0.9750	0.9521	0.9170	0.8682	0.8055	0.7307	0.6472
21	0.9993	0.9977	0.9939	0.9859	0.9712	0.9469	0.9108	0.8615	0.7991	0.7255
22	0.9997	0.9990	0.9970	0.9924	0.9833	0.9673	0.9418	0.9047	0.8551	0.7931
23	0.9999	0.9995	0.9985	0.9960	0.9907	0.9805	0.9633	0.9367	0.8989	0.8490
24	1.0000	0.9998	0.9993	0.9980	0.9950	0.9888	0.9777	0.9594	0.9317	0.8933
25	1.0000	0.9999	0.9997	0.9990	0.9974	0.9938	0.9869	0.9748	0.9554	0.9269
26	1.0000	1.0000	0.9999	0.9995	0.9987	0.9967	0.9925	0.9848	0.9718	0.9514
27	1.0000	1.0000	0.9999	0.9998	0.9994	0.9983	0.9959	0.9912	0.9827	0.9687
28	1.0000	1.0000	1.0000	0.9999	0.9997	0.9991	0.9978	0.9950	0.9897	0.9805
29	1.0000	1.0000	1.0000	1.0000	0.9999	0.9996	0.9989	0.9973	0.9941	0.9882
30	1.0000	1.0000	1.0000	1.0000	0.9999	0.9998	0.9994	0.9986	0.9967	0.9930
31	1.0000	1.0000	1.0000	1.0000	1.0000	0.9999	0.9997	0.9993	0.9982	0.9960
32	1.0000	1.0000	1.0000	1.0000	1.0000	1.0000	0.9999	0.9996	0.9990	0.9978
33	1.0000	1.0000	1.0000	1.0000	1.0000	1.0000	0.9999	0.9998	0.9995	0.9988
34	1.0000	1.0000	1.0000	1.0000	1.0000	1.0000	1.0000	0.9999	0.9998	0.9994
35	1.0000	1.0000	1.0000	1.0000	1.0000	1.0000	1.0000	1.0000	0.9999	0.9997
36	1.0000	1.0000	1.0000	1.0000	1.0000	1.0000	1.0000	1.0000	0.9999	0.9998
37	1.0000	1.0000	1.0000	1.0000	1.0000	1.0000	1.0000	1.0000	1.0000	0.9999
38	1.0000	1.0000	1.0000	1.0000	1.0000	1.0000	1.0000	1.0000	1.0000	1.0000

THE NORMAL DISTRIBUTION FUNCTION

If $Z \sim N(0,1)$, then this table gives the value of $f(z)$ where $\Phi(z) = P(Z \le z)$.

$$\Phi(-z) = 1 - \Phi(z)$$

z	0	1	2	3	4	5	6	7	8	9	1	2	3	4	5	6	7	8	9
														ADD					
0.0	0.5000	0.5040	0.5080	0.5120	0.5160	0.5199	0.5239	0.5279	0.5319	0.5359	4	8	12	16	20	24	28	32	36
0.1	0.5398	0.5438	0.5478	0.5517	0.5557	0.5596	0.5636	0.5675	0.5714	0.5753	4	8	12	16	20	24	28	32	36
0.2	0.5793	0.5832	0.5871	0.5910	0.5948	0.5987	0.6026	0.6064	0.6103	0.6141	4	8	12	15	19	23	27	31	35
0.3	0.6179	0.6217	0.6255	0.6293	0.6331	0.6368	0.6406	0.6443	0.6480	0.6517	4	7	11	14	18	22	25	29	32
0.4	0.6554	0.6591	0.6628	0.6664	0.6700	0.6736	0.6772	0.6808	0.6844	0.6879	4	7	11	14	18	22	25	29	32
0.5	0.6915	0.6950	0.6985	0.7019	0.7054	0.7088	0.7123	0.7157	0.7190	0.7224	3	7	10	14	17	20	24	27	31
0.6	0.7257	0.7291	0.7324	0.7357	0.7389	0.7422	0.7454	0.7486	0.7517	0.7549	3	7	10	13	16	19	23	26	29
0.7	0.7580	0.7611	0.7642	0.7673	0.7704	0.7734	0.7764	0.7794	0.7823	0.7852	3	6	9	12	15	18	21	24	27
0.8	0.7881	0.7910	0.7939	0.7967	0.7995	0.8023	0.8051	0.8078	0.8106	0.8133	3	5	8	11	14	16	19	22	25
0.9	0.8159	0.8186	0.8212	0.8238	0.8264	0.8289	0.8315	0.8340	0.8365	0.8389	3	5	8	10	13	15	18	20	23
1.0	0.8413	0.8438	0.8461	0.8485	0.8508	0.8531	0.8554	0.8577	0.8599	0.8621	2	5	7	9	12	14	16	19	21
1.1	0.8643	0.8665	0.8686	0.8708	0.8729	0.8749	0.8770	0.8790	0.8810	0.8830	2	4	6	8	10	12	14	16	18
1.2	0.8849	0.8869	0.8888	0.8907	0.8925	0.8944	0.8962	0.8980	0.8997	0.9015	2	4	6	7	9	11	13	15	17
1.3	0.9032	0.9049	0.9066	0.9082	0.9099	0.9115	0.9131	0.9147	0.9162	0.9177	2	3	5	6	8	10	11	13	14
1.4	0.9192	0.9207	0.9222	0.9236	0.9251	0.9265	0.9279	0.9292	0.9306	0.9319	1	3	4	6	7	8	10	11	13
1.5	0.9332	0.9345	0.9357	0.9370	0.9382	0.9394	0.9406	0.9418	0.9429	0.9441	1	2	4	5	6	7	8	10	11
1.6	0.9452	0.9463	0.9474	0.9484	0.9495	0.9505	0.9515	0.9525	0.9535	0.9545	1	2	4	4	5	6	7	8	9
1.7	0.9554	0.9564	0.9573	0.9582	0.9591	0.9599	0.9608	0.9616	0.9625	0.9633	1	2	3	4	4	5	6	7	8
1.8	0.9641	0.9649	0.9656	0.9664	0.9671	0.9678	0.9686	0.9693	0.9699	0.9706	1	1	2	3	4	4	5	6	6
1.9	0.9713	0.9719	0.9726	0.9732	0.9738	0.9744	0.9750	0.9756	0.9761	0.9767	1	1	2	2	3	4	4	5	5
2.0	0.9772	0.9778	0.9783	0.9788	0.9793	0.9798	0.9803	0.9808	0.9812	0.9817	0	1	1	2	2	3	3	4	4
2.1	0.9821	0.9826	0.9830	0.9834	0.9838	0.9842	0.9846	0.9850	0.9854	0.9857	0	1	1	2	2	2	3	3	4
2.2	0.9861	0.9864	0.9868	0.9871	0.9875	0.9878	0.9881	0.9884	0.9887	0.9890	0	1	1	1	2	2	2	3	3
2.3	0.9893	0.9896	0.9898	0.9901	0.9904	0.9906	0.9909	0.9911	0.9913	0.9916	0	1	1	1	1	2	2	2	2
2.4	0.9918	0.9920	0.9922	0.9925	0.9927	0.9929	0.9931	0.9932	0.9934	0.9936	0	0	1	1	1	1	1	2	2
2.5	0.9938	0.9940	0.9941	0.9943	0.9945	0.9946	0.9948	0.9949	0.9951	0.9952	0	0	0	1	1	1	1	1	1
2.6	0.9953	0.9955	0.9956	0.9957	0.9959	0.9960	0.9961	0.9962	0.9963	0.9964	0	0	0	0	1	1	1	1	1
2.7	0.9965	0.9966	0.9967	0.9968	0.9969	0.9970	0.9971	0.9972	0.9973	0.9974	0	0	0	0	0	1	1	1	1
2.8	0.9974	0.9975	0.9976	0.9977	0.9977	0.9978	0.9979	0.9979	0.9980	0.9981	0	0	0	0	0	0	0	1	1
2.9	0.9981	0.9982	0.9982	0.9983	0.9984	0.9984	0.9985	0.9985	0.9986	0.9986	0	0	0	0	0	0	0	0	0

ANSWERS

Unit 1: Representation of Data

Section 1: Mathematical models   p 7
D1.1: What is a mathematical model ?
1. (a) 4 n.m. (b)around 40 minutes after they leave port.
2. C, D, E

Section 2: Working with Data   p 8
D2.1: Types of data
1. QL   2. QN   3. QN   4. QL
5. D   6. C   7. C   8. D   9. C   10. D

D2.2: Ungrouped frequency tables
1. Number :   3 4 5 6 7 8 9 10
   Frequency   1 3 2 4 2 3 4 1
2. Each frequency would be 1 or 2.

Section 3: Stem-and-Leaf diagrams   p 9
D3.1: Stem-and-leaf diagrams
1. Ages of mothers   Key 3|3 = 33

3	3 5 7 7 9	(5)
4	0 0 1 8	(4)
5	0 1	(2)

2.(a) Length of feet in cm   Key 27|2 = 27.2

26	6 8 8 9 9	(5)
27	1 2 4 4 5 5 5	(7)
	6 6 7 7 7 8 8 9	(8)
28	0 0 1 1 1 2 2	(7)
29	0	(1)

(b) 29 cm

3. 40-50 days or around 6 weeks   4. 1 packet
5. (a) 28   (b) 3

D3.2: Back to back stem-and-leaf diagrams
1. (a)Ages of fathers   Ages of mothers Key 3|3 = 33

	8 7 5	3	3 5 7 7 9
9 7 6 3 2	4	0 0 1 8
	6 0	5	0 1
	1	6	

(b) The mothers are younger than the fathers.
2. (a) Brambley Road H   Stone Wall H

(4)	4 2 1 0	1	5 5 6 6	(4)
(5)	9 7 5 1 0	2	0 6 6 7 8 9	(6)
(5)	8 8 6 4 1	3	0 1 2 2 5 7 8 9	(8)
(9)	9 8 7 5 3 2 2 1 0	4	1 3 3 4 5 7 8	(7)
(6)	9 9 8 5 4 2	5	1 1 4 5	(4)
(3)	5 4 1	6	2 4 7	(3)
(2)	2 1	7	1 2 3 3	(4)

(b) Stone Wall Hospital : more people get seen earlier
3. (a)They did NOT appear to improve.
   (b) It was easier to get high marks on the mock paper.

Section 4: Tables and charts   p 12
D4.1: Information from tables
1. (a) West Midlands & Greater Manchester (b) True
   (c) 32%   (d) True: 32% in 1991 & 40% in 1891
   (e) London, West Midlands, Greater Manchester,
       Merseyside : Between 1971 and 1991 there was
       a significant drop in their populations.
2. (i) Rounding errors
   (ii) Possible features
       • overall figures show a steady decrease
       • both male and female figures showed one
         increase (1998-99)
   (iii) Number of households may have increased.

D4.2: Statistical diagrams
1. (a) France, Germany, Austria
   (b) Denmark, Finland, Sweden   (c) Lower
   (d) less
   (e) Their price levels are much lower than in the UK
2. (a) More : total for evening and night = 61% > half
   (b) Some people were not sure exactly when they
       were burgled, as they were not at home.
   (c) Morning
   (d) No: 6pm Fri —> 6am Monday = 2.5 days
       2.5 days ≈ 36% of the week.
   (e) The proportion of evening/night burglaries was
       higher in 1997, but you need to know the
       numbers, not the proportions.
3. (a) Males   (b) Females   (c) 50-59 & 60-69
4. (a) Percentage bar chart   (b) Bar chart
   (c) 1992 – 1996   (d) 1992 – 1998 : Debit cards
   (e) ATM cards ; fallen

Section 5: Histograms   p 15
D5.1: Histograms
1.

Income	width	FD	Frequency
0–150	150	0.2	30
150–200	50	0.5	25
200–300	100	0.8	80
300–500	200	0.6	120
500–600	100	1.5	150
600–1000	400	1.6	640

2. (a)

Income	width	FD	Frequency
0–150	150	0.25	45
150–200	50	1.2	60
200–300	100	0.9	90
300–400	100	1.1	110
400–600	200	0.8	160
600–1000	400	1.1	440

(b)
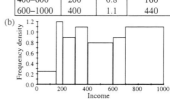

(c) Little Barding

D5.2: More about histograms
1. (a)

Length	Freq	True classes	w	FD
0 - 5	150	$-0.5 \le x \le 5.5$	6	25
6 - 10	75	$5.5 \le x \le 10.5$	5	15
11 - 20	60	$10.5 \le x \le 20.5$	10	6
21 - 36	48	$20.5 \le x \le 36.5$	16	3
37 - 60	48	$36.5 \le x \le 60.5$	24	2

(b)
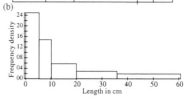

page 152

2. (a)

Distance	Freq	True classes	w	FD
0 - 1	20	$-0.5 \leq x \leq 1.5$	2	10
2 - 6	65	$1.5 \leq x \leq 6.5$	5	13
7 - 10	48	$6.5 \leq x \leq 10.5$	4	12
11 - 20	60	$10.5 \leq x \leq 20.5$	10	6
21 - 35	24	$20.5 \leq x \leq 35.5$	15	1.6
36 - 60	20	$35.5 \leq x \leq 60.5$	25	0.8

(b)
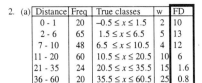

3. (a)

Number	Freq	True classes	w	FD
1 - 2	8	$0.5 \leq x \leq 2.5$	2	4
3 - 5	15	$2.5 \leq x \leq 5.5$	3	5
6 - 10	16	$5.5 \leq x \leq 10.5$	5	3.2
11 - 20	5	$10.5 \leq x \leq 20.5$	10	0.5
21 - 50	6	$20.5 \leq x \leq 50.5$	30	0.2

(b)
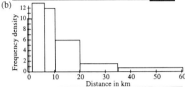

4. 16 44 52 30 12
5. (a) FD are : 2.4   3.0   3.2   1.6   0.6   0.3
   (b) age at last birthday
   (c) 0-6, 6-21, 21-51, 51-91

D5.3: Getting the words right
Task 1: 1, 2, 3,4 are samples   5 is the population
Task 2: A, D primary   B,C,E,F secondary

D5.4: Relative frequency histograms
1.
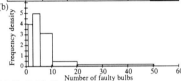

D5.5: Frequency polygons
1.
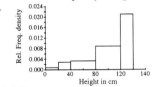
2. Both are true

Section 6: Cumulative frequency   p 20
D6.1: Cumulative frequency diagrams
1. 80 - 135 min —>150 cars   TRUE
2. 40 - 90 min —> 100 cars   FALSE
3. 30 min or less ≈ 10 cars   FALSE
4. 3 hours or longer ≈ 50 cars (just over 10%) TRUE

D6.2:Britain's population outlook
1. 68%   2. 25%   3. 6 to 7 million
4. 31-32 milllion   6. 61%, 61%, 60%
7. 32.2 million, 35.3 million, 37.2 million
8. 74 million

Section 7: Median and quartiles   p 22
D7.1: Median and quartiles
1. (a) 5   (b) 13   (c) 0   (d) 63
2. (a) 58, 68, 86   (b) 2.5, 4, 6.5   (c) 88, 90, 94
   (d) 42, 47, 63.5
3. (a) 11   (b) 38, 46, 50
4. (b) 31, 40, 56 (c) 25 (d) True

D7.2: Median and quartiles from frequency ...
1. (a) 23   (b) 0, 2, 3   2. 3, 4, 5

D7.3: Interpolation
1. (a) $20 \leq t < 30$; $30 \leq t < 50$ (b) 31.1, 44.7
2. (a) 3.73, 4.30, 4.72   (b) (i) 1999 (ii) 2000
3. (a) 36.74, 36.88, 37.03   (b) 18

D7.4: Using cumulative frequency diagrams
1. (b) ≈ 220, 350, 515   (c) (515 – 220) ≈ 295
2. (a) ≈ 150, 305, 720   (b) £305 ≤ I < £350
   (c) £150 ≤ I < £720
3. (b) ≈ 54, 62, 72 (c) ≈89 (d) ≈ 52 (e) ≈ 51   (f) ≈ 79
4. (a) £4,272   (b) £76,875   (d) ≈ £18,200
   (e) ≈ £29,000 (f) ≈ £5,000

Section 8: Median and quartiles   p 28
D8.1: What is an average ?
1. (a) £150, £135, £135
   (b) 6 out of the 8 values are less than £150, so £150
   is not representative.
   (c) The extreme value of £285 has distorted the
   calculation of the mean.   (d) median or mode
2. (a) 2.2, 2, 2   (b) 2   (c) 30 (d) 66
3. (a) 0 ≤ age < 5 (b) 8.5 (c) 8.2
4. (a) 29 & 46   (b) 33 (c) 35 (d) median or mean

D8.2: Using statistical calculator functions
2. 55.3   3. 66.75   4. 45.68   5. 26.97
6. 8, 409, 21201, 51.125
7. 9, 6735, 5040235, 748.3   8. 6, 628, 65820, 104.7
9. 3.018

D8.3: Mean and median from histograms
1. (a) 15 min   (b) 162   (d) 5 min 33 s
2. (a)   (i) 2.9 cm wide & 6.0 cm high
   (ii) 3.8 cm wide & 3.8 cm tall   (b) 38

D8.4: A shortcut to finding the mean
1. (a) (i) 6.2   (ii) 26.2   (iii) 106.2
   (b) Add 50 to the mean
2. 856   3. 132   4. (a) –0.5 (b) 199.5

Section 9: Simple measures of spread   p 33
D9.1: Range and interquartile range
1. (a)

Mary	36	25	60	57.2
James	57	18	54	59.1

(b) James' 95%   (c) Yes
(d) Mary – median   (e) James – IQR
2. (a) 240 (b) Maths   (c) Maths

D9.2: Box-and-whisker plots

1. (a)

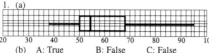

20 30 40 50 60 70 80 90 100

(b) A: True   B: False   C: False
    D: False   E: True   F: True

3. (a)

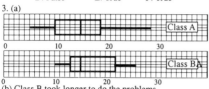

Class A

0   10   20   30

Class B

0   10   20   30

(b) Class B took longer to do the problems.
   Class A had a wider range of times.
   The spread of the middle 50% was the same for
   both classes.
   The middle value (median) was the same for both.

D9.3: A mixture of techniques

1. Test 2   2. Test 2   3. Test 2: less than 42 marks
   Test 3: less than 45 marks   4. Test 3
5. Test 1: 48, 59, 75   Test 2: 47,57, 70
   Test 3: 52, 63, 80
6.

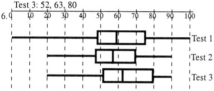

0 10 20 30 40 50 60 70 80 90 100

Test 1

Test 2

Test 3

Test 3 because it gives a good spread of marks but
students also achieve well.

D9.4: Skewness

1. (a) 7, 6, 4, 8   (b) 6.55, 5.7, 8.1   (c) (below)

50 55 60 65 70 75 80 85 90 95 100

(d) The distribution is positively skewed.

Section 10: Standard deviation   p 37

D10.1: The standard deviation from the mean

1. (a) 3   (b)

2.6	2.9	3	3.2	3.3
-0.4	-0.1	0	0.2	0.3

   (c) Negative deviations cancel out some of the
       positive deviations. (e) 0.06 (f) 0.245
2. 16, 3   3. 30.4, 4.88   5. 4.18
6. 8.8634   7. 15.576   8. 25.417
9. 165176   10. 8

D10.2: Standard deviation of tabulated data

1. (a)

3.4–3.6	3	3.5	10.5	(c)	0.5241	1.5725
3.7–4.0	5	3.85	19.25		0.1399	0.6995
4.1–4.4	9	4.25	38.25		0.0007	0.0063
4.5–4.7	8	4.7	37.6		0.2266	1.8128

   (b) 4.224   (c) 0.4045
2. 4.638; 2.56

D10.3: Using the calculator

1. 55.3 ; 5.10   2. 66.75; 3.07   3. 45.68; 4.36
4. 102.9 ; 11.034

1. 100.7 ; 0.4   Machine B, on average, is more
   accurate than A, but the errors vary more widely.
2. 57.5; 9.94   60; 14.14   59; 12.7

Section 11: Related sets of data   p 40

D11.1: What happens when ... ?

1. (a) mean = 7.8, median = 8
   (b) range = 6, SD = 2.134
2. (a) & (b) mean = 57.8, median = 58
   (c) & (d) range = 6, SD = 2.134
3. (a) & (b) mean = 520.2, median = 522
   (c) & (d) range = 54, SD = 19.206

D11.2: Related data sets

1. (a) mean = 33.76   SD = 1.05
   (b) mean = 92.28   SD = 1.05
   (c) mean = 101.28 SD = 3.15

Unit 2: Probability

Section 1: Basic ideas   p 43

D1.1: Review

1. (a) $^3/_5$ (b) $^1/_5$ (c) $^2/_5$
2. (a) $^4/_7$ (b) $^5/_7$ (c) $^3/_7$ (d) $^4/_7$
3. (a) $^1/_{26}$ (b) $^1/_{52}$ (c) $^{12}/_{13}$ (d) $^5/_{52}$ (e) $^7/_{26}$
4. (a) $^8/_{25}$ (b) $^8/_{25}$ (c) $^3/_{25}$
5. (a) $^7/_{26}$ (b) $^5/_{13}$ (c) $^8/_{13}$ 6. $^5/_{21}$
7. (a) 36   (b) $^1/_{18}$ (c) $^1/_6$ (d) $^1/_6$ (e) 0
8. (a) $^1/_8$ (b) $^{19}/_{24}$ (c) 0   9. (a) $^1/_3$ (b) $^1/_{53}$

D1.2 : Sample space diagrams

1. (a) $^1/_9$ (b) $^1/_6$ (c) $^5/_{18}$ 2. (a) $^1/_6$ (b) $^2/_3$
3. (a) $^1/_{12}$ (b) $^1/_3$ (c) $^1/_4$
4. (a) $^1/_{12}$ (b) $^1/_4$ (c) $^1/_6$ (d) $^1/_4$

Section 2: The addition rule   p46

D2.1 : Using set diagrams

1. 4   2. 18   3. 22   4. 28   5. 2
6. 30   7. $^2/_{15}$ 8. $^3/_{10}$ 9. $^{11}/_{15}$ 10. $^{14}/_{15}$
11. $^1/_{15}$ 12. 28   13. 4   14. 18   15. $^1/_7$
16. $^9/_{14}$ 17. $^1/_{14}$ 18. $^3/_{14}$ 19. $^4/_7$

D2.2 : The addition rule for probability

1. (a) $^1/_2$ (b) $^1/_2$ (c) $^1/_8$ (d) $^7/_8$ 2. $^5/_{24}$
3. 0.55   4. $^{23}/_{30}$

D2.3 : Probabilities of mutually exclusive events

1. (a) $^3/_7$ (b) $^2/_7$ (c) Yes ; 'getting a black' and
   'getting a white' are mutually exclusive.
2. (a) $^2/_7$ (b) $^5/_7$ (c) No ; 'not a white counter' and
   'a red counter' are not exclusive
3. (a) $^2/_5$ (b) $^3/_5$ (c) $^1/_5$ (d) $^2/_5$ (e) $^3/_5$
   (f) p(1 or 2) = p(1) + p(2)
   (g) p(red or 1) ≠ p(red) + p(1)
4. (a) 'dark hair' and 'red hair' are mutually exclusive
   or you can't have dark hair and red hair
   (b) 'dark hair' and 'glasses' are not mutually
exclusive or someone with dark hair may wear glasses
   (c) 0.15   (d) 0.55

Section 3: Tree diagrams   p49

D3.1 : Independent events

1. I   2. N   3. I   4. I   5. N   6. I
7. N   8. I   9. I   10. N   11. N

D3.2 : Tree diagrams
1. (a) 0.135   0.765   (b) 0.765   (c) 0.22
2. (a)

Outcomes	W, Yes	W, No	Y, Yes	Y, No
Probabilities	$^6/_{15}$	$^4/_{15}$	$^9/_{30}$	$^1/_{30}$

(b) $^7/_{10}$

D3.3 : Tree diagrams for independent events
1. (a)

Outcomes	B,B	B,W	W,B	W,W
Probabilities	$^3/_{10}$	$^3/_{10}$	$^3/_{10}$	$^1/_{10}$

(b) $^4/_{10}$ (c) $^6/_{10}$ (d) $^7/_{10}$
2. (b) $^1/_{66}$ (c) $^{13}/_{33}$ (d) $^{17}/_{22}$

D3.4 : Dependent and independent events
1. (a) $^8/_{15}$ (b) $^2/_{45}$ 2. $^8/_{15}$
3. (a) 0.01 (b) 0.18 (c) 0.19
4. (a) (i)

Outcomes	G,G	G,G'	G',G	G',G'
Probabilities	0.64	0.16	0.16	0.04

(ii) 0.32   (iii) 0.96
(b) (i)

Outcomes	G,G	G,G'	G',G	G',G'
Probabilities	0.49	0.21	0.18	0.12

(ii) 0.39

Section 4: The multiplication rule   p53
D4.1 : The multiplication rule for ind. events
1. (a) $^1/_6$ (b) $^1/_3$ 2. (a) 0.12 (b) 0.42
3. (a) $^1/_{36}$ (b) $^1/_4$ 4. (a) 0.18 (b) 0.28 5. $^1/_{1296}$
D4.2 : Using the multiplication and addition rules
1. (a) $^1/_{216}$ (b) $^5/_{72}$ (c) $^{125}/_{216}$ (d) $^{91}/_{216}$
2. (a) $^1/_{36}$ (b) $(^{35}/_{36})^{25} \approx 0.4945$ (c) 0.5055
3. (a) $^1/_9$ (b) $^2/_9$ (c) $^8/_9$ (d) $^1/_9$
4. (a) 0.36 (b) 0.48 (c) 0.16
5. (a)(i) $^{364}/_{365} \approx 0.9973$ (ii) $^{364}/_{365}$ x $^{363}/_{365} \approx 0.9918$
(b) 0.8831 (c) 0.1169

Section 5: The multiplication rule   p55
D5.1 : Conditional probability
1. (a) $^{11}/_{30}$ (b) $^1/_6$ (c) $^1/_{10}$ (d) $^4/_{15}$ (e) $^8/_{14}$ (f) $^8/_{11}$
(g) $^5/_{11}$ (h) $^6/_{19}$
2. (a) $^1/_4$ (b) $^1/_{13}$ (c) $^1/_{13}$ (d) $^1/_4$ (e) $^1/_{13}$
3. (a) $^{12}/_{25}$ (b) $^{13}/_{25}$ (c) $^{15}/_{25}$ (d) $^7/_{25}$ (e) $^1/_{15}$ (f) $^8/_{13}$
(g) $^1/_2$ (h) $^1/_2$
4. (a) $^3/_7$ (b) $^4/_7$ (c) $^5/_7$ 5. (b) $^4/_{12}$
D5.2: The multiplication rule for dependent events
1. (a) $^5/_9$ (b) $^2/_9$ (c) $^{24}/_{45}$
2. (a) $^7/_{11}$ (b) $^7/_{10}$ (c) $^{21}/_{55}$ (d) $^{26}/_{55}$
3. (a) $^1/_{17}$ (b) $^{13}/_{204}$ (c) $^{13}/_{51}$ (d) $^{12}/_{51}$

Section 6: Putting it all together
D6.1 : Probability relationships and tree diagrams
1. (a) 0.28 (b) 0.3 (c) 0.2 (d) 0.6 (e) 0.24 (f) 0.34
2. (a) 0.4 (b) 0.1 (c) 0.24 (d) 0.28 (e) 0.72 (f) 0.6
3. (a) $^4/_7$ (b) $^1/_7$ (c) $^3/_7$ (d) $^4/_7$
4. (a) $^1/_5$ (b) $^1/_3$
5. (a) 0.5 (b) 0.35 (c) 0.21 (d) 0.7 (e) 0.3 (f) 0.09
D6.2 : Probability rules and relationships
1. (a) 0.14 (b) 0.2 (c) 0.5 2. (a) $^1/_5$
(b) $^4/_7$ (c) $^3/_5$
3. (a) 0.1 (b) 0.39 (c) 0.6 (d) 0.36 (e) $^{12}/_{13}$
4. (a) 0.2 (b) 0.5 (c) $^1/_3$ (d) 0.4 (e) 0.5
5. (a) $^1/_{10}$ (b) $^{11}/_{20}$ (c) $^2/_5$
6. (a) $^1/_6$ (b) $^1/_2$ (c) $^1/_8$
D6.3 : Conditional probability problems
1. (a) $^{33}/_{95}$ (b) $^{48}/_{95}$ (c) $^{11}/_{19}$ 2. (a) 0.525
3. (i) (a) $^3/_{20}$ (b) $^{13}/_{120}$ (ii) $^{10}/_{13}$
4. (a) 0.020392 (b) 0.9804

(c) 98% of those who test are non-carriers, so the
test is NOT SUITABLE.
5. (i) 0.0064 (ii) 0.9568 (iii) 0.778
6. (a) $q - 0.25$ (b) $\dfrac{2}{12q - 3}$ (c) $^{13}/_{20}$
7. (i) $^1/_{28}$ (ii) $^1/_{13}$ 8. (i) $^1/_7$ (ii) $^5/_7$
9. (a) $^{115}/_{150}$ (b) $^{119}/_{150}$ (c) $^{31}/_{150}$ (d) 30
(e) P(a female employee is paid weekly) (f) 0.5
10. (a) (i) $^1/_4$ (ii) $^5/_{24}$ (iii) $^1/_6$
(b) not independent since P(A and B) ≠ P(A) x P(B)
11. (a) 0.04675 (b) 0.363
12. (i) (a) $^1/_2$ (b) $^1/_6$ (c) $^1/_{12}$ (d) $^1/_8$ (e) $^1/_3$
(ii) (a) $^1/_7$ (b) $^1/_{288}$ (c) $^5/_{288}$ (d) $^1/_5$

Section 7: Permutations   p62
D7.1 : Factorials
1. (a) 6 (b) 2 (c) 120 (d) 720
2. (a) 30 (b) 1320 (c) 336 (d) 380
3. (a) $\dfrac{7!}{4!}$ (b) $\dfrac{20!}{17!}$ (c) $\dfrac{15!}{9!}$
4. (a) 56 (b) 105 (c) 420 (d) 715
5. (a) 495 (b) 35 (c) 36
D7.2 : Permutations of distinct items
1. (a) 5040 (b) 60 (c) 6720
2. (a) 20 (b) 35 (c) 35 (d) 6
3. (a) $\dfrac{n!}{(n-2)!}$ (b) $\dfrac{(n-1)!}{(n-4)!}$ (c) $n!$ 4. (a) 24 (b) $^1/_{24}$
5. 362 880
D7.3 : Permutations with repetitions
1. 12 2. 20 3. 720 4. 20 160 5. 3360
6. (a) 10 080 (b) 2 520 (c) $^1/_4$
7. (a) 1 260 (b) 280

Section 8: Combinations   p65
D8.1 : Combinations
1. (a) 35 (b) 5 (c) 1
3. (a) 56 (b) 120 (c) 12
4. 20 5. 15 6. 10
7. (a) 10 626 (b) 1 771
8. (a) 15 504 (b) 190
10. (a) 2 (b) 70 (c) $^1/_{35}$ (d) $^{34}/_{35}$
11. (a) 715 (b) 0.026 (c) 0.974
D8.2 : The multiplication rules
1. 686 000 2. 163 350 3. 360 4. 1 260
5. 756 6. (a) 36 (b) 84 (c) $^3/_7$
7. (a) 56 (b) 24 (c) 24 (d) 48

Section 9: Adding complications   p68
D9.1 : Permutations with restrictions
1. (a) 3 360 (b) 360 (c) 2 520
2. (a) 360 (b) $^1/_2$ (c) $^2/_3$ 3. (a) 210 (b) $^2/_7$
D9.2 : Permutations with repeats
1. (a) 3 36 (b) 512 2. (a) 256 (b) 24 (c) 12 (d) 8
3. (a) 256 (b) 56 (c) $^7/_{32}$
D9.3 : Keeping them apart
1. (a) 11! or 39 916 800 (b) 967 680 (c) 8 467 200
2. (a) 3 632 428 800 (b) 259 4559 200 (c) 0.071
(d) 39 916 800 (e) 0.011 (f) 0.126
D9.4 : Adding permutations
1. (a) (i) 60 (ii) 120 (iii) 180 (b) 360 (c) 60 (d) $^1/_6$
2. (a) 840 (b) 240 (c) 120
E9.5 : Miscellaneous problems
1. (a) 720 (b) 15 2. 0.6 3. 72

page 155

4. (a) 480 (b) 720
5. (a) $\frac{4}{35} \approx 0.1143$ (b) $\frac{6}{35} \approx 0.1714$ 6. 0.387
7. (a) 0.24 (b) 0.049 (c) 0.094 (d) 0.216
8. (a) 12! = 479 001 600 (b) 103 680 (c) 0.00022
(d) 3 628 800   9. 110

Unit 3: Discrete Random Var.

Section 1: Probability distributions   p 74

D1.1: Discrete random variables
1. (b)

t	0	1	2	3
$P(T = t)$	$\frac{1}{8}$	$\frac{3}{8}$	$\frac{3}{8}$	$\frac{1}{8}$

2. (b)

x	0	1	2	3	4	5
$P(X = x)$	$\frac{6}{36}$	$\frac{10}{36}$	$\frac{8}{36}$	$\frac{6}{36}$	$\frac{4}{36}$	$\frac{2}{36}$

3. (b)

r	0	1	2
$P(R = r)$	$\frac{3}{28}$	$\frac{15}{28}$	$\frac{10}{28}$

4. (b) (i)

x	2	3	4	5	6	7
$P(X = x)$	$\frac{1}{36}$	$\frac{2}{36}$	$\frac{3}{36}$	$\frac{4}{36}$	$\frac{5}{36}$	$\frac{6}{36}$

x	8	9	10	11	12
$P(X = x)$	$\frac{5}{36}$	$\frac{4}{36}$	$\frac{3}{36}$	$\frac{2}{36}$	$\frac{1}{36}$

(ii) $\frac{5}{18}$

(c) (i)

z	1	2	3	4	5	6
$P(Z = z)$	$\frac{23}{36}$	$\frac{7}{36}$	$\frac{3}{36}$	$\frac{1}{36}$	$\frac{1}{36}$	$\frac{1}{36}$

(ii) $\frac{11}{12}$

5.

x	0	1	2	3
$P(X = x)$	$\frac{20}{84}$	$\frac{45}{84}$	$\frac{18}{84}$	$\frac{1}{84}$

6.

x	1	2	3	4	6	9
$P(X = x)$	$\frac{1}{36}$	$\frac{1}{9}$	$\frac{1}{6}$	$\frac{1}{9}$	$\frac{1}{3}$	$\frac{1}{4}$

7.

m	1	2	3
$P(M = m)$	$\frac{1}{3}$	$\frac{8}{33}$	$\frac{14}{33}$

E1.2: Probability distribution challenge
1. (b)

d	0	1	2	3
$P(D = d)$	0.38	0.3	0.12	0.2

D1.3: Probability distributions and the Σ notation
1. $\frac{1}{4}$ 2. 0.1
3.(a)

s	1	2	3	4	5	6	7	8
$P(S = s)$	$\frac{1}{6}$	$\frac{1}{12}$	$\frac{1}{6}$	$\frac{1}{12}$	$\frac{1}{6}$	$\frac{1}{12}$	$\frac{1}{6}$	$\frac{1}{12}$

(b) $\frac{1}{3}$

5. A quadratic equation gives $c = 0.3$ or -0.8
Since c is a probability, $0 < 0.3 < 1$, so only one value of c, that is 0.3

D1.4: Cumulative distribution functions
1. (a) 0.7 (b) 0.55   (c) 0.8
2.

x	3	4	5	6	7	8
$P(X = x)$	0.2	0.05	0.11	0.24	0.15	0.25

3. $a = \frac{1}{4}, b = \frac{1}{4}, c = 0, d = \frac{1}{4}$

D1.5: An alternative notation
1. $\frac{1}{5}$ 2. (a) $\frac{3}{7}, \frac{5}{7}$ (b) $\frac{2}{7}$ (c)

x	1	2	3	4
$P(X = x)$	$\frac{1}{7}$	$\frac{2}{7}$	$\frac{2}{7}$	$\frac{2}{7}$

3. (a) $\frac{1}{8}$ (b) $\frac{3}{4}$

D1.6: Putting it all together
1. (a) $\frac{1}{6}$ (b)

s	2	3	4	5	6	7
$P(S = s)$	$\frac{1}{12}$	$\frac{1}{6}$	$\frac{1}{4}$	$\frac{1}{4}$	$\frac{1}{6}$	$\frac{1}{12}$

2. (a)

g	0	1	2
$P(G = g)$	$\frac{5}{28}$	$\frac{15}{28}$	$\frac{2}{7}$

(b) $\frac{23}{28}$

3. (a)

c	0	1	2	3
$P(C = c)$	0.44706	0.42354	0.11946	0.00995

(b) $\frac{23}{28}$

E1.7: Miscellaneous Challenges
1. (a) 0.2 (b)

x	0	1	2	3	4	5
$P(X = x)$	0.2	0.1	0.12	0.22	0.11	0.21

2. (a) 21 (b) $\frac{4}{21}$ (c)

a	20	30	60	70	100
$P(A = a)$	$\frac{6}{21}$	$\frac{4}{21}$	$\frac{8}{21}$	$\frac{2}{21}$	$\frac{1}{21}$

3. (a) 0.1 (b) $\frac{11}{30}$ (c) $\frac{5}{11}$

Section 2: Expectation and Variance   p 79

D2.1: Expected frequency of an outcome
1. 100
2. (a) 65 (b) 20 (c) 5 (d) 130 (e) 80 (f) 180
3. (a) 50 (b) 150   (c) 300   (d) 350
4. (a) 0.7828   (b) 563.6 boxes
5. (a) 1.04 weeks   (b) 21.84 weeks

D2.2: Expectation
1. 4.4   2. 4   3. 6   4. 1
5. (a) $\frac{7}{3}$ (b) 7   6. (a) 0.15 (b) 4.2
7. $\frac{41}{26}$ 8. $7\frac{5}{6}$ 9. (a) gain of 3.13p
(b) Customers made an average gain of 3.13p, so management made an average loss of 3.13p.

D2.3: Methods for calculating variance
1. 3 ; 4.75   2. 1 ; 3.7   3. 2.75 ; 0.3875
4. 0.3875   5. $3\frac{2}{15}$; 2.516   6. 5.15 ; 7.4275

D2.4: Problems with expectation and variance
1. (a)

b	0	1	2
$P(B = b)$	$\frac{5}{18}$	$\frac{5}{9}$	$\frac{1}{6}$

(b) $\frac{8}{9}$

2. 1 ; 2   3. (a) £$\frac{10}{9}$ (b) £20   (c) £12
4. 2.375 ; 0.7344   5. 2
6. (a) 0.26 ; 0.7158 (b) 260   (c) 9.74
(d) order from Bright Light - less faulty bulbs
7. Choose "trad" idea – expected profit higher
[zany : £260 000 trad: £290 000]   8. £12

Section 3: Expectation of a linear ...   p 85

D3.1: Linear functions of random variables
1. (a) 10 (b) 36 (c) 7 (d) 9 (e) –5 (f) 81 (g) 9
2. (a) $\frac{3}{2}$; $\frac{3}{4}$ (b) 4, 4, 3, $\frac{3}{16}$ (c) totals almost identical
(d) Mary's are more widespread than Robert's
3. $a = 5$ $b = 2$

Section 4: The Binomial Distribution   p 86

D4.1: Introducing the binomial distribution
1. $P(X = x) = {}_3C_x\,(\frac{1}{6})^x(\frac{5}{6})^{3-x}$ $x = 0, 1, 2, 3$
2. $P(Y = y) = {}_4C_y\,(\frac{1}{4})^y(\frac{3}{4})^{4-y}$ $x = 0, 1, 2, 3, 4$
3. 0.3294; 0.0165

D4.2: The binomial distribution
1. (a) 5   (b) 6   (c) 45
2. (a) 0.2304   (b) 0.0768   (c) 0.01024
3. (a) 0.2621   (b) 0.24576 (c) 0.001536
4. (a) 0.124   (b) 0.2873   (c) 0.6593
5. (a) 0.2683   (b) 0.6746   (c) 0.9964

D4.3: Cumulative binomial distribution tables
1. (a) 0.4617   (b) 0.1954   (c) 0.9944
2. (a) 0.0055   (b) 0.7759   (c) 0.0777
3. (a) 0.5634   (b) 10
4. (a) 0.9999   (b) 0.9999   (c) 0.0176

D4.4: Binomial expectation and variance
1. (a) 3.5 ; 2.275 (b) 0.7515   2. 13 ; 4.55
3. 1.25 ; 1.0897

D4.5: Is a binomial model suitable ?
1. Binomial, assuming $p = \frac{1}{6}$ constant; $n = 20$
2. Not binomial – n is not fixed
3. Binomial, with $n = 12$, assuming $p = \frac{1}{6}$ constant.
   In fact, P(parking space is empty is likley to depend on the time of day and is unlikely to be constant.
4. Binomial, $n = 20$, $p = 0.6$
5. Not binomial
6. Binomial, with $n = 10$, assuming $p = 0.1$ assuming the days of absence occur INDEPENDENTLY which is unlikely.

D4.6: Putting it all together
1. $p = 0.1$; 0.1384
2. (a) 0.5987   (b) 0.9990   (c) 0.0115
3. (a) $p = 0.06$ (b)

Pred f.	147	44	6	0.5	0	0
Actualf.	148	45	6	1	0	0

   a good match
4. (a) 0.0536   (b) 0.0243
5. (a) 0.201   (b) 0.0064   (c) 120 ; 2
6. (a) 4.8; 0.98 (c) 0.655   (d) 0.737
7. (a) 0.00157 (b) 0.085

Section 5: The Geometric Distribution   p 91
D5.1: Introducing the geometric distribution
1. $P(X = x) = (\frac{35}{36})^{x-1}(\frac{1}{6})$ $x = 1,2,3,...$
2. (a) $P(X = x) = (\frac{7}{8})^{x-1}(\frac{1}{8})$ $x = 1,2,3,...$
   (b) $P(X = x) = (\frac{3}{4})^{x-1}(\frac{1}{4})$ $x = 1,2,3,...$
D5.2: The geometric distribution
1. (a) 0.144   (b) 0.0864   (c) 0.2304
2. (a) 0.343   (b) 0.657   (c) 0.7599
3. (a) 0.0655   (b) 0.9345   (c) 0.4096
4. (a) 0.0588   (b) 0.1073   (c) 0.0769
5. (a) 0.0819   (b) 0.1073   (c) 0.8322
6. (a) 0.0105   (b) 5
D5.3: Geometric expectation
1. $3\frac{1}{3}$ 2. 1.382   3. 5 4. £10   5. 2
D5.4: Miscellaneous geometric problems
1. (a) (i) 0.0384 (ii) 0.0256(iii) 0.064 (iv) 0.064 (d) $\frac{5}{3}$
2. (a) 0.1   (b) (i) 0.081 (ii) 0.6561 (iii) 0.4095
   (iv) 0.4550
3. (a) $\frac{1}{6}$ (b) 0.5787   (c) 0.5981   (d) 0.4822
   (e) 0.1122(f) 0.0003   (g) 0.965   (h) 21
4. (a) 0.0670 (b) 0.6651 5. (a) 0.8210 (b) 0.7799

Section 6: The Poisson Distribution   p 95
D6.1:The Poisson distribution
1. (a) 0.0842   (b) 0.2650   (c) 0.5595
2. (a) 0.1003   (b) 0.5960   (c) 0.4040
3. (a) 0.0842   (b) 0.5665
4. (a) 0.0183   (b) 0.07326 (c) 0.2381   (d) 0.9084
5. (a) 0.3680   (b) 0.1340   (c) 0.4405   (d) $n = 3$
6. (a) 0.0498   (b) 0.1494   (c) 0.2440   (d) 0.8008
7. (a) 0.1353   (b) 0.5665   (c) 0.0644
D6.2:The Poisson as an approx. to the binomial
1. (a) (i) 0.1485   (ii) 0.1486   (b) (i) & (ii) 0.0062
2. (a) $n = 500$, $p = 0.005$ (b) 0.2570   (c) 2.5
   (d) 0.2565
3. (a) 0.1045   (b) 0.1057   (c) Yes   (d) 0.1
4. (a) 0.0099   (b) 0.3594
   (c) The second, since, for the first n is too small.

Section 7: The Normal Distribution   p 98
D7.1: Meet the normal distribution
1. C   A   B   2. X
D7.2: Normal distributions
Task 1:   161.524, 5.928
D7.3: The standard normal distribution
1. (a) 0.7881   (b) 0.8888   (c) 0.9986   (d) 0.9772
2. From $-\infty$ to zero, 0.5 of the total area is shaded
3. (a) 0.0668   (b) 0.2144   (c) 0.5685
4. (a) 0.0179   (b) 0.1915   (c) 0.2327
   (d) 0.0668   (e) 0.738   (f) 0.3475
5. (a) 1.96   (b) –0.675
6. (a) 0.44   (b) –0.58 (c) –2.51 (d) 2.62   (e) –0.1
D7.4: Probs of non-standard distributions
1. (a) $Z = \frac{1}{5}(X - 30)$; 0.9772
   (b) $Z = \frac{1}{4}(X - 12)$; 0.0668
   (c) $Z = \frac{1}{6}(X - 7)$; 0.3085
   (d) $Z = \frac{1}{20}(X - 100)$; 0.2417
   (e) $Z = \frac{1}{6}(X - 17)$; 0.2417
   (f) $Z = \frac{1}{2.5}(X - 76)$; 0.8621
2. (a) 0.8413   (b) 0.0228   (c) 0.4962
   (d) 0.9544   (e) 0.1587   (f) 0.8621
3. 9.503
D7.5: Deriving mean and SD from given probs
1. 3.552   2. 38.63   3. 1.4   4. 6.25
5. 20.27   6. 40.64, 22.73   7. 2.822, 0.2872
D7.6: Normal distribution problems
1. 0.4502   2. 0.62%   3. 0.589 4. 6.792

Section 8: Random Sampling   p 104
D8.1: Random samples of a population
1. Yes
2. It would take too long and, if the mixing was not thorough each time, the results would not be random.
3. 3rd person in 7BJ; 2nd person in 13PJ
4. (a) out of range (b) already got it
5. $759 \div 50 \approx 15$
6. All numbers must be equally likely to be chosen – and 7-15 cannot be trhown with a dice.
7. (c) 351 - 999 are out of range
8. (b) $350 \times 3 = 1050$, so 50 people would only be allocated 2 numbers.

Section 9: Dist. of the Sample Mean p 106
D9.1: Sampling and sample means
1. $E(\overline{X}) = 5$ 2. (b) 6   (c) 6   3. (b) 614   (c) 14
4. (b) 5   5. (a) 0, $\frac{7}{6}$
D9.2: Dist. of the sample mean from a normal pop
1. (a) $\overline{X} \sim N(35, 1.25)$ (b) 0.9963   (c) 0.1856
2. 0.39   3. 21   4. (b) 0.0032   (c) 0.1682
D9.3: The Central Limit Theorem
1. (a) 0.2592   (b) 0.0091
2. (b) 3.5   (d) 0.0581   (e) 0.9046
3. 40

Unit 4: Corr. and Regression

Section 1: Correlation   p 112

D1.1: Scatter graphs and correlation
1. Graph A = Set R   Graph B = Set P   Graph C = Set Q
2. (a) strong +ve corr.   (b) poor/no corr.
   (c) strong +ve corr.   (d) strong –ve corr.
   (e) no corr.   (f) poor –ve corr.
   (g) strong +ve corr.   (h) strong +ve corr.

D1.2: Measuring correlation
1. $\Sigma x = 696$ $\Sigma y = 648$ $n = 12$ $\bar{x} = 58$ $\bar{y} = 54$; 149.3
2. $\Sigma x = 696$ $\Sigma y = 648$ $\Sigma(x - \bar{x})^2 = 4372$
   $\Sigma(y - \bar{y})^2 = 3046$ $r = 0.491$ 3. $r = 0.491$
4. Each represents the total deviation from the mean which is zero.

D1.3: The product moment correlation coefficient
1. Strong +ve, 10, 160, 40, $r = 1$
2. Strong –ve, 10, 674, –82, $r = -0.9988$
3. Weak +ve, 10, 29.2, 5, $r = 0.293$
4. No correlation, 25.2, 12.8, 2.4, $r = 0.105$

D1.4: Calculation methods
1. 0.154   2. –0.219   3. –0.305   4. 0.005   5. 0.295
6. (a) 1   (b) 1   (c) all points lie on a straight line

D1.5: Using calculator functions
2. 0.7033   3. –0.2352

D1.6: Working with real data
Case 1: –0.472   Case 2: 0.962

D1.7: Scaling data
1. $r = 0.0255$

Section 2: Regression   p 119

D2.1: Finding the line of best fit
1. (a) 0.36   (b) $y = 0.36x + 7.4$ (c) ≈ 1160
2. (a) $y = 19.96 + 0.3x$ (b) 87
3. $y = 424.7 - 33.9x$ 4. $y = 1.625 + 0.3125x$
5. $y = 3.662x - 3.144$
6. (a) $y = 6.84 - 0.064x$ (b) 4.3 min
   (c) There is no guarantee that the reaction will be at the same rate at higher temperatures.

D2.2: Using calculator functions
1. (a) 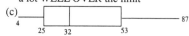   (b) $E = 0.00767T - 2.136$
        (c) $t = 0.9998$; extremely accurate
        (d) 4.76
   (e) The rod may not continue to extend at the same rate at higher temperatures.
2. (a) 0.9617 (b) $P = 49.15 + 0.578G$ (c) 36 points
   (d) The calculated value is only an estimate

D2.3: The two regression lines
1. $y = 5.362 + 9.638x$ $x = -0.05 + 0.0974y$
2. $y = 0.348 + 1.435x$ $x = -6 + 3y$
3. $V = 343.6 - 18.94t$ $t = 16.33 - 0.405V$
4. $p = -3.203 + 1.526m$ $m = -3.178 + 4.493p$

D2.4: Making predictions
1. (a) (i) $y = 29.375 + 0.4828x$ (ii) 62%
   (b) (i) $x = 19.93 + 0.6615y$ (ii) 68%
2. (a) (i) $x = 180.3$ $\sigma = 15.6$ (ii) $y = 175.1$ $\sigma = 22.8$
   (b) $r = -0.3522$; not very reliable
   (c) $y = 268.5 - 0.518x$; $x = 222.2 + 0.2395y$
   (d) 170   (e)   180

---

3. (a) $\Sigma x = 384$ $\Sigma y = 967$ $\Sigma x^2 = 15\,916$ $\Sigma y^2 = 81\,429$
   $\Sigma xy = 34\,459$ $x = 32$ $y = 80.58$
   (b) $y = 49.48 + 0.9689x$ (c) 08.13   (d) 0.9857
   (e) $x = -48.82 + 1.003y$ (f) 08.11

Section 3: Dependent/Independent Var. p 125

D3.1: Dependent and independent variables
1. (a) $y = 0.267 + 3.011x$ (i) 106 cm   (ii) 46 cm
   (b) 301.4   (c) $x = 100$ is way oputside the experimental range of values and the linear relationship may not still hold here.
2. exp. var. = load ; response var. = compression
3. (a) time t (b) distance d (c) 4.2 s   (d) 40.54 m
4. (a) $h = 1.651 + 1.543r$ (b) 63h

Section 4: Spearman's Rank Correl. p 127

D4.1: Rank correlation
1. (a)

Rank 1:	6	4	7	5	3	4	8	1
Rank 2:	8	5	6	3	1	2	7	4

(b)   (c) $r = 0.738$

D4.2: Spearman's rank correlation coefficient
1. (a) & (b) $r_s = -0.257$ 2. (a) & (b) $r_s = 0.257$
3. (a)

Rank 1:	4	2	5	3	1	6
Rank 2:	4	1	6	3	2	5

(c) strong agreement as to rank order
4. (a) 0.965   (b)   0.929   (c) reasonably good
   (d) very good
5. (a) 0.5772   (b) 0.6   (c) No - since, in each newpaper, the schools' scores are all close together.

D4.3: Ranming methods
1. $r = 0.63$ 2. $r = 0.68$

D4.4: Ranking without data
1. (a)

x	1	2	3	4	5	6
y	6	2	4	1	5	3

(b) –0.257

2. (a)

x	1	2	3	4	5	6
y	3	5	2	4	1	6

(b) 0.143

3. (a) 1   (b) –1
4. 3   4   6   7   1   5   2

REVISION ANSWERS
Unit 1: Representation of data
1. (b) (i) £16, 500   (ii) 0.21 (c) 0.073
2. (a) 11, 9, 8, 1   (b) 14 min, 6 min, 23 min
   (c) 21 min
   (d) & (f)
   (e) positive skew
   (g) Train journeys from Shefton are much more consistent/reliable - smaller spread of times
3. (b) very few JUST OVER the limit of 35 kg a lot WELL OVER the limit
   (c)

(d) HISTOGRAM shows better the High Number just below the weight limit and the very small number just over the weight limit.
4. (a) 15, 2 (b) 50, 20   (c) $5x + y$, $2x$
5. (i) HISTOGRAM
   (ii) Individual data values are not known
   (iii) median = 69 or 70, IQR = 7.8 or 8 marks
   (iv) No influence on median or IQR.
       Mean increases by 0.2
6. (i) English   (ii) Science   (iii) Science

(v) Danny's diesel consumption is much lower than average
(vi) Diesel consumption depends on the weight of the load, which is independent.
4. 0.357 ; X and Y most in agreement ;
   prizes to B, A, C
5. (i) −0.8646   (ii) −0.9048
   (iii) (a) PMcoeff. will change
        (b) Spearman's rank correlation coefficient will stay the same

Unit 2:Probability
1. (i) 0.64   (ii) 0.75
2. (i) 0.36   (ii) 0.48   (iii) 0.07776 (iv) 0.92224
3. 0.32, $^7/_{15}$
4. 0.345
5. 0.3888
6. (a) 0.3   (b) P(B/aA) ≠ P(B) so not independent
   (c) 0.42

Unit 3:Discrete Random Variables
1. 2.3, 5.9 ;

r	1	2	3	4	6	9
P(R = r)	0.04	0.12	0.2	0.09	0.3	0.25

2. (i) 0.25   (ii) $2^1/_3$; $1^7/_{18}$
3.

r	0	1	2	3
P(R = r)	0.30	0.34	0.20	0.16

   (i) 1.22   (ii) 4.2116   (iii) 0.36
4. (i) 0.3177   (ii) 0.6471
5. 0.2 ; 0.096
6. (a) (i) 0.3671   (ii) 0.31146
   (b) P(diamond) would not remain constant
7. (a) X ~ B(20, 0.2)   (b) 0.0115   (c) 0.0867
8. (i) Y ~ Geo($^1/_6$)   (ii) 30 (iii) 0.2326
9. X ~ Geo($^1/_{11}$)   (i) 0.0683   (ii) 0.3855
   (iii) 11 & 110
10. (a) 0.1653   (ii) 0.2694
11. (a) (i) 0.99885   (ii) 0.00109   (c) 0.5503
12. (i) 46.48%   (ii) 0.532 m   (c) 1.00 m
13. 15, 47
14. (a) (i) 4.947%   (ii) 0.0048% (I & II not satisfied)
    (b) (i) 105.3 ml   (ii) 106.45 ml ; 106.45 = smallest acceptable value
    (c) (i) 103.3 ml ; 3.9823 ml
       (ii) Overhaul now because as soon as σ increases, the conditions will not be met.
15. (a) (i) 0.1887   (ii) 0.5619
    (b) 0.5348   (c) 0.23555

Unit 4:Correlation and Regression
1. (i) $r = 0$ (ii) strong, positive correlation
2. (i) $a = 3.07$, $b = 1.17$
   (ii) When x is dependent on y or when y is the controlled variable.
3. (ii) $y = 7.356 − 0.0002217x$
   (iii) Gradient b represents the decrease in diesel consumption for every 1 kg load increase
       Intercept = Diesel consumption when empty
   (iv) 30 000 is outside the range of the data and almost certainly could not be carried by the lorries.